THE BITTER AND THE BOLD

BY:

C.M. BYRD

TABLE OF CONTENTS

ABOUT THE AUTHOR

Crysta Byrd stands as a towering figure of resilience, a woman forged in the crucible of unimaginable hardship, her life a testament to the raw, unyielding power of the human spirit to rise from the ashes of trauma. Born in the humid embrace of Ponchatoula, Louisiana, Crysta's story is no mere biography—it is an epic, a saga of survival, a battle cry etched in ink and tears, resonating with the weight of a life reclaimed from the jaws of betrayal, violence, and systemic failure. At thirty-six, with blonde hair streaked with the gray of battles fought and green eyes that blaze with a defiance honed over two decades, she is not just a mother, writer, or survivor—she is a force, a beacon for those lost in the dark, a voice that refuses to be silenced. Her book, *The Bitter and The Bold*, is not simply a memoir; it is her soul laid bare, a map of scars and triumphs, a lifeline flung to others who bear the same wounds. To understand Crysta is to walk through the fire of her life, to feel the pulse of her pain and the thunder of her courage, a journey that begins in the innocence of a sixteen-year-old girl and culminates in the indomitable woman she has become.

Crysta's story begins in the small-town sprawl of Ponchatoula, where the sticky heat of December 2005 clung to her like a premonition. At sixteen, she was a spark of mischief, her blonde hair frizzing in the Louisiana humidity, her green eyes alight with the reckless thrill of youth. She was not the star of the high school clique nor an outcast, but a vibrant in-betweener, part of a tight-knit crew—Candace, Cami, and sometimes Caitlin—bound by laughter and the shared rebellion of sneaking into dive bars. That fateful night, when she slipped into an Irish pub with her friends, she was a girl chasing adventure, unaware that the world was about to shatter her. The encounter with "Don," a thirty-year-old predator cloaked in charm, marked the end of her innocence. The assault that followed—on a grimy couch in a shadowed house—fractured her soul, leaving her to stumble home, scalding her skin in a shower that could not wash away the violation. Yet, even in that moment of devastation, the seeds of her resilience were sown. She confided in Cami, her anchor, and buried her secret, a sixteen-year-old girl building a fragile armor of silence to protect what remained of her world.

The discovery of her pregnancy in January 2006 was a seismic blow, a second violation that tethered her to her rapist through the life growing inside her. Alone in her bathroom, clutching a drugstore test, Crysta faced a choice that would define her: erase the child and perhaps the pain, or embrace the unknown. Her decision to keep Jada—felt in the tiny flutters against her palm—was an act of defiance, a mother's love igniting in the ashes of her trauma. At seventeen, she gave birth to Jada in a Baton Rouge hospital, holding her daughter's eight-pound miracle against her chest, her green eyes weeping with joy and terror. Jada became her light, her reason to breathe, a beacon that guided Crysta through the suffocating whispers of Hammond's gossip mill, where she was branded a scandal, a teen mom with a fabricated story of a vanished boyfriend. She graduated high school early, plunged into college, and worked diner nights, grease on her skin and secrets in her soul, building a life atop a lie that shielded her from the truth she could not yet face.

The truth, however, has a way of clawing free. In 2011, at twenty-two, the small-town rumors reached Don, and the secret Crysta had guarded for five years erupted. A subpoena for Jada's DNA test forced her to relive the violation, driving her daughter to Baton Rouge with a lie—"Just a checkup"—as her heart broke under the weight of powerlessness. The confirmation of Don's paternity was a gut punch, but the true devastation came in the Tangipahoa Parish courthouse, where his pursuit of custody—despite the rape—unveiled a system blind to her pain. The 50/50 custody ruling was a betrayal that ignited a warrior within her. Crysta became a shark, as her lawyer Tom instructed, learning to hide, to fight, to survive in a courtroom where her voice was muted, and Don's smirk was a constant wound. She endured his control—his inspections of Jada's appearance, his threats to exploit any misstep—each moment a test of her resolve, each trial a wound to her spirit, yet she stood firm, her love for Jada a fire that no gavel could extinguish.

By 2015, at twenty-six, Crysta's pain had festered into nightmares and panic attacks, but a counselor's words—"You can still report it"—

sparked a cry for justice. Filing the rape report with the Tangipahoa Parish Sheriff's Office was a moment of hope, a bold step toward reclaiming her truth, only to be crushed by the system's silence. The report languished for seven years, a victim of Don's wealth and connections—his company, Gumbeaux Digital Branding, tied to the Ponchatoula Police—a shield that rendered him untouchable. Crysta's despair was palpable, her green eyes wild with fury as she stormed the station, only to be dismissed as a nuisance. Yet, even in this abandonment, her resolve hardened, her bold spirit vowing to scream louder, to fight harder, for Jada and for herself.

The years that followed were a descent into isolation and fear. Don's control over Jada—banning friends, monitoring calls, tearing pages from her diary—was a slow strangulation of her daughter's light, mirrored by his threats to Crysta: "I've got connections. I can take her anytime." Each encounter left her trembling, sixteen again, pinned under his power, but she refused to break. The courtroom became her battlefield, where she faced Judge Jeffrey Cashe's sealed records and Don's polished lawyers, who twisted her life into a narrative of instability. The ultimate injustice came in March 2022, when an ex parte order stripped Jada away, granting Don full custody and forcing Crysta to pay $117 monthly child support, backdated to 2015—a debt that felt like blood money, a mother's love turned into a transaction with her rapist. The pain of those supervised visits, four hours every other Saturday, was a knife to her heart, yet she clung to Jada's blue-green eyes, her blonde curls, a lifeline in the darkness.

Crysta's redemption began with a phone call from WBRZ's Chris Nakamoto in May 2022, a moment that shattered her silence and unleashed a media storm. Her raw confession on air—"He raped me at sixteen, now I pay him for my daughter"—ignited global outrage, unsealing Cashe's records and forcing a partial reversal: Jada was placed with a third party, a fragile victory that left Crysta both relieved and enraged. The world's roar—tweets of "Justice for Crysta," advocates like Stacie Triche from SAVLIV35—became her armor, a reminder that she was not alone. By 2023, Jada was emancipated and returned to Crysta, their bond mending through tentative smiles and shared silences on their porch, a slow, fierce healing that mirrored Crysta's own journey in therapy, where she unraveled the PTSD and lies that had rewired her soul.

Today, Crysta Byrd is a warrior reborn, her blonde hair a banner, her green eyes a lighthouse for survivors. At thirty-six, she speaks at shelters and book signings, her voice a thunderclap demanding reform, envisioning "Jada's Law" to protect others from the horrors she endured. Her writing—*The Bitter and The Bold* and the forthcoming *Failed and Derailed*—is a rebellion, a testament to her refusal to be defined by Don's violence or the system's betrayal. She is a mother, fiercely protective of Jada, now nineteen, whose art and resilience mirror her own. She is a friend, trusting again in the hazel-eyed confidante who held her through the darkest nights. And she is a survivor, her scars a map of battles won, her heart a furnace of love and defiance.

Crysta's life is no fairy tale—it is a saga of bitter losses and bold triumphs, a cliffhanger where the fight continues. Don's appeals loom, the DA's review of her rape case drags on, but she stands undaunted, her pen a sword, her story a war cry. For Jada, for survivors, for the sixteen-year-old girl who swore no one would know, Crysta Byrd rises, a phoenix from the ashes, her legacy a promise that the bold will always outshine the bitter, that love and truth will prevail, no matter the cost. She is not just an author—she is a revolution, and her story is only beginning.

DEDICATION

March 2025, Ponchatoula, Louisiana. The night is thick, heavy with the weight of a thousand unspoken truths. My desk is a battlefield, littered with crumpled tissues, half-drunk coffee gone cold, and a flickering lamp that's seen me through too many sleepless hours. My blonde hair falls in tangled strands, catching the dim glow, and my green eyes—God, they're wet again, burning with tears that won't stop, tears that carry the ache of twenty years. My pen trembles in my hand, ink smudging as I write this, my heart screaming to the heavens. This is for you—every soul who kept me alive, who gave me a reason to fight when the darkness tried to swallow me whole. This is my dedication, my vow, my raw and bleeding altar to those who held me up when I was too broken to stand.

To Jada, my daughter, my heartbeat, my everything. You're eighteen now, your blonde curls catching the Louisiana sun, your blue-green eyes holding a fire I pray I helped kindle. From the moment you were born in August 2006, a tiny miracle in a world that had already tried to crush me, you were my why. At sixteen, I carried you in secret, my body a shield against the shame of that night in 2005. At twenty-two, I fought for you in courtrooms that reeked of betrayal, my voice shaking as I faced Don's smirk, knowing he'd stolen half of you. At thirty-two, I lost you to his lies, my screams echoing in an empty house as you were torn away. But you, Jada—you fought too. At fifteen, you whispered truths about his abuse, your courage a blade against his control. At seventeen, you emancipated yourself, choosing me, choosing us, and now, at nineteen, you're sketching your future, free of his shadow. Every tear I've shed, every night I've raged, every time I've clawed my way back from despair—it's been for you. You are my light, my bold, my reason to keep breathing. This book is yours, Jada, a testament to the love that no court, no lie, no monster could break.

To my best friend, my anchor, my warrior with sandy hair and hazel eyes that never flinched from my pain. You were there when I collapsed, when the weight of Don's threats and the system's betrayal crushed me. You held me as I sobbed, my blonde hair a mess, my green eyes hollow, whispering, "You're not alone, Crysta." You were there for Jada when I couldn't be, your calm resolve, a sanctuary when my mind was a warzone. You stood beside me in court, your presence a shield against the sharks circling my life. Your laughter, your fierce hugs, your refusal to let me give up—they stitched me back together when I was unraveling. This is for you, for the nights you stayed up with me, for the days you fought for me when I had nothing left. You are my family, my bold, my proof that love can survive the bitterest storms.

To my aunt, who always tried to be there for me from afar. You may not have lived locally, but when I was out of money and at my wits end, you made sure I had the means to keep fighting. Thank you for every court date you drove in to make and every dime you sent to make sure Jada was safe.

To the survivors, my tribe, my scarred and fierce kin. You're out there, reading this, your hands trembling as mine do now. I see you—eighteen, thirty, forty-five, men and women, any gender, your hearts carrying wounds no one else can fathom. Your letters, your stories, your quiet hugs at speaking events—they've meant the world to me. You've told me of your own nights like 2005, your own battles in courtrooms or silence, your own Jadas you fight for. You've shown me that we're not alone, that our scars are not our shame but our strength. This book is for you, a cry to rise, to speak, to be bold together. We've been through the fire, but we're still here, our voices a chorus that will shake the heavens. I'm with you, always, in every word I write, in every tear I shed, in every step we take toward the light.

The lamp flickers, threatening to die, but I keep writing, my pen a blade carving truth into the dark. This is my dedication, my soul laid bare, a promise to Jada, to my friend, to you, survivors, that I will never stop fighting. The bitter has shaped me, but the bold defines me. This is for us—our scars, our rage, our love, our unbreakable will to rise. My tears fall, the night stretches on, but I am not afraid. This is our story, and it's only just begun. Let's turn the page.

PREFACE

I sit here, pen trembling in my hand, the weight of this truth pressing down on me like a thousand stones piled atop my chest. The truth--was it consensual? That's what people ask me now. That's what people want to know, but I'm not going to answer that question for you. The truth—it's not some noble, shining thing I've chosen to carry. No, it's a parasite, a leech that's burrowed into my soul, feeding on my silence, growing fat on my fear. For years, I've let it fester there, locked away in the dark corners of my mind, a prisoner I refused to acknowledge. I never wanted to write this story. I never wanted to drag these memories kicking and screaming into the light, to relive the moments that broke me, reshaped me, and left me gasping for air in a life I barely recognize. But here I am, because silence is no longer an option—it's a slow, suffocating death, and I refuse to let it claim me any longer.

Why now? Oh, how I've wrestled with that question, night after night, staring at the ceiling as the shadows danced like ghosts of my past. I used to think that if I kept my head down, if I played by the rules, if I built a life so fragile yet so carefully guarded that not even a whisper of wind could topple it, I'd be safe. Safe—what a cruel illusion that word is. Trauma doesn't vanish because you turn your back on it; it lingers, a shadow that stretches longer with every step you take. I've spent years pretending it wasn't there, pasting smiles on my face, nodding through conversations, burying the screams that clawed at my throat. But I'm tired—so damn tired—of pretending. I want to be free. I want to rip this parasite from my chest and let it bleed out on these pages. And more than that, I want you—yes, you, reading this—to feel that freedom too. If you've carried a truth too heavy to speak, I'm giving you permission now: let it out. Step into the light. There's no shame here, only survival.

But let me warn you—this isn't some tidy tale of triumph, wrapped up with a pretty bow and a soundtrack of hope. This is messy, jagged, raw. It's rage that burns so hot it blisters my skin, grief that drowns me in waves I can't outrun, and loss that carves hollows in my bones. This is the story of a girl who was shattered before she even had a chance to live, a girl who clawed her way through the wreckage and came out the other side—not whole, not healed, but alive. If you've walked a path like mine, I hope these words wrap around you like a lifeline, whispering that you're not alone. And if you haven't, I beg you to listen, to feel, to understand the weight of what it means to survive when the world tries to bury you alive.

The truth--- I believe it lies in the little details.

So, again, was it consensual? Yes, no, maybe? I think I'll let you decide for yourself. After reading this, if you decide that it was, then I'm fine with you making that judgement call because for me, that question doesn't even matter. For me, all that matters is that my child is safe, and I did what I had to do to make that happen. The end. Period.

CHAPTER 1
A NIGHT IN 2005

The air that night was a living, breathing thing, a thick, damp beast that wrapped its suffocating arms around Ponchatoula, Louisiana, on December 15, 2005, mocking any dream I'd ever had of a crisp, storybook Christmas. I was sixteen years old, Crysta Byrd, standing on the cracked pavement of my sleepy little town, my frizzy blonde curls plastered to my neck in the muggy haze, my green eyes flickering with a restless spark I couldn't yet name—a fire caught somewhere between innocence and a darkness I didn't see coming. There was no snow here, no delicate flakes drifting down to soften the edges of the world, just a sticky warmth that pressed against my skin like a secret I couldn't shake, a confession I didn't know I'd soon be forced to hear, a weight that clung to me like a shadow I couldn't outrun. I trailed behind Candace Bennett and Camille "Cami" McMorris, my wild-hearted sisters in chaos, my anchors in a storm of reckless abandon I didn't even know I was chasing, as we made our way toward an Irish pub that glowed like a grimy lantern in the heart of our small, suffocating world. Caitlin Lovings, the fourth piece of our jagged little crew, was home sick that night, her absence a quiet ache we brushed aside in our fevered hunger for something—anything—to make us feel alive, to break the monotony of this town that felt like it was closing in on me every single day. My heart pounded in my chest, a wild, untamed drumbeat of freedom and danger, and for that fleeting moment, I felt untouchable, invincible, a girl teetering on the edge of everything, my sneakers scuffing the pavement as if I could kick away the weight of my small-town life. God, how wrong I was—how blind, how naive, how utterly unprepared for the abyss that was waiting to swallow me whole.

It all started hours earlier, in the sacred, cluttered haven of Candace's bedroom, a space that thrummed with the restless pulse of our teenage souls, a cocoon where we could be ourselves away from the prying eyes of Ponchatoula. The three of us—Candace, Cami, and me—sprawled across her unmade bed like leaves scattered by a careless wind, our legs tangled in the kind of easy closeness that only comes from being young and trusting, from not yet knowing how fragile that trust could be. That room was our rebellion made real: posters of bands with screaming guitars plastered the walls, their edges curling in the relentless humidity, a chipped vanity mirror catching our flushed, laughing faces, and a tiny TV flickering in the corner, its fake fireplace glowing with cheap, orange flames—a Louisiana Christmas mirage that mocked the damp heat seeping through the cracked window, a heat that never let up, not even in December. Down here in the swamp-soaked belly of the South, we didn't get snow or the comforting snap of real logs burning in a hearth; we got a humidity that sank into your bones, a weight that clung like a second skin, a sorrow you couldn't outrun no matter how fast you moved. That night, it slithered into the room, thick and heavy, mingling with the sweet, desperate scent of Candace's vanilla candle, its wax melting slow and mournful in its little glass jar, pooling like tears I didn't know I'd soon be shedding, tears that would mark the end of the girl I was and the beginning of something broken.

We were a mess of giggles and chaos in that moment, our voices tumbling over each other in a symphony of restless joy, bubbling up from somewhere deep and untamed inside us, a spring breaking through dry earth after years of drought. I can still feel the rough denim of Candace's jeans brushing against my bare legs as we swapped clothes, her oversized hoodie swallowing me up, soft and worn from a hundred nights just like this, nights where we'd laugh until our sides hurt and dream of a world beyond these streets. The cool slick of her cherry lip gloss smeared across my fingers as I swiped it on, laughing at my reflection in that chipped mirror, my wild curls bouncing as I tossed my head back with a confidence I didn't fully own, a lightness I borrowed from the air around me, from the energy of the girls beside me. Cami sat cross-legged next to me, her hazel eyes wide and shimmering with a nervous kind of wonder, her fingers twisting the hem of her faded T-shirt as she watched us with a smile that trembled on the edge of fear, like she could sense something I couldn't, something lurking just beyond the horizon of our laughter. We were alive—electric—in a way only sixteen can be, teetering on the brink of something vast and dangerous, our hearts racing with a hunger we couldn't name but felt in every trembling inch of our bodies, a hunger that gnawed at me, that whispered of escape, of freedom, of a life bigger than the one I'd been handed. Ponchatoula's sleepy streets were a cage, a prison I'd been born into, and in that room, we were free, if only for a stolen breath, a fleeting moment before the world crashed down.

Candace was the wildfire of us three, a spark that could set the whole world ablaze with a single glance, a force of nature I couldn't help but follow. Her wit cut like a knife, sharp and bright, her tongue even sharper, slicing through the ordinary like it was nothing more than tissue paper, leaving me in awe of her every time she spoke. She leaned back on her elbows, dark hair spilling over her shoulders like ink bleeding across a page, her smirk a dare that made my chest tighten, a challenge I couldn't resist. "Ben's in town," she said, her voice low and thick with thrill, a secret she dangled like a weapon, knowing it would pull us all in. Her older brother, Ben—the rugged border patrol guy who chased shadows near the Canadian line—was a myth we whispered about, a storm who blew into Ponchatoula and vanished just as fast, leaving us breathless in his wake, a figure larger than life in our small, suffocating world. "He called me," she went on, her eyes gleaming with a fire that sent a rush of awe and fear and reckless joy flooding through me, a tidal wave that drowned out every doubt I might've had. "Wants to meet at the pub." The words hung there, curling around us like smoke, pulling us into a night that felt bigger than our small lives, a night that promised something wild, something forbidden, something I couldn't yet fathom. "Just tell Mom we're seeing Ben at a restaurant," she added, tugging on a pair of ripped jeans with a casual defiance that made my heart ache with admiration, her fingers quick and sure as she zipped them up, her movements a dance I'd watched a hundred times but never tired of. It wasn't a lie—not really, not in the way that mattered. The pub served greasy burgers and fries by day, a thin thread of truth we could stitch into our fragile alibi, and oh, the thrill of it—the way it pulsed through me like a second heartbeat, wild and intoxicating, a taste of rebellion that coated my tongue and made my blood sing.

Cami's breath hitched, a soft sound that broke the spell for a second, a reminder of the fragility beneath our facade. She chewed her bottom lip, her eyes darting to the bedroom door like Candace's mom might storm in at any moment, her disapproval a detour to shatter our rebellion, a force we all feared but never spoke of. "What if we get busted?" she whispered, her voice shaking with a thousand what-ifs, her hands twisting that faded shirt until it stretched thin, her fingers betraying the nerves she tried to hide. My heart lurched for her, for the fear I knew so well but buried deep beneath my cocky grin, a mask I wore to keep the shadows at bay, to convince myself I was stronger than I felt. "We won't," I shot back, bold and brash, sixteen and invincible, tossing my hair like it could banish every doubt, every danger lurking in the corners of our plan, like I could will it away with sheer force of will. "Ben's got us covered." I believed it—God help me, I believed it with every tear I'd ever swallowed, every dream I'd tucked away in the quiet of my small-town nights, every prayer I'd whispered into the humid dark when no one else was listening. Ben was our shield, our savior, the older brother none of us deserved but all of us needed, a towering figure who could bend the world to his will—or so I thought, so I hoped, so I clung to with every ounce of my trembling, youthful heart. I'd have followed Candace into the jaws of hell itself if she'd asked, my loyalty a flame that burned bright and blind, a fire that would soon consume me, a blaze I didn't see coming until it was too late.

We weren't the glossy cheerleaders with their practiced smiles and perfect ponytails, nor the burnouts with their ash-stained fingers and hollow, haunted eyes—we were something else entirely, something raw and undefined, caught in the tender, treacherous space between innocence and ruin, a place I didn't even know existed until that night carved it into me. The good "bad" girls, we called ourselves in hushed, reverent tones, rule-benders with hearts too big for the cages we'd been born into, souls too wild for the narrow streets of Ponchatoula, too restless to stay still. We chased freedom like it was a firefly flickering just beyond our grasp, its light a fleeting promise in the humid dark, a prize I could almost taste, almost touch, a glittering, tear-soaked dream dangling before us, teasing us with its closeness. I can still hear the creak of Cami's beat-up sedan as we piled in, the engine coughing and sputtering to life like it, too, was reluctant to let us go, its groan a warning we didn't heed, a plea we ignored in our rush to break free. We peeled out into the night with a screech of tires that felt like a battle cry, a declaration of our defiance, our hunger, our desperate need to be more than what this town had made us, more than the girls we'd been told we had to be. The radio crackled to life, a pop song bursting through the static, its sugary beat thrumming through me, a melody that sank into my bones, a tune I'd hum for days—weeks—years—until it became a scar, a haunting echo burned into the marrow of my memory, a reminder of the night I lost myself.

My skin prickled with sweat as we drove, the damp heat pressing against me like a hand I couldn't shake, a relentless presence that seeped into my pores and made my clothes cling to my body, a weight I couldn't escape. My heart pounded a frantic drumbeat, a wild rhythm of anticipation and terror and untamed, tearful hope, each thump a reminder that I was alive, that I was here, that I was hurtling toward something I couldn't yet see, something I wasn't ready for. Ponchatoula blurred past us in a watercolor smear of sleepy streets—the gas station where we'd sneak Slurpee's on sticky summer afternoons, its neon sign buzzing faintly in the dark; the church where my grandma dragged me every Sunday, her hymns a chain I longed to break, their weight a burden I'd carried since I could walk; the life I'd known 'til then fading in the rearview like a ghost I wasn't ready to mourn, its outlines soft and hazy in the humid night, a past I thought I could leave behind with a single reckless night. I was invincible that night—or so I thought, my laughter spilling out of me like a river breaking its banks, a shield against the shadows I couldn't see creeping closer, darker, hungrier than I'd ever imagined, shadows that would soon have names, faces, hands I'd never forget. We were three girls on the edge of everything, teetering between the safety of our yesterdays and the thrilling, tearful unknown of our tomorrows, and I didn't know—God, I didn't know—that the night would mark me, scar me, shape me in ways I'd spend a lifetime unravelling, a wound I'd carry like a secret tattooed beneath my skin, a pain I'd bury deep until it clawed its way back out.

Candace's room was where it started, a cocoon of chaos and dreams, a place where I could still feel the girl I'd been—wild, hopeful, unbroken—but the road, the road was where it truly began, where the weight of our choices settled into my chest like a stone I'd carry forever, a burden I didn't yet feel but would soon come to know intimately, a heaviness that would define me. I can still smell the vanilla of that candle, its sweetness a faint memory against the bitterness to come; I can still hear Cami's shaky breath, a prelude to the fear that would soon consume us all; I can still feel the pulse of that pop song thrumming through me, a heartbeat of joy as we hurtled into the dark, the wind whipping through the cracked windows like a lover's desperate touch, tugging at my curls, pulling me forward into the unknown. Candace's smirk lit the way, a beacon in the night, and in that moment, with the tires screaming against the pavement and my laughter echoing in my ears, I thought we'd catch it—freedom, or maybe just the echo of who we wanted to be, who we could've been if the world had been kinder. I thought we'd win. I thought we'd soar.

But the shadows were waiting, patient and unyielding, their jaws poised to snap shut, and oh, how they'd teach me what it meant to run, what it meant to fall, what it meant to break, lessons I'd learn in the hardest, cruellest way imaginable.

The Irish pub rose up before us like a specter in the night, its dim lights bleeding into a haze of cigarette smoke that hung thick and heavy in the air, a shroud that swallowed us whole as we stepped inside, a fog that blurred the edges of everything I thought I knew. The sour tang of stale beer assaulted my senses, soaking into the walls, the floor, the very fabric of the place, mingling with the faint, greasy scent of fries long gone cold, a smell that stuck to me like a second skin. The jukebox whined in the corner, a twangy country tune scratching at my nerves, its mournful notes a stark contrast to the wild pulse of my heart, a sound that felt out of place in the chaos I was diving into. Ben was there, thirty and towering, his broad shoulders filling the space like he owned it, his laugh too loud as it cut through the din, a booming sound that made Candace light up as he clapped her on the back, a brotherly gesture that made me ache for something I didn't have. Beside him stood Jason Babine, his buddy from way back—dark hair falling into dark eyes that pierced the smoky gloom, a smirk curling his lips that sent a shiver racing down my spine, a tremor I couldn't place but felt deep in my gut, a warning I didn't know how to heed. They were men, real men, with jobs and scars and lives we couldn't fathom, a world apart from the girls we were, and yet there we stood, drawn into their orbit like moths to a flame we didn't yet know would burn us, a flame I didn't see until it was too late.

Candace vouched for the bartender, a grizzled man with a lazy nod who didn't blink as we slid into the booth, no IDs, just blind teenage bravado and a hunger for the forbidden, a hunger that gnawed at me, that pushed me forward even as my instincts whispered to turn back. My sneakers stuck to the floor with every step, peeling up with a faint, wet sound that made my stomach twist, but I felt the thrill of it—the reckless, intoxicating taste of something wild on my tongue as someone slid me a beer I didn't ask for, its amber surface catching the dim light like liquid gold, a temptation I couldn't resist. Cami sipped hers slow, her movements tentative, her eyes darting around the room as if she could sense the danger I couldn't yet see, a danger I was too caught up in the moment to notice. Candace chattered on about her boyfriend Ashton, her cheeks flushing a soft pink when Cami teased her about "doing it," her laughter bright and carefree in a way that made my heart jump with a smile of my own. I just soaked it in, sixteen and riding the high, my green eyes darting around the pub like I owned the place, my curls bouncing with every tilt of my head, my confidence a fragile shield against the storm I didn't know was brewing, a storm that would break me before the night was through.

The second Jason's eyes hooked into mine, it hit me like a bolt of thunder ripping through the smoky haze—a stare so sharp, so fierce, it sliced through the noise and pinned me where I sat, my breath catching in my throat, a jolt that stopped me cold. My heart tripped over itself, a scared little bird fluttering wild in my chest, while he stared me down, sizing me up with a look that peeled me open, layer by layer, in ways I didn't even know to fear yet, ways I wouldn't understand until it was too late. He was smooth—Lord help me, he was too smooth—slipping closer with that crooked grin splitting his face, all sharp edges and charm with something that felt ugly, something rotten, hiding just beneath the surface, a darkness I couldn't see but felt in the pit of my stomach. His voice came low and thick, dripping like molasses over broken glass, as he dangled the words: "Need a ride? Cami's calling it a night." She'd mumbled it moments before, her voice half-lost in the pub's roar, tired and ready to go, her shoulders slumping as she rubbed her eyes, a signal I should've taken as my cue to leave too. He jumped on it, keys rattling in his hand like a warning bell tolling in the distance, a sound that should've stopped me cold, that should've sent me running back to the safety of my girls. "I'll take care of her," he said, smooth as silk, and my gut twisted up tight—a sour, sick feeling that crawled up from somewhere deep and dark inside me, clawing at my insides, begging me to listen, to run, to scream. I didn't. I couldn't. I was sixteen, dumb as a bag of hammers, and all I managed was a shaky, "Sure," my voice so small it drowned in the noises around us, a whisper swallowed by the night, a decision I'd replay in my head for years, picking at it like a wound that wouldn't heal.

Candace and Cami, my lifelines, my girls, they just waved me off with quick, careless smiles, caught up in their own little world, laughing and drifting away like I wasn't about to step off a cliff into the abyss, like they didn't see the edge I was teetering on. They didn't feel it—the shift in the air, the way it thickened around me, heavy and oppressive, like I couldn't breathe right, like the world was closing in. They didn't hear the scream I kept locked up tight in my throat, clawing to get out, a cry I didn't dare let loose—not then, not yet, not when I still thought I could handle it. I was too young, too soft, too full of this dumb, trembling hope that people weren't as cruel as they could be, that the world wasn't as dark as it would soon prove itself to be, a hope that blinded me to the truth staring me in the face. So, I went with him, my sneakers dragging on the busted-up pavement outside, my breath catching in jagged little gasps as the night closed in around us like a fist, tight and unyielding, a grip I couldn't escape. The pub's wild pulse faded behind me, its lights dimming in the distance, and then it was just me and him—Jason, with his keys and his straight face and this heavy, awful thing I didn't even know I'd agreed to, a weight that settled over me like a shroud I couldn't shake, a nightmare I was walking into with my eyes wide open.

I couldn't stop thinking about it later—Lord, I chewed on it till it tore me up inside, a wound I'd pick at for years, bleeding fresh every time I closed my eyes, every time I let my mind wander back to that moment. That jingle of his keys, sharp and cold, rang in my ears like a song I'd never unhear, a haunting melody that followed me into the dark, a sound that still echoes in my nightmares. Candace and Cami didn't catch it, didn't feel that shift in the air, didn't see the way his eyes darkened, the way his face twisted, into something hungrier, something that should've sent me running. They didn't hear the scream I swallowed, the panic I buried beneath my trembling voice, the fear I didn't have a name for yet, a fear that was growing, clawing, taking root. I was too young, too blind, too desperate to prove I could handle this, and so I followed him out, a stupid kid too naive to see the jaws snapping shut around her, too trusting to recognize the trap until it was sprung, too lost to save herself.

His truck was a monster lurking in the shadows, a big, dark thing that waited for us in the parking lot, its hulking frame swallowing me whole as I climbed inside, a beast that felt alive, that felt like it knew what was coming. The leather seats were cold against my legs, sticking to my jeans through the fabric, sending a shiver racing up my spine that wouldn't quit, even with the thick, wet heat of Louisiana pressing in from outside, a heat that made everything feel heavier, slower, more inescapable. The air inside stank—something sour and wrong, maybe sweat, maybe spilled beer, maybe something nastier, something I didn't have a name for yet but felt deep in my bones, a stench that clung to me like a second skin, a smell I'd never forget. My hands shook as I fumbled with the seatbelt, my fingers clumsy and slick with sweat, the click of the buckle a faint noise in the chaos of my racing thoughts, a sound that grounded me for a split second before the panic crept back in. Outside, Ponchatoula's streets whipped by in a blur of shadows and quiet, the damp air sneaking in through the cracked window in the early am hours, heavy with the scent of moss and decay, a reminder of where I was, of how far I'd strayed from the safety I'd known. At sixteen, I didn't have much experience with alcohol—just a sip here and there at a party or two—so when that beer hit me, it hit hard, and fast. The world started spinning, a dizzy whirl that made my stomach churn, and I couldn't stop talking—Lord, I couldn't stop—words tumbling out of me in a frantic rush, spilling over each other like water from a broken dam, a flood I couldn't control. School, the bands I loved, stupid little stories from my sixteen years—anything, everything, a desperate stream of noise to push back the dark feeling eating me alive, the dread that coiled tighter with every passing second, the fear that was growing louder, sharper, more real.

But then Don spoke up—Don, not Jason, because Jason stayed silent, just like always, his hands locked on the wheel, knuckles white, gripping it hard like he was holding something back—or holding something in, a tension I didn't understand but felt all the same. Don was in the truck too, a friend of Jason and Ben's I barely noticed at the pub and didn't speak to much until now, sitting in the back, his voice cutting through the silence like a warm breeze, soft and easy, a lifeline I didn't know I needed. "Hey, Crysta, you're a riot, you know that?" he said, chuckling lightly, his tone friendly, almost comforting. "Tell me more about that band you like—what's their deal? You sound like you could be their biggest fan." I latched onto it, grateful for the distraction, babbling about music as the world tilted and spun around me, my words slurring but my heart clinging to his kindness. He kept talking, asking questions, laughing at my funny answers, his voice steady and warm, making me feel like maybe this wasn't so bad, like maybe I wasn't so alone in this drunken, spinning mess. "You've got a real way with words, even three sheets to the wind," he teased, and I managed a weak laugh, my head lolling against the seat, the sound of his voice anchoring me just enough to keep the panic at bay.

"Where are we going?" I finally choked out, my voice breaking apart, slurring as I gripped the door handle, the world a blur of dark trees and empty roads outside, a blur that made my stomach roll even harder. Don leaned forward, his tone gentle, almost protective, a softness that wrapped around me like a blanket. "Not home yet, kiddo," he said, and I could hear the smile in his voice, a warmth that felt genuine, that felt safe. "You're pretty drunk, and I don't want you getting in trouble with your mom. She'd have my head if I dropped you off like this—I remember when I was your age, parents don't understand. Let's just chill for a bit, okay? I'm looking out for you, I promise." I believed him—God, I wanted to believe him, needed to believe him. His words felt like he understood me, a promise that someone cared, and in my drunken haze, I thought he was being nice, that he was watching out for me like a big brother might. I nodded, my head heavy, my vision swimming, trusting he meant it, that he was keeping me safe, that this detour was for my own good. “Okay,” I mumbled, my voice thick, my thoughts muddled, and I let myself sink into the seat, clinging to that trust like it was all I had left.

We pulled up to Don and Jason’s house, roommates I deducted then; a sagging, grimy thing at the edge of town, its warped porch groaning beneath his heavy steps as if it, too, wanted to collapse under the weight of what it had seen. Don helped me out of the truck, his hand steady on my arm as I stumbled, the world lurching beneath me, my legs shaky and weak. “Easy there, champ,” he said, his voice soft, almost playful, and I clung to that kindness like it was a rope pulling me out of the spinning dark. But then the beer caught up, and I doubled over, throwing up in the bushes outside, my stomach heaving as the world spun faster, a violent whirl that left me gasping. Don was there in an instant, gently holding my hair back, his hand light on my shoulder, his touch careful, considerate. “You’re okay, Crysta,” he murmured, his tone soothing, steady, like a parent calming a scared kid. “Just let it out. I’ve got you—don’t worry, I’ve seen worse than this.” I wretched again, tears stinging my eyes, my throat burning, but his calm voice made me feel like I could trust him, like he was taking care of me in a way no one else had that night, a kindness I latched onto with everything I had left.

Inside, he guided me to the couch, the room dim and stale, the air thick with rot and despair, a heaviness that pressed down on me even through the haze. He disappeared for a moment, then came back with a glass of water and a napkin, pressing them into my trembling hands. "Here, clean yourself up," he said, his smile small but warm, his eyes crinkling at the corners like he genuinely cared. "Sip that water slow—you'll feel better soon, I promise. You're tougher than you look, you know that?" I wiped my mouth, sipping the water, my head still spinning but my heart settling a little, the coolness of the glass grounding me. I thought he was being nice, a good person helping me through this mess, and I let myself relax, just for a second, believing he meant well, that he was the safety I'd been searching for all night.

But then Jason was there, closer than before, his presence heavy and dark, a shadow that loomed over me as I sat on that creaky couch, the cushions sinking beneath me. He looked at Don and announced, "I'm calling it a night. The keys are on the counter if you need them." I felt relieved that he was going to bed, and I started to relax a little more. Don and I chatted some more about my life as he assured, I'd be okay, then I started to get very sleepy. I assumed it was from the effects of the alcohol, so I laid my head back onto the arm of the couch. After a few moments of lying there with eyes closed heavy with sleep, he leaned in, his breath hot against my face, and when I realized what he was doing, I turned my head, rejecting the kiss, my stomach twisting with unease, a cold jolt cutting through the drunken fog. "No," I mumbled, my voice weak, slurred, but he backed off—for a moment. I felt uncomfortable, a little scared, the room tilting as my haze sharpened into something colder, something sharper, something that made my chest tighten. Then he tried again, and I opened my mouth to say no, clearer this time, my voice trembling but firm, but he smashed his lips against mine, cutting me off, his weight pinning me down. My body went stiff, fear exploding in my chest, sharp and icy, a terror that froze me in place. I couldn't get a word out, couldn't scream—his mouth was a gag, his hands rough as they tugged at my pants, pulling them down despite what I thought was resistance. I shook my head, side to side, begging him to stop without words, my eyes trying to fight open with panic, my heart slamming against my ribs, but he didn't care, didn't see me, didn't acknowledge the no I was screaming inside. His weight held me there, too strong, too heavy, and I couldn't push him off, couldn't fight back. My arms failing me, then froze, my strength draining as he kept going, rough and painful, a violation I couldn't stop, a nightmare I couldn't wake from. After a while, I gave up trying to move—knew I wouldn't win even if I could, knew he was too strong—and just lay there, limp and broken, letting him do what he wanted, my mind screaming while my body went silent, a surrender that carved a hole in me I'd never fill.

When it was over, he pulled away, and suddenly he was tender again, like nothing had happened, like he hadn't just shattered me. He went to the bathroom, and I could hear him moving around in there and I was terrified, but I still couldn't move. When he returned, he grabbed my clothes off the floor, setting them gently on my legs, his touch soft now, a cruel contrast to what I'd just endured, a gentleness that mocked me. He kissed my cheek, light and sweet, and said, "Take your time getting dressed. I'll bring you home when you're ready." His voice was calm, casual, like he hadn't just torn me apart, like this was normal, like I wasn't sitting there trembling, violated, destroyed. I sat there, my hands shaking, my young brain spinning, confused and questioning my own sanity, my own reality. How could he act so normal, so kind, after that? It didn't make sense, and that confusion burrowed deep, twisting my thoughts into knots, making me wonder if I'd imagined it, if I'd somehow misunderstood what had just happened between us.

Don drove me home after, chatting like we were old friends, his voice warm and easy again, a tone that clashed with the cold emptiness inside me. "Well, this was fun," he said, glancing at me with a grin, his eyes bright in the dark. "Hope your mom isn't too mad you're out this late on a school night—? I'd hate to be on her bad side." The truth is my mom wouldn't care. She doesn't care much about what I do or where I go. She's fine as long as I don't bother her too much and check in occasionally. Every couple of days would do. He chuckled, joking, "I could write you an excuse if you've got too bad a hangover tomorrow—I'm tight with your principal, you know. Could say you were helping me with some community project or something. What do you think?" I stared out the window, numb, my eyes still heavy and blinking closed for long moments at a time. His words distant, and his friendliness a mask I couldn't trust anymore, a lie I saw through too late. He was a wolf in sheep's clothing, fooling everyone in this town, even me, until that moment, until the truth broke through the haze and left me raw. I saw it now—he was a monster pretending to be good, a predator who'd played me perfectly, and I'd fallen for it, hook, line, and sinker, a naive kid who'd trusted too much, who'd believed in kindness that wasn't real. Jason wasn't the danger after all, it was him.

I stumbled out a few blocks from Momma's house, the little yellow light a beacon I didn't deserve anymore, a home I felt I'd lost the right to claim. My trembling fingers fumbled for my phone, dialling Cami's number by muscle memory, and when her voice answered, soft and steady, a comfort in the dark, I managed only a whisper— "I need you"—a broken thread of sound she somehow understood, a plea she didn't question, didn't hesitate to answer. Her headlights pierced the darkness soon after, cutting through the night like a blade, and she was there, pulling up beside me, her quiet presence a comfort as I slipped away from that house, a wraith fleeing a tomb I'd never meant to enter, a grave I'd walked into willingly. She didn't press me with questions, didn't demand explanations—just drove, her silence a balm to the chaos shredding my chest, the only thing keeping me from dissolving entirely into the void that yawned inside me, a void that threatened to swallow me whole.

Once I felt sober enough, I crept into Momma's house like a thief, past her sleeping form sprawled on the living room couch, her snores a cruel, oblivious melody underscoring the devastation I carried in my bones, a sound that mocked the ruin I'd become, that highlighted how alone I was in this. The bathroom became my sanctuary—I turned the shower as hot as it would go, the scalding water beating against my skin like a penance, steam rising in thick clouds as I tried to purge him from me, to wash away the rancid stench of him, the bruises of his hands, the violation he'd carved into my flesh, the memory of his weight, his breath, his cruelty. I scrubbed until my skin was raw, blonde hair plastered against my face like wet ropes, green eyes burning with tears I'd exhausted, until I collapsed onto the tile, drenched and shivering, my body a trembling wreck as I vowed to bury this night where no one else could find it, a secret I'd lock away in the vault of my heart, a truth I'd hide behind a brittle smile. Cami became my confidante, the sole keeper of my pain, her gentle voice a fragile thing as dawn crept through the window, its grey light cold and unforgiving, illuminating a girl I no longer recognized, a stranger staring back at me from the mirror, a ghost of who I'd been.

"This is who I am now," I whispered to the empty air, my voice a faint echo of the person I'd been just hours before, a girl who'd laughed in Candace's room, who'd dreamed of freedom, who'd thought she could outrun the shadows. The world beyond kept turning, indifferent to the wreckage I'd become, never trusting anyone ever again, its rhythm unbroken while I lay shattered, a sixteen-year-old casualty of a night I'd never outrun, a night that had taken everything I was and left me hollow. That night, Crysta Byrd didn't just suffer—she died, not in the physical sense, but in every way that mattered, her spirit snuffed out beneath the weight of Don's hands, her laughter silenced, her dreams drowned in the humid dark, her innocence stolen and discarded like it was nothing. What emerged from her ashes was a husk, a walking wound, a bitter seed of pain I'd conceal for years, its roots twisting through the fissures of my broken heart, whispering a haunting refrain that would echo through the rest of my days: this was only the beginning of the unravelling, the first thread pulled in a tapestry of grief I'd spend a lifetime trying to mend, a story I'd carry like a scar no one else could see.

CHAPTER 2
THE SECRET I CARRIED

Here I am, Crysta Byrd, sixteen years old, a trembling wisp of a girl caught in the suffocating grip of a Louisiana winter that won't relent, its damp, oppressive breath seeping through the cracked window of my bathroom on this fateful January day in 2006. The air hangs heavy, a shroud of humidity that clings to my skin like a second sorrow, and my bare feet press against the chipped beige tiles—cold, unforgiving, each jagged edge a tiny blade slicing into my soles as if the earth itself wants to punish me for what's happened. My hands, oh, my poor, fragile hands—still the hands of a child, not yet hardened by the cruelties of the world—shake uncontrollably as they grip that flimsy plastic stick, that cheap, cruel harbinger of doom we call a pregnancy test. It's so light, so insignificant in its design, yet it weighs more than my soul can bear, heavier than the dreams I've nursed in the quiet corners of my heart, heavier than the entire sky pressing down on this ramshackle house in Ponchatoula.

And then I see them—two pink lines, stark and merciless, slashing across the little window like a judge's gavel crashing down on my life. They burn into my retinas, an indelible brand of shame and terror, and in that moment, the world I've built for myself—oh, how delicately I'd woven it!—shatters like glass under a hammer. Gone are the visions of prom night, the sequined dress I'd sketched in my spiral notebook, the laughter of friends as we twirled beneath cheap gymnasium lights. Gone are the college brochures I'd hidden under my mattress that would take me away from here, their glossy pages promising a future where I'd be someone, something more than a girl from a nowhere town. Gone is the lightness of being sixteen, the innocence of stolen kisses and whispered secrets, replaced by a weight so crushing I can barely breathe. My chest heaves, my lungs clawing for air, but all I can feel is the drowning—the suffocating, relentless tide of fear pulling me under.

My blonde hair, wild and untamed, a frizzy halo in this godforsaken humidity, clings to my face, matted with the saltwater rivers streaming from my eyes. Those eyes—green, once sparkling with a fire my grandma called "trouble in the makin'"—are now wide, glassy pools of panic, staring into a void I can't escape. I catch my reflection in the streaked mirror above the sink, and I don't recognize the girl looking back—cheeks flushed and blotchy, lips quivering, a stranger wearing my skin. Above me, the bathroom's single bulb flickers, a dying pulse casting jagged shadows across the peeling paint, turning the walls into a prison of dancing ghosts. Beyond the locked door, my bedroom waits—a sanctuary turned traitor—where posters of boy bands plaster the walls, their glossy perfection a cruel mockery of the chaos I'm drowning in. Nick Carter's blue-eyed smirk, Justin Timberlake's cocksure grin—they leer down at me from their paper thrones, untouched by the filth and despair that have invaded my life, their smiles a taunt I can't unsee.

The sobs come then, unbidden, unstoppable—a torrent of sound that tears from my throat, raw and jagged, like the cries of some wounded, caged beast. They ricochet off the tiles, the walls, the ceiling, filling the tiny space with the echoes of my breaking. I am broken. I am pregnant. I am alone. The words hammer inside my skull, a litany of horror I can't outrun, a secret so monstrous it feels like it's eating me alive from the inside out. My body—my own body—has betrayed me, turned against me, harboring this thing, this life I didn't ask for, forced upon me in a moment of weakness I can't even speak aloud. My hands, still clutching that damned test, fling it away in a surge of desperation, hurling it into the rusted trash can where it lands with a pathetic thud. I grab fistfuls of crumpled tissues—stained with mascara, snot, the debris of my unravelling—and bury it deep, as if shoving it out of sight could erase the truth gnawing at my guts, as if I could smother the reality that's already begun to reshape me, cell by cell, into someone I never wanted to be.

But it's there, undeniable, a parasite of fate I can't expel, and as I sink to the floor, my knees buckling under the weight of it all, I wrap my arms around myself—small, frail, a girl trying to hold together a life that's already slipping through her fingers. The bathroom, this grimy little box, is my fortress now, my battlefield, my confessional, and I am its lone occupant, a sixteen-year-old prisoner of a life I didn't want. Outside, the world spins on, oblivious—cars rumble down the street, my mama's voice hums faintly from the kitchen, the neighbor's dog barks at nothing—but in here, time has stopped, frozen in the moment those two pink lines rewrote my story. I am Crysta Byrd, and this is where my childhood ends, on a cold tile floor, with a secret too colossal to bear, and a heart too broken to fight.

The stage of my existence stretches before me, rickety and worn, a sixteen-year-old girl drowning in the masquerade that school has twisted into—a cruel, unrelenting theater where I'm forced to wear the mask of Crysta, the version of myself I can barely recognize, the one who once laughed without the sound catching in her throat, whose heart didn't pound with dread at every fleeting shadow. The bell shrieks, sharp and merciless, and I trudge into algebra class, my sneakers scuffing the linoleum as though dragging the weight of my shattered spirit. I collapse into my seat, the desk icy against my shaking hands, clutching my pencil like it's the only tether keeping me from drifting away, scratching out equations that blur before my eyes—x's and y's that might as well be ancient runes for all the meaning they hold. My mind is a swamp, dense and choking, and the teacher's voice is a faint murmur beneath the thunder of my own fear.

My friends circle around me like fading constellations, their light dim and unreachable. Candace, with her sly giggles slicing the air, leans across the aisle, whispering about some boy's lopsided grin, her brown hair bouncing with every snicker. Cami, dear Cami, with her quiet loyalty woven into the way she glances my way, her hazel eyes gentle and probing, as if she senses the tempest raging beneath my surface but can't find the words to breach it. They prattle on about weekend dreams—movies, milkshakes, stolen kisses behind the bleachers—and I nod, forcing my lips into a hollow curve, a frail imitation of the Crysta they still see. Their voices hum, a distant buzz I can't connect to, because every part of me is screaming, clawing, pleading to be heard, yet I'm silent, locked in this performance where I'm both the player and the captive.

My body has turned Judas, betraying me at every cruel twist. Mornings are a gauntlet: nausea coils my stomach into knots so fiercely I crumple over the toilet, heaving until my throat is raw and my eyes brim with tears I can't justify to Momma. Exhaustion seeps into my bones like molten lead, heavy and unyielding, slowing my steps through these flickering hallways until I'm wading through a mire. And then there's the swell—the subtle, undeniable rounding beneath my ribs, a secret I've smothered beneath oversized sweatshirts swiped from Sasha's closet, my older sister, steeped in the faint scent of her perfume and stale smoke. I pull the fabric taut, a desperate armor against the reality pressing in, but it's there, growing, nudging against my refusal with every breath I take.

Mirrors have become my enemy, and I dodge them like they're blades poised to slice away the last shred of who I was. When I catch a glimpse by mistake—in the smudged glass of the bathroom door, in the glint of a locker—I recoil, because the girl glaring back isn't me. Her green eyes, once alive with mischief, are stormy now, swirling with a dread that gnaws at my core. Her face is pale and drawn, cheekbones stark against skin that's lost its warmth, just an admirer of the Crysta who giggled at the pub mere weeks ago, confident and teasing the world like it couldn't break her. Now, she's a stranger, a hollowed-out figure burdened with too much, and I despise her—despise her trembling, despise the way she murmurs my secret in every faltering breath.

Nights, though—nights are the deepest abyss, a plunge into a torment I can't escape. I lie awake in my narrow bed, the springs groaning beneath me, the ceiling whirling above like a kaleidoscope of shadows that twist and coil until they form his shape—Don's shape. His face etches itself into the dark, a cruel portrait: his icy eyes gleaming with something wild, his smirk a jagged edge, his hands—those hands—that pinned me down, that stole my breath and my light. I feel them still, ghostly weights pressing my wrists, and my pulse hammers, a frantic rhythm against my ribs. My palms slide to my stomach, hesitant, horrified, tracing the faint curve beneath my nightshirt, and panic rises like a flood—crashing, strangling, unmerciful. Will this baby wear his face? Will its eyes echo his, cold and piercing like the ones in my dreams? Will its tiny form carry his mark, his malice carved into its essence, a living shadow of the night I can't erase?

My breath stutters, shallow gasps that scrape my throat raw, and my chest constricts until I'm certain it'll collapse, crushing me under the enormity of this secret I can't outrun. Sixteen—just sixteen—and I'm sinking, submerged in a tide of my own creation, a captive in this fragile, swelling skin that no longer feels like home. The darkness closes in, thick and smothering, and I can't speak it—not to Candace, not to Cami, not even to the shadows that hold me through these endless hours. It's mine alone, this weight, this fear, this life stirring within me, and I'm lost in it, a girl unanchored, adrift in a masquerade where the mask is fraying, and the truth is tearing its way out.

It was a bitter, bone-chilling evening in late February when the world as I knew it began to unravel, thread by fragile thread, in the dim glow of Momma's kitchen. The air was thick. She was heating up a frozen dinner for us in the microwave, we were barely getting by, and Mom didn't cook. She was raising me and my older sister solo in a house that creaked with every gust of wind. I sat there at our chipped wooden table, my fork nudging peas in restless circles, their vibrant green mocking the grey storm brewing inside me. My appetite had vanished weeks ago, replaced by a gnawing dread that clung to my ribs like damp moss. I should have been showing more than I was, and I knew it wasn't healthy for me, but the stress I was under was completely consuming me and my non-existent appetite. Momma, though—oh, she wasn't one to miss a thing. Those brown eyes of hers, sharp as a hawk's and twice as relentless, sliced through the flimsy curtain of my silence like it was nothing but tissue paper. "Crysta, what's wrong? You haven't been yourself lately." she demanded, her voice a tight wire stretched to snapping, laced with that fierce, unyielding love that had carried us through every bruise life dealt us.

I tried to hold it in—Lord knows I tried—but her gaze was a blacksmith's hammer, and I was glass, brittle and trembling, ready to break. I knew I would have to tell someone eventually, so I decided I would start here. A step I wasn't ready to take, but then again, I don't know if I ever would be ready. The words tore out of me, jagged and raw, like I'd ripped them straight from my chest. "I'm pregnant," I sobbed, my voice cracking into a thousand shards, tears streaming hot and fast down my cheeks, pooling in the hollow of my throat. My hands shook as I clutched the edge of the table, nails digging into the wood, anchoring me to something—anything—solid. But the rest, the deeper wound, the truth clawing at my throat—it wouldn't come. I couldn't say it, couldn't let "rape" spill into the air between us, couldn't paint the shadow of that thirty-year-old monster who'd never admit to what he'd done. Maybe he didn't realize what he'd actually done to me, who'd stolen me in a moment I'd never reclaim. So, I lied. I stammered out a flimsy tale of a boyfriend—some vague, crush I had on a boy closer to my age, a fiction I spun from desperation because the real story was a blade too sharp, too heavy to wield. My green eyes, wide and glassy, darted to hers, pleading for her to believe me, to not dig deeper into the truth I was drowning in.

Her reaction was a wildfire. First, fury—her face flushed crimson, eyes blazing like twin suns, her lips parting as if she might scream or curse the heavens themselves. I braced myself, my heart thudding so loud I swore she could hear it, a frantic drumbeat of shame and fear. But then, oh then, the storm broke, and her features softened, melting into something tender, something fierce in its gentleness. She crossed the kitchen in two strides—her worn socks whispering against the linoleum—and pulled me into her arms. I collapsed against her, my sobs muffled in the soft cotton of her blouse, the faint scent of lavender soap wrapping around me like a cocoon, a shield against the chaos tearing me apart. She held me tight, rocking me like she did when I was five, when nightmares were just shadows under the bed, not living, breathing horrors etched into my skin. She cried, "Oh, Crysta, this isn't ideal," she murmured, her voice a low, steady hum against my ear, "but we'll figure this out."

We sat there for what felt like hours, her arms a fortress, my tears soaking through her shirt, the world shrinking to just us—me and Momma against it all. She didn't press, didn't pry, just let me spill what I could. And then, in a voice soft but firm, she offered me an escape. "You don't have to keep it," she said, her hand stroking my tangled blonde hair, smoothing it down like she could smooth away the pain. "There's a clinic. We can go. You can take your life back. No one has to know." Abortion—an out, a chance to erase him, to scrub his mark from my body, to pretend those trembling, violating hands had never touched me. I nodded, numb, my mind spinning with the possibility, but I would know. Could I live with that knowledge? I pictured it: an exam room, a quick end, a world where I could breathe again, where my reflection didn't scream "victim" back at me in the mirror. It wasn't an option for me though, I already knew I wanted this baby, and I loved it the moment I found out I was pregnant, despite the fear and the unknown.

That same night, I called my Dad. I didn't have the best relationship with him. He was a hot headed, ill-tempered man, and I had a feeling how this would go, but I wanted to rip the band aid off and get it over with. "Dad, I'm pregnant," I blurted out after he asked how I was doing. He was furious as suspected, "What?? Ga Damnit! I really thought you were smarter than this, what were you…" and I hung up the phone before he could finish his sentence with no intention of calling him back anytime soon. Mom says I'm old enough now that I can choose to have him in my life or not, and right now, I'm choosing me. He can judge me and scold me, but I don't have to listen to it.

Then came March, a month that crept in quiet and cold, wrapping the earth in a hesitant thaw. It was one of those endless nights, the kind where the darkness presses against your chest, when everything changed again. I lay in my narrow bed, the quilt pulled tight around me, my hand resting on the faint curve of my belly—stretch-marked already, a map of what was happening inside me. And then I felt her. My baby. I just found out that it was girl a week ago. A flutter, so soft at first, I thought I'd imagined it, like butterfly wings brushing against my soul. My breath caught, my heart stuttered, and I pressed my palm harder, chasing that whisper of life. There it was again—tiny, insistent, alive. My daughter. I decided to name her Jada. Tears welled up, hot and fierce, spilling over as I stared at the ceiling, my blonde hair fanning out across the pillow like a halo, my green eyes shimmering with a flood I couldn't stop. A tidal wave crashed through me—not fear this time, not shame, but love, raw and overwhelming, stitching itself into every broken piece of me.

"I already love you," I whispered, my voice a trembling thread in the stillness, barely audible over the thud of my own pulse. "I'll keep you safe, baby girl." The words were a vow, a promise, a defiance I hadn't known I could muster. She was mine—not his, never his. He didn't get to claim her, didn't get to taint this fragile, fluttering miracle growing inside me. Every kick, every pulse, was a thread pulling me back together, mending the fractures he'd left behind. I chose her—my Jada, my redemption, my reason. And in that moment, with tears soaking my pillow and my hand cradling her presence, I found something I thought he'd stolen forever, myself.

The air in Ponchatoula hangs thick, heavy with the scent of pine and judgment, a small-town crucible where every glance is a spark, every whisper a flame licking at my heels. I'm Crysta Byrd, sixteen years old, and already the gossip mill has me in its jaws, tearing at me with teeth sharpened by boredom and righteousness. I feel their eyes—those small-town eyes—drilling into me as I walk down Main Street, my sneakers scuffing the cracked pavement, my head bowed against the weight of their stares. "Crysta Byrd, pregnant at sixteen," they hiss, their voices weaving through the aisles of the Piggly Wiggly, slithering between the pews at First Baptist, curling around me like smoke I can't escape. They don't say it to my face—not yet—but I hear it in the way Mrs. Henderson's lips tighten when I pass her cart, in the way Pastor Jim's sermons on sin seem to linger a little too long in my direction. Their pity stings worse than their scorn, a bitter, rancid pill I choke down with every forced smile, every "I'm fine, thank you" I toss back on auto pilot to keep them at bay.

I've built a lie to shield me, a fragile fortress of half-truths and shadows. A boyfriend, I tell them—some faceless boy, a fling who "isn't around anymore" in a hurry, a story so vague it's a ghost, so flimsy it trembles under the slightest scrutiny. I spin it out in the diner when the old timers ask, their coffee cups steaming, their curiosity cloaked as concern. "Oh, you know how it is," I say, my voice a tightrope I walk with trembling legs, "young love, gone before it started." It's armor, this lie, a rusted breastplate I strap over my chest to keep the truth from spilling out.

Because the truth—the real truth—is a jagged shard lodged in my throat, a word I can't speak, won't speak: *rape*. I'm hesitant to even call it that at this point, the night still so confusing to me. All I know is that I was too young, too intoxicated to consent. To say the word, would be to crack myself wide open; to let the shame I've buried deep behind my stormy green eyes flood out like a dam breaking, drowning me in its black, churning tide. So, I hold it in, lock it away in a vault where no one can reach, not even me, and I carry on, my smile a mask, my heart a battlefield. Even when my own friend, Caitlin, who wasn't there the night it happened, home sick, taunts me. I forget what the argument was about, but ended in a dig about me being pregnant, "Well, if you could have kept your legs closed." It hurts, I don't want to fight with her, but I snap back with words that are also unkind, and we don't speak for a while. I've developed a sharp tongue as is my defense mechanism to the cruelty of my peers. I also distance myself from my friends and family even more after that day because I realized that that's what they all think of me. A whore, who couldn't keep her legs closed and did this to herself. It's my fault, not his. I'm to blame for my "misfortune".

May comes like a storm rolling in off the Gulf, wild and relentless, and I graduate high school early, a diploma clutched in my sweating hands like a talisman against the chaos inside me. I chose not to walk across that stage. I couldn't imagine me in a loose black gown, the fabric billowing around me, hiding the swell of my belly—her, the life growing beneath my skin, the secret I both cherish and dread. I did attend the graduation but sat in the audience instead. The auditorium echoes with applause, my classmates' cheers a distant roar, a sound I can barely hear over the thunder of my own pulse, the nausea clawing up my throat, the pride warring with the terror in my chest. I did it, I think, my jaw tight, my eyes burning. I did it despite them, despite me, despite everything. But the triumph is fleeting, a candle flickering in a gale, because the road ahead looms vast and uncharted, and I'm just a girl, sixteen and pregnant, with a lie for a compass and a dream for a map.

College crashes into my life like a wave, and I dive in headfirst, Southeastern University my sanctuary, my salvation. Full-time, they say—used text books stacked high on my desk, pages dog-eared and stained with thumb prints and smudges, my nights a blur of lectures and notes and the relentless hum of ambition driving me forward. I'm building something, I tell myself, my pen scratching across paper, my mind racing to outrun the past. Something for her, for us, a future carved out of the rubble of my choices, my secrets. I study until my eyes ache, until the words swim on the page, until the weight of my belly pulls me down like an anchor. But I don't stop—I can't stop—because stopping means sinking, and I've already come too far to let the tide take me now.

By night, I trade my textbooks for a grease-stained apron, the diner my second battlefield, a fluorescent-lit purgatory where the air smells of fried onions and desperation. I balance trays of burgers and coffee, my arms trembling under the weight, my legs screaming with every step, the ache a constant companion as my belly grows, stretching the fabric taut. The clatter of plates is a chaotic symphony, forks scraping, voices rising, the buzz of the overhead lights a relentless drone that burrows into my skull. I'm Crysta Byrd—sixteen, pregnant, a secret festering in my soul—and I move through it all like a ghost, pouring every ounce of myself into this grind, this fight. The regulars watch me, their eyes soft or sharp depending on the day, and I wonder what they see: the scandal, the fallen girl, or something more, something I can't yet name. "You're a hard worker, Crysta," Old Man Tate says one night, his voice gravelly, his tip a crumpled five slipped under his plate. I nod, my throat tight, because hard work is all I have left to give, the only currency I can trade for a chance at redemption.

She's coming soon, I know it—the kicks against my ribs, the flutter of her life inside me, a reminder of everything I've lost and everything I still might gain. I don't know how I'll do it, how I'll be her mother when I'm still a child myself, how I'll keep the lie alive when she looks into my eyes and sees the truth I've hidden. But I will. I'll carry her through the whispers, through the shame, through the nights when the diner's lights flicker and my bones ache and the weight of it all threatens to crush me. I'll build us a life, brick by brick, shift by shift, page by page, until the girl I was—the scandal, the secret—fades into the woman I'll become. Because I'm Crysta Byrd, and this is my story:

raw, ragged, and mine, a tapestry of pain and promise stitched together with every trembling step I take into the unknown.

By summer, sprawled across the weathered boards of our sagging porch in the thick, suffocating embrace of a Louisiana day, the sun a tyrant in the sky, its golden rays clawing at my skin as if to peel back the layers of my weary, fractured self, I feel the weight of time pressing down on me. The cicadas—oh, those relentless, screaming cicadas woven in the trees—shriek their endless anthem, a chorus that reverberates through the humid air and into the marrow of my bones. My college textbooks, dog-eared, highlighted, and heavy with the promise of a future I can scarcely imagine, lie in a haphazard pile beside me, their pages whispering dreams I'm too exhausted to chase. The diner shifts—those grueling, soul-sapping hours—have carved hollows beneath my green eyes, eyes that once sparkled with a girlhood now buried beneath the weight of my reality. I'm huge now, my body no longer my own, a swollen vessel stretched taut with life, etched with silvery stretch marks that map the terrain of my sacrifice. I was barely a hundred pounds when I became pregnant, and now I'm about 20 pounds heavier. Eight of it from the human growing inside of me. And yet, within me, Jada moves—real, alive, a miracle soon to burst forth—and every flutter, every tiny kick, ignites a spark in my chest, a wildfire of hope that roars through the icy tendrils of fear threatening to strangle me.

It's late July now, and I'm eight months pregnant, my belly a heavy, undeniable presence that shifts my center of gravity and my entire world. Candace shows up one humid evening, her brown hair pulled back in a messy bun, her grin as sly as ever, like she's still the girl who whispered about boys in algebra class. "Wanna hang out?" she asks, leaning against the porch railing, her voice light but her eyes sharp, taking me in—me, the swollen shadow of who I used to be. I hesitate, the weight of my body and my secrets anchoring me to the spot, but she doesn't wait for an answer. "Come on, let's cruise," she says, jingling the keys to her sleek little sports car, a cherry-red thing that growls like it's alive. I nod, slow and uncertain, hauling myself up with a grunt, my hands braced against the porch boards.

We hit the road, windows down, the hot wind whipping my blonde hair into a wild tangle as she guns the engine, tearing through Ponchatoula's sleepy streets. The town blurs past—Main Street's cracked pavement, the Piggly Wiggly's faded sign, the oak trees dripping with Spanish moss—and for a fleeting moment, I feel it: normalcy. A breath of the old Crysta, the one who laughed too loud and dreamed too big, slipping through the cracks of the girl I've become. The radio hums some pop song I can't place, and Candace taps the wheel, chattering about nothing—gas station gossip, a new guy in her life that has taken her time so she isn't around as much anymore—her voice a murmur I cling to, letting it pull me out of the swamp in my head. My hands rest on my belly, Jada kicking softly as if she feels it too, this rare, fragile lightness, and I almost smile, almost believe I can hold onto it.

Then she says it, casual as a tossed pebble, rippling through my calm like a stone through still water. "Ben's in town again," she says, her eyes flicking to me, gauging my reaction. "I wanna swing by the bar, see him for a few. You can wait in the car—y'know, because of your condition." My condition? I think the words sting like a slap, a reminder of how she sees me now, fragile, broken, a girl who can't step into a smoky bar like the rest of them. But I swallow it down, nod stiffly. "Yeah, that's probably best," I mutter, my voice flat, my fingers tightening around the seatbelt strap as we pull into the gravel lot outside the Rusty Anchor.

She's gone maybe ten minutes, the car growing stifling even with the windows cracked, the night air seeping in like a warning. I sit there, sweat beading on my forehead, Jada shifting restlessly inside me, and I try to breathe through the rising tide in my chest. I'm growing increasingly uncomfortable in the cramped passenger seat of her tiny sports car, shifting my weight from one side to the other. When Candace slides back into the driver's seat, her cheeks flushed and her eyes bright, she drops the bomb. "Don asked about you," she says, tossing it out like it's nothing, like his name isn't a knife twisting in my gut. I tense, every muscle locking up, my breath catching as she keeps going. "I told him you couldn't come in 'cause you're real pregnant now." She laughs, light and careless, but I'm spiraling, panic clawing up my throat like a living thing. He knows. He knows I'm pregnant. My hands press hard against my belly, protective, possessive, as if I can shield Jada from him through sheer will.

I don't want her to see it—the terror, the storm breaking inside me—so I force my face still, my voice steady. "Nothing," I say when she asks what's wrong, my lips trembling around the lie. "I just didn't think he'd remember me, that's all." It's weak, flimsy, but she lets it drop, cranking the engine as we peel out of the lot. My mind races, a frantic loop: He knows I'm pregnant, but maybe he won't think it's his. Maybe he's heard the boyfriend rumors, the lie I've spun for the town. Maybe I'm still safe. Maybe Jada's still mine alone. But the maybe's choke me, each one a noose tightening around my neck, and I stare out the window, the town blurring past again, normalcy gone, replaced by the cold, creeping dread that's my constant shadow now.

My hands tremble now as they cradle my belly, my breath hitching as I steel myself against the storm I know is coming. My green eyes, fierce and unyielding, blaze with a mother's primal roar, a defiance born of love and terror intertwined. "You're enough," I whisper to her, my voice cracking like brittle glass, the cicadas' relentless drone swallowing the dread that coils tight in my gut, a serpent ready to strike. Am I saying it to her or am I really saying it to myself, always worried I won't be. It scares me more than I'm willing to admit that I will still be this teenage wild child and won't be the mother she deserves. The secret I carry—it's a brick, a crushing, unyielding weight pressing down on my chest, a burden I've borne alone for months, its edges sharp and unforgiving. But Jada—she's my spark, my bold, my reason to drag myself from the abyss each morning. I picture her in the quiet moments, her face forming in my mind's eye—blonde like me, her hair a cascade of sunlight, her eyes, oh God, I pray they're mine, those green mirrors of my soul, not his, never his. And I vow it, fierce and unyielding, my heart hammering against my ribcage: I'll carry this alone, forever if I must, for her. The bitter—it's suffocating, a darkness that claws at my throat, threatening to swallow me whole—but the bold blazes brighter, a flame forged in the crucible of love and grit, and I am Crysta Byrd—sixteen, fractured, a girl splintered by circumstance, but fighting, always fighting, my heart a battlefield where Jada reigns supreme, my tiny, unborn queen.

The days stretch on, long and sticky, each one a gauntlet I must run, a test of my endurance, my resolve, my very will to survive. I'm a ghost in my own life, haunted by that night—the night that stole me from myself—his hands, his breath, the lie I've spun like a fragile web to shield us both from the truth. But Jada, she's my tether, my lifeline, pulling me back from the precipice every time I teeter too close to the edge. I sit in lecture halls, surrounded by peers who laugh and chatter, their lives untouched by the shadows that cling to me. My notebook fills with scribbled notes I barely absorb, my pen moving mechanically as my mind drifts to her kicks, her presence within me a quiet rebellion against the shame that gnaws at my edges like a ravenous beast. At the diner, I pour coffee with a steady voice, smiling at the regulars—those old men with kind, crinkled eyes, the truckers with their tired, road-worn grins—playing the part of the girl they think they know. But when I'm alone, wiping down counters slick with grease, my hands shake, betraying me, the weight of my secret pressing harder with every passing week, every tick of the clock bringing her closer to the world—and him closer to us.

I'm terrified, a bone-deep fear that claws at my insides, that he'll come for her, that he'll see her—her blonde hair, her tiny, perfect face—and claim what's mine, what he has no right to touch, no right to taint. My green eyes catch my reflection in the diner's smudged windows as the sun dips low, painting the sky in hues of fire and blood, and I barely recognize the girl staring back—older, harder, a stranger forged in the crucible of a life I never chose. I was forced to grow up too fast, a mother before I'd even learned to be a woman, my youth stripped away like peeling paint on this rotting porch. But I keep going, stacking textbooks with trembling fingers, counting tips in crumpled bills and loose change, whispering to Jada in the stillness of night when the house is quiet, when Momma sleeps down the hall, oblivious to the war raging in my soul. "We'll make it, you and me," I tell her, my voice a fragile thread, my tears falling silent as they soak into the pillow, each one a testament to the love and the terror that battle within me.

She's coming soon—I can feel it deep in my bones, a certainty that pulses with every kick, every restless tumble she makes inside me. Jada's movements are fierce now, insistent, like she's clawing her way into the world, demanding to be known, and I cling to that promise with every fiber of my trembling soul. My hands, calloused from diner shifts and nights spent scrubbing floors, splay across the curve of my belly, protective, possessive, a shield against the shadows that loom too close. Don's out there—I know he is. His name is a splinter lodged in my heart, his knowledge of her an eventual certainty I can't outrun, a threat that lingers in the corners of my mind like smoke I can't wave away. He doesn't deserve her, doesn't deserve us, but I see his eyes in every stranger's glance, hear his voice in the wind that rattles the screen door. I'm building walls, though—brick by brick, mortar mixed with my own blood and tears—erecting a fortress with every textbook I devour, every tip I pocket, every lie I spin to keep us hidden and safe.

"You're my everything, my sweet girl." I murmur, my voice a cracked whisper as I rock back and forth, blonde hair tumbling into my face, clinging to my damp cheeks like a veil I can't lift. The words are a reassurance, grounding me as the sobs rise, a tide I fight to hold back because if I let them break free, they'll drown me. I'm drowning already, aren't I? The secret I carry is a chain, heavy and cold, wrapping tighter around my neck with every passing day, every sidelong glance from the neighbors, every question I dodge with a smile that feels like a lie. It's a chain reaction that I can't control. One lie leads to the next that leads to the next. But Jada—she's my wings, my salvation, a flutter of hope beneath my ribs that lifts me when I'm sure I'll sink. I'll bear this weight—alone, silent, fierce—for her, forever if I must, because she's the light piercing through the storm I've become.

The bitter taste of it all is a tempest I can't outrun, a howling gale of regret and rage and sixteen years of breaking beneath a world that doesn't bend for girls like me. I'm Crysta Byrd, shattered and stitched back together with spit and stubbornness, my heart a battlefield where love and loss wage their endless war. The nights are long, the diner's fluorescent lights buzzing like a chorus of judgment as I pour coffee and count change, my feet throbbing, my spirit frayed. But the bold in me—it's a fire, a roaring blaze that refuses to gutter out, fueled by the daughter who's already my everything, my reason, my redemption. I study until my eyes burn, I work until my hands tremble, I lie until my tongue tastes of ash—all for her, all for the life I'll claw out of this dirt and despair to give her. The porch holds me as the stars wheel overhead, and I rock, I whisper, I endure, because Jada's coming, and I'll be ready—broken, yes, but unbowed, a mother forged in the crucible of my own silent war.

CHAPTER 3

JADA, MY LIGHT

It's August 29, 2006, exactly one year after hurricane Katrina, one of the worst storms these parts have ever seen. It's no wonder she would be born on this day. Strong and fierce she would be, and there would be more hurricanes to come, always crashing through on her birthday. She would always complain about plans being ruined and having to hunker down or evacuate. I've just turned seventeen at the beginning of the month, a fragile, fractured soul sprawled across a hospital bed in Baton Rouge, Louisiana, my body no longer my own but a tempest-torn battlefield, slick with sweat and shuddering under the weight of a pain I never knew could exist. The air is thick, heavy with the metallic tang of blood and the sharp, biting sting of antiseptic that claws its way into my lungs with every ragged breath I manage to steal. My water broke at 6am this morning, and I've been in labor for almost twelve hours now. My screams—oh, those screams—rip from my chest like a caged beast clawing for freedom, echoing off the sterile white walls, bouncing back to me as if to remind me there's no escape from this crucible of agony. Above me, the fluorescent lights hum and flicker, their cold, relentless glow buzzing like a swarm of wasps, taunting me, daring me to break beneath their indifferent stare. My blonde hair, once a source of quiet pride, is now a sodden, tangled mess, plastered to my forehead in damp, heavy strands, a curtain I can't part no matter how I twist or thrash. My green eyes—those wide, wild mirrors of my soul—are darting, frantic, searching for something, anything, to anchor me: the nurse's steady, unshaken gaze, the ceiling tiles I've counted a hundred times over in a desperate bid to calm my mind as my body betrays me. I vow to never do this again. It's too painful, too horrible to endure a second time.

My hands, trembling and slick with sweat, clutch the icy metal bed rails with a ferocity that turns my knuckles bone-white, my chipped nails digging crescent moons into my palms as another contraction crashes over me. It's a tidal wave, a merciless, roiling force that starts deep in my core and surges outward, tearing through muscle and sinew, splitting me open in ways I never imagined a body could endure. I'm breaking—shattering—my breath hitching in jagged gasps as I think, with a clarity that cuts like a blade, *This is it. This is where I end.* A girl too young, too fragile, too hollowed out by the ghosts of the past to bear this unbearable weight. My legs tremble uncontrollably, my back arches against the thin mattress, and I'm drowning, sinking beneath the relentless tide of pain, my vision blurring at the edges as the room spins and tilts. I'm not strong enough. I've never been strong enough—not since that night in 2005 when the world turned dark and cruel, when my body became a crime scene, when shame sank its claws into me and refused to let go. I'm seventeen, and I'm dying, I'm sure of it. 'I would probably be a horrible mother anyway,' I think as my heart is hammering so hard it might burst free from my chest and leave me empty. I hear the nurse demand one more big push, and I bite down and do it even when I have no strength left. I give one final blast of energy directed straight to the core of me.

But then—oh, then—the storm breaks, and she arrives.

The nurse moves with a quiet grace I can barely comprehend, her hands steady where mine are shaking, and she lifts this tiny, wriggling creature from the wreckage of my body. Eight pounds of pure, unadulterated miracle, swaddled in a scratchy hospital blanket that scratches at my raw nerves even from a distance. Time doesn't just slow—it stops, suspended in the humid, antiseptic air, and my breath catches, a sob and a laugh tangling together in my throat like vines, choking me with their intensity. I can't believe it did. It feels like an eternity that I was in agony, but it's finally over and I get to see what the cause of it was. I reach for her, my arms trembling so violently I'm terrified I'll drop her, terrified I'm not enough—not now, not ever—to hold something so precious, so perfect. Jada. My Jada. The nurse places her in my arms, and the weight of her—solid, warm, *real*—grounds me like nothing else ever has. Her blonde wisps of hair, fine as spider silk, catch the flickering light, shimmering against her pink scalp, and her eyes—those blue-green pools, unfocused yet piercing—blink up at me, fierce and unyielding, as if she's already staking her claim on this chaotic, broken world.

I clutch her to my chest, my fingers curling around her tiny frame, and her heartbeat—oh, that heartbeat—thuds against mine, a fierce, steady rhythm that drowns out the cacophony of my fears. It's a drumbeat, a sounding board, a song of life so vibrant, so defiant, that it washes away the shadows that have clung to me like damp rot since that night in 2005. Its violation—had carved a hollow space inside me, a wound I thought would never heal. The shame, the secret I carried like a stone in my gut, the whispers I imagined behind every glance—they'd defined me, reduced me to a ghost of the girl I'd once been. But now, with Jada in my arms, her warmth seeping into my skin, her breath a soft huff against my collarbone, it all dissolves. The pain, the past, the poison—it melts away in the heat of her presence, in the weight of her tiny body pressed against mine. She's perfect, and I realized then that she's not his, but not mine either. She is her own person. She is beautifully made by God, and I am just her keeper and protector; in that sacred, fragile moment, I'm reborn in the precious light of her being.

Tears stream down my cheeks, hot and unstoppable, carving rivers through the sweat and grime as I sob—raw, ugly, beautiful sobs that shake my whole body. They drip onto her blanket, dark splotches blooming against the faded fabric, and I start to sing in a whispered hum Somewhere Over the Rainbow. My voice cracks, breaks, but I keep singing it, needing to hear it, needing her to hear it, needing the universe to know she's here, she's real, she's everything. The love that floods me is overwhelming, burning, a force so deep and untamed it terrifies me to my core. It's a wildfire, consuming every doubt, every fear, leaving only ash and this fierce, unshakeable certainty: I am her mother. I was forged in fire, tempered by pain, and now, holding her, I am whole—not despite the scars, but because of them. My heart pounds, a drumbeat of devotion, and I know, with every fiber of my being, that I will fight for her, bleed for her, live for her. Jada. My Jada. My redemption, my reason, my light in the endless dark.

Sitting in a quiet hospital room, the antiseptic smell stinging my nose, the fluorescent lights buzzing faintly overhead like a chorus of restless insects, and yet none of it matters—not the ache in my body, not the exhaustion pulling at my limbs—because she's here. The nurse, a kind-eyed woman with a voice like honey, leans over and murmurs something about how beautiful she is, how perfect, her words floating past me like a breeze I can't quite catch. I nod, I think, but I'm not really listening. How could I? My entire world has narrowed to this tiny, fragile creature cradled in my arms, her skin so soft it feels like a whisper against mine, her chest rising and falling in a rhythm that's both foreign and familiar, like a song I've always known but never heard until now. Her eyes—those breathtaking blue-green pools—flicker open for just a moment, and I swear they see me, really see me, straight through the chaos and the scars and the shame I've carried like a second skin. Her fingers, so impossibly small, curl around my own, a grip so weak and yet so fierce it yanks me back from the precipice I've been dangling over for months. I'm seventeen, a child myself in so many ways, but in this moment, I'm her mother—her everything—and the weight of that truth crashes over me like a tidal wave, pulling me under and lifting me up all at once.

I can still feel it, you know. That night. The memory of it clings to me like damp rot, festering in the corners of my mind no matter how hard I try to scrub it away. His couch, sagging and stained, the springs digging into my back. The air thick with stale beer and his breath, heavy and hot against my neck. The way my body went limp, my mind drifting up and out, hovering somewhere above me as if I could escape the weight of him, the violation of him. I didn't scream. I didn't fight. I just… floated. And when it was over, when he rolled off me and muttered something I didn't hear, I pulled myself together—piece by jagged piece—and stumbled home, the night pressing in around me like a bruise. I didn't tell anyone. Not Mom, not my friends, not even myself, not really. I buried it deep, locked it away, let it gnaw at me in silence. But now, here, with Jada in my arms, that darkness feels smaller, less invincible. She's rewriting me, line by line, breath by breath. Her existence doesn't erase what happened—it can't—but it's a light, a blazing, defiant light, and it's burning through the shadows I've been drowning in. I laugh, a raw, trembling sound that catches in my throat, tears streaming down my face as I clutch her closer. The nurse pats my shoulder, her touch gentle, and then she's gone, leaving us alone—me and my daughter, my redemption, my reason. I stare into her eyes, my green ones meeting her blue-green ones, and I whisper a promise, a vow that sears itself into my very soul: *I'll protect you. I'll fight for you. I'll be enough for you.* The pain of labor fades, the room grows still, and for the first time in months, I feel it—hope, fragile but real, blooming in my chest like a flower breaking through cracked earth.

A few days later, we come home. Home to Hammond, to our little house squatting on the edge of town like it's ashamed to be seen. My grandmother has taken me in now, and I'm grateful. It's a small place, but better than Mom's with peeling paint and floors that groan under every step, walls so thin they might as well be paper, letting every sound bleed through. Grammie's late-night TV shows hum in the background, the neighbor's barking dog, my own ragged breaths when the nightmares still come. We pile in, me and Jada and Grammie, a trio bound by blood and necessity, and I'm hit with the reality of it all: I'm a kid raising a kid. Seventeen years old, my blonde hair tangled and wild from days without a proper brush, my green eyes shadowed with exhaustion, and I'm fumbling through this new life like I'm blindfolded. The first diaper I try to change slips off her tiny hips, a lopsided mess, and I curse under my breath, my hands shaking as I try again. There are so many products and items that I'm learning to use, when and how to make sure she doesn't get rashes or colic or any of the other things babies sometimes get. The breastfeeding starts out okay until my nipples start to become raw, cracked and bleeding. I suffer through the pain and continue to feed her despite my urge to stop and just give her a bottle. She needs feeding every 1-2 hours in these early days, and it's grueling. I can't leave her to do anything and luckily I've been able to take time off from work and school. And the nights—God, the nights. They stretch on forever, an endless loop of wakefulness, my body screaming for rest while Jada's cries pierce the dark like shards of glass. The first time it happens, that full-on wail that echoes through the house, I bolt upright, heart hammering, and scoop her up, pacing the tiny living room in a frantic dance. My bare feet slap against the cold linoleum, my voice cracks as I beg her to hush, *please, hush, baby, please*, tears pricking my eyes because I don't know what I'm doing, because I'm terrified, I'll fail her. Grammie's there then, her scent washing over me like a balm, her arms steady as she takes Jada from me. "It's okay, hush sweet girl." She rocks her, humming softly, and I watch, perched on the edge of the couch, my knees drawn up, learning the curve of her sway, the rhythm of her calm.

And then it happens—Jada coos. It's a small sound, a delicate little bubble of noise rising from her chest, but it hits me like thunder. I collapse back against the cushions, my breath hitching, my green eyes softening as I stare at her in Grammie's arms. She's magic. Pure, unadulterated magic. That gummy smile, the way it splits her face wide open, unguarded and bright in the light of the dim lamp—it's an electric shock to the heart, a tether always pulling me back to shore every time I start to drift too far into the dark. Each time she looks at me, each time her tiny hand brushes mine, the weight of that night, that couch, that suffocating silence—it lifts, just a fraction, just enough. I'm still broken, still jagged around the edges, but with her, I'm something more. I'm her mother. I'm her world. And as I sit there, watching her drift to sleep, her lashes fanning out against her cheeks, I feel it deep in my bones: she's my salvation, my reason to keep going, my light in a darkness I thought would swallow me whole.

The sun hangs low over this tired little town, a bruised orange smear across the horizon, casting long shadows that stretch like accusing fingers across the warped boards of our front porch. I'm seventeen, but I feel a hundred years older, my bones aching with secrets, my skin prickling under the weight of eyes I can't escape. Hammond's watching—always watching. The houses that squat across the street, curtains twitching every time I step outside, silhouettes a hulking judge in the window, peering down on me like I'm some fallen girl in a sermon that's itching to get preached. I can feel the gazes clawing at me as I wrestle Jada's stroller over the uneven gravel, her tiny hands clutching the frayed blanket I've wrapped her in, her blonde curls catching the last gasps of daylight like a halo I don't deserve to give her. She's two now, my whole world squeezed into this fragile, giggling bundle, and I'd burn this town to ash before I let anyone take her from me. But they're all watching—Hammond, the neighbors, the ghosts of my past—and I'm drowning in the flood of their stares.

The neighbors lean over their sagging fences, chain-link and splintered wood groaning under their weight, their whispers slicing through the humid air like dull knives. “Poor Crysta,” they murmur, their voices thick with that syrupy pity that makes my stomach churn. “Teen mom, no dad around, what a shame.” I push Jada’s stroller harder, the wheels rattling against the cracked sidewalks, my sneakers scuffing the concrete as I try to outrun their words. I see it in their eyes—some glint of judgment masquerading as concern, some smug satisfaction that their lives didn’t splinter like mine did. Mrs. Carter with her drooping hydrangeas, Mr. Tillman with his rusted pickup, they stand there clutching their iced tea glasses, their lips pursed as if they’re sucking on the sourness of my story. I want to scream at them, to tell them they don’t know me, don’t know the fire that keeps me upright, but I just grip the stroller handles tighter, my knuckles whitening, and keep moving. Jada babbles something soft and sweet, her voice a light pulling me back from the edge, and I force a smile for her, my green eyes burning with a defiance I can barely hold onto.

High school feels like a lifetime ago, but its echoes stalk me everywhere. The grocery store is the worst—those harsh lights flickering overhead, casting everything in a sickly glow, while my old classmates linger by the chip aisle or the soda coolers, their laughter dying the second they spot me. I’m balancing Jada on my hip, her chubby arms flailing as she reaches for a box of cereal we can’t afford, while I clutch a basket of ramen packets and apple sauce, the cheapest kind that smells like cardboard and guilt. They don't say anything—not out loud—but their stares are loud enough, scorching holes in the back of my faded tank top. There's Tara, who used to sit behind me in algebra, her perfect ponytail swinging as she whispers to some boy I don't recognize. There's Jake, who asked me to homecoming once, his eyes sliding over me now like I'm a stranger who wandered into the wrong story. I graduated early, clawed my way out of those claustrophobic halls with a diploma clutched in my shaking hands, but they still see me as the girl who fell apart. I shift Jada higher, her warmth against my chest the only thing keeping me from shattering, and I mutter under my breath, "We're fine," as if saying it loud enough will make it true.

Sundays are their own kind of hell. The church looms at the end of Main Street, its steeple stabbing the sky like a warning, and I drag myself through those double doors because it's what you do here—because maybe, just maybe, I can find some sliver of peace in the pews. But the church folks, they're the worst of all. They cluck their tongues as I slip in late, Jada squirming in my arms, her little dress already wrinkled from the walk. "Bless her heart," they coo, their voices dripping with that sanctimonious drawl that makes me want to claw my way out of my own skin. They don't mean it—not really. It's a dagger wrapped in velvet, a way to say "poor thing" without getting their hands dirty. I sit in the back, my head bowed, pretending to listen to the preacher drone on about forgiveness while their sideways glances pin me to the bench. I can feel their questions simmering beneath the hymns—where's the father? What kind of girl lets this happen? I want to stand up, to shout that Jada's not a mistake, that she's the only thing I've ever done right, but I just hug her closer, her curls tickling my chin, and let the lie I've built hold me together.

That lie—it's my armor, but also my prison. I've woven it so carefully, thread by thread, until it's a story I can almost believe myself. "Her father's gone," I tell them when they ask, my voice steady even as my heart hammers against my ribs. "Some boy, close to my age, had problems of his own when he found out. Couldn't handle it." It's vague enough to keep them from digging, sharp enough to make them nod and back off, their curiosity sated for another day. I wield it like a blade, flashing it with every forced smile I plaster on my face, every time I duck my head to avoid their probing eyes, every "she's all I need" I fling back at their endless questions. It's flimsy, this shield of mine, patched together with half-truths and desperation, but it's fierce too—a mother's love turned weapon, guarding the secret that gnaws at me day and night. I'm terrified, bone-deep and breathless, that someone will look too closely, will see him in her features—those eyes that shone blue in the sun that don't match my green ones, that stubborn little chin that juts out just like his did when he spoke to me that night. They'll unravel it all, the truth I've buried so deep it's choking me, strangling me in the quiet hours when Jada's asleep and I'm alone with the ghosts I can't outrun. But they don't—not yet—and I cling to that fragile mercy for as long as I can.

I hold Jada tighter, her small body pressed against mine as we navigate this world that feels like it's waiting to swallow us whole. My green eyes blaze when I catch their stares, daring them to judge her worth, to weigh her against the mistakes they think I've made. She's a part of me in a way nothing else ever has been, a piece of my soul walking around outside my body, and she's enough. No, she's more than enough—she's everything, the sun and the storm and the air I breathe. My heart roars with it, a primal, wordless howl that drowns out their whispers, their pity, their sanctimony. Let them watch. Let them talk. I'll carry her through this fire, through their eyes and their tongues and their small, small minds, because she's my daughter, my miracle, my fight. And as long as I have her, I'll keep going—past Hammond's window, past the fences, past the grocery store and the church and every last one of their judging stares—until the day I can finally breathe free of the secret that's killing me, until the day I can tell her she's everything I'll ever need, and mean it with every shattered, defiant piece of me.

She grows fast—too fast—and I'm there for every fleeting, precious moment, every milestone that stitches the tattered remnants of my soul back together with threads of light. It's spring now, the world outside our sagging little house blooming with a tentative hope I'm only just beginning to feel again, and there she is, my Jada, crawling across the worn rug that's seen too many tears, her chubby little hands slapping the faded fibers as she chases dust motes swirling in a golden shaft of sunlight. I'm down there with her, on my knees like I'm praying—maybe I am—my heart pounding with a love so big it hurts, and I'm laughing, laughing so hard my sides ache and my lungs burn, a sound so raw and wild I didn't even know it was still inside me, buried under all that wreckage he left behind. Her giggles rise like music, high and sweet, and I'm grinning so wide my face might split, my eyes stinging with tears I don't bother to hide because they're not the bitter kind anymore—they're hers, they're ours.

She babbles at me—"ba-ba-da!"—a string of glorious nonsense that's better than any symphony, and I talk back, my voice pitching up high and silly, a ridiculous duet that bounces off the walls of our tiny house and fills it with something so close to joy I can almost taste it, like sugar on my tongue after years of ash. I'm eighteen, too young to feel this old, but she's my tether, my lifeline, pulling me up from the abyss with every crooked smile, every time those blue-green eyes—half his eyes, damn him, but hers now, hers forever—lock onto mine and see me, really see me, like I'm the whole world. And I am, for her. I have to be.

August creeps in, heavy with heat and the weight of another year survived, and it's her first birthday—August 2007, a date carved into my bones. I'm broke, God, so broke, my hands cracked from diner shifts where the coffee burns and the tips don't come, my body screaming from late nights hunched over textbooks in a college library that smells like mildew and desperation. But I scrape it together—every penny, every dime I've hoarded like a dragon with its gold—and I make her a cake. Chocolate, her favorite, because I've watched her eyes light up at the tiniest smudge of it on my finger, her little tongue darting out like a kitten's. The cake's lopsided, a disaster of flour and hope, but it's ours, and I carry it to the kitchen table with a pride that swells in my chest until I can barely breathe.

She's in her highchair, clapping those sticky hands, and Mom's there too, her laughter a soft echo of what it used to be before everything fractured, before he tore us all apart and left me to pick up the pieces. I light a single candle, its flame trembling like my heart, and we sing—off-key, loud, alive—and Jada squeals, her voice piercing the air like a bell. I help her smash her fists into that cake, chocolate frosting smearing across her round cheeks, her nose, her curls, and I'm right there with her, my fingers plunging into the mess, smearing it on her forehead like war paint as she shrieks with delight. My laughter erupts again, wild and unstoppable, mingling with Mom's chuckles and Jada's joy, and it's a rare, wild happiness, a moment so pure and bright it slices through the shadows that still cling to me like smoke. Then that night, I sing to her again, only its Somewhere Over the Rainbow like I did on the day she was born.

I look at her, my baby, my miracle, and I feel it deep—a mother's primal roar, a love so fierce it's a living thing inside me, clawing its way out. I'd die for her in a heartbeat, my blood spilling red and hot without a second thought. I'd kill for her, my hands steady and sure, no hesitation, no remorse. I'd tear the world apart, brick by brick, bone by bone, until nothing stood between her and safety, her and happiness. He's a ghost now, a shadow I've locked away in the darkest corner of my mind, his name a curse I won't speak, his memory a wound I refuse to let fester. He broke me, shattered me into a thousand jagged pieces, but she—she's the sun, blazing through my darkness with a heat that sears and heals all at once.

Every giggle that spills from her lips is a balm, soothing the raw edges of my spirit. Every hug, her tiny arms wrapping around my neck like she'll never let go, is a brick laid in the foundation of something new, something stronger. Every time she reaches for me, her fingers grasping, her eyes trusting, she rebuilds what he destroyed, piece by painstaking piece. I'm not whole yet—maybe I never will be—but with her, I'm more than the sum of my scars. With her, I'm a mother, a warrior, a survivor, and every beat of my heart screams her name—Jada, Jada, Jada—a rhythm that keeps me alive, keeps me fighting, keeps me here, in this worn little house where the rug is threadbare but the love is endless.

The years blur—2008, 2009, 2010—and I'm twenty-one, then twenty-two, still in that cramped house, still fighting to make ends meet, still watching her grow into this wild, beautiful thing. She's walking now, running, her blonde hair a halo of curls that catch the light as she spins in our backyard, chasing fireflies on sticky summer nights. I'm exhausted—diner grease in my hair, college textbooks piled on the table, my body aching from late shifts and early mornings—but she's magic, a spark that keeps me going. I tuck her in every night, her little body curled under a quilt Grammie sewed, her breath steady as I brush her hair back, whispering, "I love you most, always." It's a ritual, a vow, and every time I say it, my heart swells, a mix of joy and fear I can't shake. The lie's held—five years strong, the secret locked tight in a vault behind my green eyes—but I feel it, a storm brewing, a shadow stirring in the distance. I don't know how, I don't know when, but I sense him out there, waiting, his presence a chill that creeps into my bones on quiet nights like this.

It's 2011 now, spring turning the air thick and green, and I'm twenty-two, standing over Jada's bed, watching her sleep. She's five, her blonde hair splayed across the pillow like a golden crown, her blue-green eyes closed, her chest rising and falling with a trust that breaks me open. I've kept her safe, kept us whole, but the world feels unsteady, like the ground's shifting beneath me. I lean down, kiss her forehead, my lips lingering on her warm skin as I whisper, "You're my light, Jada, and no one's taking you from me." My voice trembles, my hands shake, and I feel the tears prick my eyes—not just from love, but from the dread I can't name. The night's quiet, the cicadas humming outside, but I'm not—I'm a mother on edge, my heart racing, my resolve hardening into something fierce, something bold. He's out there, I know it, and the lie I've carried, the secret I've buried, it's a ticking bomb I can't defuse. But for now, she's here, and I'll fight 'til my last breath to keep it that way.

I step back, my bare feet silent on the floor, and sink into the rocking chair by her bed, the one Mom used to rock me in when I was small. My blonde hair falls into my face, my green eyes glisten in the dim glow of her nightlight, and I let the tears come—slow, silent, a release I don't often allow. I see that night in 2005, feel his hands, hear my own screams, and it's still there, a wound that won't heal, a scar that throbs with every beat of my heart. But then I look at Jada, my daughter, my miracle, and the pain shifts—it doesn't vanish, but it bends, molds itself around the love I have for her, the strength she's given me. I'm not just surviving anymore; I'm fighting, clawing my way through the chaos for her, for us. She's my my anchor, my sun in a sky that's been dark too long, and as I sit there, rocking gently, I feel it—a fire kindling in my chest, a bold, unyielding flame that says I'll face whatever comes, I'll burn it all down if I have to, because she's worth it. She's everything.

The clock ticks past midnight, the house creaks, and I wipe my tears, my breath steadying as I watch her sleep. “I’ll protect you,” I whisper again, my voice stronger now, a promise carved into the air between us. The shadow of him, the threat I feel looming—it’s real, it’s close, but I’m not sixteen anymore, not helpless, not alone. I’m Crysta Byrd, twenty-two and fractured, a mother forged in love and pain, and Jada’s my light, my reason, my fight. The night stretches wide, the world spins on, but here, in this tiny room, it’s just us—her and me, the bitter and the bold, holding fast against the storm I know is coming. And I pray I’ll be ready, God help me, I hope I’ll be ready.

CHAPTER 4
THE TRUTH SPILLS OUT (2011)

I'm Crysta Byrd, and if I close my eyes tight enough, I can still feel it—the chipped, uneven linoleum of our kitchen floor in Hammond, Louisiana, pressing its cold, jagged edges into the soles of my bare feet like a cruel reminder of everything I couldn't escape. It's spring 2011, and I'm twenty-two years old, though I feel ancient, worn down to the bone by a weight so crushing, so relentless, it's a miracle my legs don't buckle beneath me. The air in that tiny kitchen hangs heavy, thick with the sharp, biting scent of lemon dish soap that coats my nostrils and mingles with the faint, earthy scratch of Jada's crayons as they scrape across a crumpled sheet of paper on the table behind me. My blonde hair clings to the damp curve of my neck, plastered there by sweat that beads despite the pitiful excuse for a breeze slipping through the cracked-open window. My green eyes—those wild, restless windows to a soul that's been battered and bruised—dart to her every few seconds, unable to resist the pull of her presence. She's five years old, my entire world, my everything—her blonde curls bouncing softly as she colors a rainbow so bold, so alive, it feels like a defiance against the dark, churning storm raging in my chest. She's humming, her little voice weaving a melody she's dreamed up all on her own, threading through the stillness like a fragile thread of light, and I grip it with every ounce of my being, desperate to hold on.

I'm standing at the sink, hands plunged into lukewarm water, scrubbing a plate that doesn't need scrubbing, just to keep myself braced to something real, something solid. The sponge squeaks against the ceramic, a grating sound that echoes the tension coiled tight inside me. Jada's crayons scratch on, her humming unbroken, and for a fleeting moment, I let myself believe we're safe here—just the two of us in this quiet, sacred space, untouchable by the shadows that have haunted me since the day she was born. My heart beats steady, a fragile rhythm I've fought to maintain for her sake, because she's the only thing that's ever made sense in a life that's felt like a series of storms tearing through me, leaving wreckage in their wake.

But then it comes—the phone rings, a shrill, piercing wail that rips through our delicate bubble of peace like a jagged blade slicing through silk. My heart doesn't just skip; it slams against my ribcage, a sickening thud that reverberates through my whole body. I freeze, sponge still in hand, water dripping from my trembling fingers, but I force myself to keep moving, scrubbing harder, pretending I don't hear it, I'll let the machine get it. Behind me, Jada doesn't flinch—her crayons keep dancing, her humming unbroken—and I cling to that sound like it's the last thing keeping me afloat. Then, in the living room, Grammie's footsteps shuffle across the threadbare carpet, slow and deliberate, and when she picks up the receiver, her voice drops into that low, taut register I've come to dread. It's the tone that's marked every disaster in my life, every moment when the ground's fallen out from under me, and it twists my stomach into a knot so tight I can barely breathe. My knuckles bleach white against the sponge, my breaths shallow and ragged, and I will myself to stay here, in this kitchen, with Jada's rainbows and her soft little song, safe from whatever's clawing at the edges of our world.

However, the universe doesn't care about my pleas. Grammie's silhouette looms in the doorway, a ghost against the dim light spilling from the living room, and when I turn to face her, I see it—her face, pale as a shroud, drained of all color, her dark eyes wide and glistening with something I can't bear to name. Fear? Dread? Regret? It's all there, swirling in those familiar depths, and it hits me like a punch to the gut, stealing the air from my lungs. She doesn't move, doesn't speak for what feels like an eternity, and I stand there, rooted to the spot, the plate slipping from my hands to clatter into the sink with a hollow, echoing crash. I pick it back up and turn to her, her voice finally breaks the silence, it's a guillotine dropping, sharp and merciless, severing the fragile thread I've been clinging to: "Someone's asking about Jada. I told them you'd have to call them back. Do you know what it's about?"

In that instant, the world tilts, and I'm falling—falling into a void I've spent five years running from, a darkness I've poured every ounce of my strength into keeping at bay. My eyes snap to Jada, still coloring, still humming, oblivious to the way my heart is shattering against the cold linoleum beneath me. She's my light, my reason, my everything—and now, someone's come to tear her away. I don't have to call them back to know what they want.

The plate doesn't just fall—it slips, slick and treacherous, from fingers that have forgotten how to hold steady. It's a slow, agonizing descent, like watching my life unravel in real time, and when it hits the cracked linoleum of our tiny kitchen, it explodes. A sharp, deafening crash, a thousand jagged pieces scattering like the fragments of my sanity, slicing through the quiet afternoon and straight into the marrow of my bones. My chest caves in, a hollow ache blooming where my heart used to beat, and I can't breathe—my lungs seize, my throat burns, and suddenly I'm not Crysta, twenty-two, standing in this cramped house where Jada and I share a room and the second-hand dreams. I'm sixteen again, trapped on that sagging couch in the dim glow of a TV I don't remember watching, his hands—Don's hands—crushing me, pinning me, stealing pieces of me I'll never get back. His breath, sour and hot against my neck, his smirk a blade carving itself into my memory, a brand I've carried for six endless years. The shadow I buried under the weight of this small town's dirt and gossip, praying it'd stay dead. But it didn't. The whispers—those cruel, venomous whispers that slither through diner booths and church pews—found him. They dug him up, dragged him back, and now he knows. He *knows*.

Jada's voice cuts through the haze, soft and clear like a bell ringing in a storm. "What's wrong, Mommy?" she asks, her blue-green eyes—*half his* eyes, damn him, God forgive me—lifting from the rainbow she's been coloring, all bright streaks of joy on a page I wish could be her whole world. She's five, my miracle, my anchor, her tiny hands smudged with crayon wax, her innocence a light I've fought to protect since the moment she first cried in my arms. I force a smile, but it's shaky, brittle, like glass about to shatter. My lips quiver as I kneel beside her, brushing a strand of her blonde hair—my hair—behind her ear. "Nothing, baby," I whisper, my voice a threadbare lie, fraying at the edges. "Just a clumsy momma, that's all." She giggles, satisfied, and goes back to her colors, oblivious to the tempest roaring inside me. But I'm not okay. Inside, I'm screaming—a wild, scared howl that starts in the pit of my gut and claws its way up, tearing at my ribs, my throat, my everything. It's a sound no one hears but me, a cry I've muffled for years, and now it's breaking free because he's back. Don's back, and I'm not ready—not for him, not for the fight I can feel brewing like a storm on the horizon, dark and unstoppable.

The days after that moment blur into a fever dream, a nightmare I can't claw my way out of. Time bends and warps, each hour heavy with dread, each minute a fresh wound. It's a muggy Tuesday when the subpoena arrives, presented to me by an officer I don't recognize, like a snake coiled to strike. I'm sitting in a rocking chair in the living, and I see it from the window first, a crisp white envelope stark against the dark uniform, and my stomach drops, a cold sweat prickling my skin. I stumble outside in my faded flip-flops, the concrete burning under my feet, and snatch it up with hands that won't stop trembling. My chipped nails catch on the seal as I rip it open, and the words inside hit me like a fist to the gut—black ink on stark white paper, cold and official, demanding Jada's DNA. Demanding proof of the secret I've carried like a stone in my chest since that night in 2005, a truth I've guarded with every fiber of my being. His name reaches out from the paper like a cold, black rush of wind. My knees buckle, and I'm back inside before I know it, pacing our cramped living room, the carpet worn thin under my frantic steps, a reminder of all the nights I've walked this same path, worrying, hiding, surviving.

My blonde hair's a mess, a wild tangle spilling into my face, and I shove it back with fingers that shake so bad I can barely feel them. My green eyes—burn with tears I can't let fall, not here, not now. She's on the floor, my little girl, surrounded by her toys, their plastic smiles mocking me as she hums a tune she made up, her laughter a melody so pure it rips me open wider than any wound. I grab my phone, the screen cracked from a drop I couldn't afford to fix, and I'm dialling lawyers I can't pay for, my voice breaking as I plead into the void. "Can I fight this? Please, somebody, tell me I can stop it!" I'm begging, raw and desperate, my breath hitching as the words spill out. But I'm nobody—just Crysta, the college student, single mom. I'm just me, the girl slinging steak and eggs at the diner for tips that don't cover the bills, drowning in college loans I took out dreaming of a better life I feel like I'll never reach. The voices on the other end are clipped, impersonal, a chorus of receptionists, "No, the attorney won't speak with you without a consult." A consult that would cost a hefty fee. The words echo, a death knell, and I choke on a sob, swallowing it down as my mind spins, tumbling back to that night, to the couch, to the weight of him, to the moment I became a vault for this horrible, unshakable truth.

I sink to the floor beside Jada, my back against the wall, my hands pressed to my face as if I can hold myself together by sheer will. She looks up, tilting her head, her tiny brow furrowing. "Mommy, are you sad?" she asks, and it's a dagger, twisting deep. I shake my head, force another smile, and pull her into my lap, burying my face in her hair, breathing in the scent of crayons and baby shampoo. "No, baby," I murmur, my voice thick, "Mommy's just tired." But it's a lie, and it tastes bitter on my tongue. I'm not tired—I'm terrified, unravelling, a woman on the edge of a war I never wanted. Don's out there, and he's coming for us, for her, and I don't know if I'm strong enough to stop him. All I know is I'll fight—God help me, I'll fight with everything I have, because she's worth it, my Jada, my light, and I'll be damned if I let him take her from me.

How did it come to this? How did the threads of life—once so tightly woven with hope and grit—unravel into this jagged, chaotic mess? Standing in the doorway of Jada's room, breath catches in the chest like a trapped bird, watching her tiny hands orchestrate a perfect little world with her horse figurines. She's humming softly, her chestnut curls bouncing as she arranges a mommy horse, a daddy horse, a baby horse—all of them smiling, all of them safe. The heart twists, a slow, agonizing wrench, because the truth looms heavy: there's no choice, no escape from the path forced upon this soul. The drive to New Orleans stretches ahead like a plunge into some fiery abyss, and as Jada is buckled into her car seat, the Louisiana humidity presses against the windows, thick and oppressive, a suffocating shroud mirroring the weight within. The whole way there, I try to calm my nerves by thinking: Maybe he really is a good person who made a mistake. Maybe he just wants to see his child because he wants to be a good dad. Maybe this could be a good thing. Maybe she needs a father to help take care of her. Maybe I don't have to do this alone anymore. All of these thoughts are supposed to be comforting me, but I'm not fully convincing myself as I still feel tight and my stomach is in knots.

Her little hand slips into a larger one, warm and trusting, and she tilts her head up, those blue-green eyes—so untainted—sparkling with innocent wonder. "Where are we going, Mommy? Why are we at the doctor? Am I sick?" she asks, her voice a melody of softness and curiosity. A smile is forced, the jaw clenched so tight it throbs, and the lie spills out like poison: "Just a checkup, baby." Each syllable cuts deeper, slicing through until there's nothing but bleeding inside, because this isn't a journey to safety—it's leading her straight into the jaws of a trap that can't be unmade.

The lab is clean, cold, a stark contrast to the heat outside, and Jada is held close on a lap as the technician swabs her mouth. She squirms, giggling a little, then looks up, confused but still trusting—always trusting the one she sees as her rock, her protector. My chest tightens until breathing feels impossible, and suddenly the mind reels back to sixteen, to that suffocating winter of 2005. The weight of him—Don—pins down, hands shaking as the world shatters on that couch. The memory is blinked away, clutching Jada closer as the swab disappears into its vial, whispering, "I'm sorry, I'm so sorry," into her curls. The voice cracks, tears streaming hot and relentless down cheeks, soaking into her hair as she pats my face with her chubby little hand, oblivious to the storm unleashed, to the truth buried for six long years. Weeks crawl by, each day a torment, until the envelope arrives—white, crisp, official. It's torn open with trembling fingers, and there it is in black ink: 99.97% probability of paternity. His. Don's. The room spins, bile surges up the throat, and a collapse onto the bed follows, the paper crumpling in a fist as sobs rack the body. I knew it would be, but part of hoped it would say something different somehow. The truth fought so hard to bury claws its way free, a snarling beast rising from the grave, and the realization hits—he's her father, biologically, undeniably. That shadow from nightmares, is reborn now, his presence seeping into this life like a stain that can't be scrubbed away. I keep repeating. Maybe he's not all bad. Maybe he regrets it. Maybe he made a mistake. It's all I have to hold onto when my thoughts go to the worst.

Summer 2011 dawns heavy and unrelenting, the Louisiana heat a noose tightening around the neck as a step is taken into the Tangipahoa Parish courthouse. I'll be twenty-three soon, but the soul feels ancient, worn down by the weight of survival, of motherhood, of secrets. The thrift-store dress—cheap polyester, a faded blue that's seen better days—clings to skin, damp with sweat, outlining every curve in a way that leaves a sense of nakedness, exposure. The hem is tugged at, hands unsteady, but there's no hiding here. My blonde hair is pulled back into a ponytail so tight it yanks at the scalp, a sharp, grounding pain clung to because it keeps the crumbling at bay, keeps the terror clawing inside from dissolving everything. Green eyes—wild, frantic, a wildfire trapped behind glass—dart around the room, taking in the polished wood, the murmur of voices, the weight of judgment hanging in the air. And then he's there. Don. Thirty-six now, standing in a suit that reeks of money and manipulation, his ice blue eyes locking on across the courtroom. That smirk—it's the same one, the one that pinned me down six years ago, the one that stripped me bare and left me trembling, broken, a girl forced to claw her way back to life. The stomach lurches, a violent sea of nausea threatening to drown, and hands tremble in the lap, nails digging into palms until the sting of blood is felt. But the chin is forced up, the spine stiffening, a mother's defiance roaring through like a tidal wave. I'm naïve, still recognizable—but I'll be damned if he takes her too. Jada is the light, the reason, and no courtroom, no DNA test, no ghost from the past will rip her away. Not while there's still breath in my lungs.

My world is crumbling beneath me, piece by jagged piece, as I sit in this buzzing courtroom, my heart pounding like a war drum in my chest. He wants custody—custody of Jada, my little girl, my light, the one pure thing that came from the darkest night of my life. She's five years old now, with her blue-green eyes that mirror mine and blonde curls that tumble wild and free, and he thinks he can claim her. Him—the man who pinned me down, who stole my freedom, my dignity, my everything. I can still feel his weight, the suffocating press of him, the way my screams turned to ash in my throat that night six years ago. "He raped me!" I want to shriek it, let it rip through this suffocating silence, let it echo off the cold, grey walls until everyone hears the truth. It's a wail that lives inside me, endless and secret, clawing at my skull, begging to be let out. But Tom, my lawyer, stops me. He's a rough-edged man, all gravelly voice and cigarette-stained fingers, someone I stumbled across through a friend of a friend when I had nowhere else to turn. I scraped together a retainer fee from family and extra shifts at the diner. His hand clamps down on my arm, heavy and insistent, his breath sharp with coffee as he mutters, "Not now, Crysta, not here." He feels my anxiousness, and I bite down hard, my teeth grinding, my voice trapped behind a wall of fear and shame as I sit there, trembling.

The courtroom feels like a war zone, and I'm unarmed, defenceless against the enemy across from me. His lawyers strut like peacocks, their suits crisp, their shoes gleaming as they click across the tile floor. They're vultures in human skin, picking at my bones with every word they sling. They twist my story, painting me as some wild, reckless teenager who spread her legs and begged for trouble—a slut, a liar, a girl who deserved what she got. I was sixteen then, barely more than a kid myself, and now I'm on the brink of twenty-three, a mother carved from survival, sitting here like a statue forged from rage and terror. My green eyes burn, darting to the empty space where Jada should be—thank God she's not here, safe with my sister for now—but she's everywhere in my mind. Her ghost hovers over every lie they spit, every smug glance they throw my way. I can see her so clearly: her tiny hands clutching her favorite stuffed bunny, her giggles filling our cramped house, her trust in me so absolute it breaks me apart. And then the judge's gavel crashes down—50/50 custody—and it's not just a sound, it's a gunshot, a bullet tearing straight through my heart. I wasn't ready for this. We barely fought back. I didn't think this could happen. Not to me, I'm a good mom. I don't break the law, I don't do drugs, and I keep my head down and live a quiet life of the mundane. I stagger inside, my heart splintering, my breath catching as the room tilts. Biology wins. Justice loses. His smirk stretches wide, a predator's grin, and I'm unravelling, my legs giving out as I stumble into the hallway.

I rush to the bathroom where no one can see me, and the sobs come then, raw and jagged, tearing free from my throat so violently I can't breathe, can't think. I collapse against the wall, my knees buckling under me, my hands clawing at the air as their words echo in my ears: "He's her father." Father? That word is a blade twisting in my gut. He's no father—he's a monster, a thief who stole my innocence, a nightmare that refuses to fade. And now he's been handed half her life, half my soul, like it's nothing, like she's some prize to be split down the middle. He doesn't know her favorite color, or her favorite snack, he doesn't know her at all. I wiped my eyes and walked out, I see him then, as we're leaving, his shadow looming too close. At first, I think maybe he'll say something nice to put me at ease like, "I didn't want it to be this way, but you kept her from me so I had no choice, and I hope we can put that behind us and co-parent together." After all, I could have said something earlier, but no, I let my fear of him get the best of me. He leans in, his breath hot and rancid against my ear, his voice a low, venomous hiss: "I'll see her soon." It's a promise, a threat, and it snaps something deep inside me. The threads of who I am—Crysta, the fighter, the mother—fray and break one by one. I picture his hands on her, my baby girl, Jada, torn from me and handed to him like a trophy in his sick, twisted game. My mind reels, spinning into a dark place where I'm screaming, clawing, fighting to keep her safe, and I don't care what it costs me.

That night, I'm in her room, the air thick with the sweet, familiar scent of her strawberry shampoo—a smell that's anchored me through every storm. She's asleep, tucked under a blanket I've pulled too tight around her small, fragile body, her chest rising and falling with a peace I can't touch. Her blonde curls spill across the pillow like a halo, her blue-green eyes hidden behind soft lashes, and she's so beautiful it hurts, an ache that burrows into my bones. I don't deserve her trust—not tonight, not after today, not after letting him slither back into our lives like the snake he is. My knees hit the hardwood floor beside her bed, a dull thud that echoes in the quiet, and I clutch the edge of her mattress, my knuckles white, my nails digging into the fabric. "I'll kill him before he hurts you," I whisper into the dark, my voice a broken, desperate thing. The tears come then, hot and relentless, streaming down my face, soaking the blanket, my blonde hair falling forward like a shield to hide the wreckage of me. I'm a mother on fire, my love for her a wildfire roaring through my veins, fierce enough to burn this whole damn town to ash if it meant keeping her safe. But I'm terrified—terrified of what he'll do with his half of her life, terrified of what I've already lost by letting this happen, terrified of the monster I might have to become to stop him. My hands tremble as I reach out, brushing a curl from her forehead, and I swear to her sleeping form, to the universe, to whatever god might still be listening. I'll fight. I'll bleed. I'll break myself apart before I let him take her from me.

I've been carrying this lie for six years, a festering wound I've dressed up in pretty stories and half-smiles, pretending it didn't burn every time I spoke it aloud. I told myself I was protecting her—my little girl, with her wide blue-green eyes and curls that bounce like sunlight—but the truth has claws, and it's ripped through that fragile façade now, leaving me bleeding and exposed. It's all out there, the boyfriend who vanished into the night like a ghost, the silence I wrapped around that horrible moment when everything changed. I see it replaying behind my eyelids every time I close them: her tiny hand clutching mine at that DNA test, her voice—so small, so trusting—asking, "Mommy, why are we here?" And me, choking on my own cowardice, forcing out, "Just a checkup, baby," when I should've told her the truth. That lie sliced me open deeper than any knife ever could, and I've been bleeding ever since, a mother who failed her daughter, who let the monster back into our fragile little world. The guilt is a stone lodged in my chest, heavy and unyielding, pressing down until I can't breathe. Last night, I collapsed beside her bed, my forehead pressed to the cool edge of her mattress, her soft breathing a rhythm I don't deserve. My sobs shook the silence, tears soaking her blanket as I whispered, "I'll fix this, baby, I swear I will." But how? How do I mend a break this deep, a betrayal this raw, when I'm just twenty-three—a girl who should be chasing dreams under neon lights, laughing at college parties, falling into first loves—yet here I am, drowning in the wreckage of a night I can't erase, fighting a war I never signed up for?

The first exchange came too fast, a punch to the gut I wasn't ready for. It was a muggy morning outside, the air thick and sticky, pregnant with the threat of rain. Jada's outfit was a pair of shorts and a big t-shirt around her knees, a burst of yellow against the grey haze of my world, and I held her hand so tight I worried I'd leave marks on her soft skin. My green eyes—wild, panicked—darted to the horizon as his truck rolled into view, sleek and black, a predator stalking its prey. The engine growled to a stop, and there he was: Don, thirty-six, towering over us both, his smirk a jagged blade twisting in my stomach. I trembled, my knees threatening to buckle, but I forced myself to kneel to her level, my blonde hair falling into my face as I whispered, "Be good, baby," my lips brushing her forehead. She smelled like strawberry shampoo and innocence, her eyes sparkling as she looked at me confused, oblivious to the storm raging inside me. She didn't want to go; I had to pick her up and put her in the truck myself as she cried. I watched, frozen, as he looked her over—her curls, her tiny sneakers—like she was some prize he'd won, not my daughter, not the piece of my soul he was stealing. My breath came shallow, ragged, as he shot me that nod—smug, victorious, bragging sentence. "I've got her now." As they drove away, I hear him yell at her, "Knock it off!" as she cried in the back seat. The gravel crunched under his tires as he drove off, her little hand waving from the window, and something inside me shattered. I stumbled back to my car, my fists slamming against the hood, a scream ripping from my throat—"No, no, NO!"—because this wasn't just a moment, this was my new reality, a hell I couldn't escape, and all of my hopes I muttered to myself on the way to the DNA test turned out to be hollow and just plain wrong. I couldn't fool myself any longer as I drove home with tears blurring the road, my mind spiralling—picturing her in his house, his hands too close, his voice in her ears—and the rage exploded, a mother's fury igniting every nerve. My blonde hair whipped in the wind through the open window, my green eyes hardened into steel, and I swore to myself, my voice a low growl, "He won't win this. He won't take her from me."

Days later, I found myself in Tom's office, a cramped, suffocating cave buried under stacks of yellowing files and the ghosts of a thousand lost fights. The air was thick with cigarette smoke, curling around his grizzled face like a shroud. He leaned forward, his voice rough as the gravel in the parking lot outside, and barked, "Crysta, you're in a war now. He's a shark—cold, calculating—and you've got to sharpen your teeth if you're gonna survive him." I sat there, timid and terrified, a girl who still felt like a kid herself, staring down a predator I couldn't outrun. But Tom didn't let up—he drilled me, his words hammering into me like nails. "Say less, Crysta. Hide more. Trust no one—not a soul. They'll take anything—your words, your tears, your whole damn life—and twist it 'til you're the criminal. They'll make it seem like you're a threat to your own daughter. Shut it down. No parties, no drinking, no nothing. Your soft heart will get nothing but run over in this world." I nodded, swallowing the panic clawing up my throat, my hands trembling as I rehearsed testimony after testimony. Hours bled into each other, my voice growing steadier, colder, my green eyes turning to ice as I learned to choke back the tears threatening to spill. I was forging myself in that smoky room, molding a fighter out of a girl who'd never known how to win— just a placid, go with the flow type, but I had to now, for her. Tom laid it bare: Don's game was control, manipulation, using Jada like a weapon to break me apart piece by piece. I could see it already, the way he'd looked at her that day, inspecting her like she was his property, the way his eyes lingered on me—a hunter savoring the chase, knowing I was cornered. I'm too young, damn it, a girl who should be sketching out a future— maybe a little apartment with plants on the sill, with a lover that doesn't leave scars—but instead, I'm here, battling shadows from a past I can't outrun. I'm her mom, though, her shield, her everything, and I'll become whatever it takes—shark, warrior, liar—to keep her safe from him. My heart pounds with the weight of it, but I lift my chin, staring into the abyss of this fight, and whisper to myself, "I won't let him win. Not her. Not us."

The truth slipping out isn't just a moment—it's a fracture, a seismic shift that cleaves my life into before and after, a chasm I can't bridge. His charisma, his money, his influence—it's a weapon in his hands, a cudgel he'll swing to take her from me. I lie awake at night, the ceiling spinning above me, picturing her with him, her laughter fading under his shadow, and I'm sobbing into my pillow, "I should've run, I should've fought harder." But I was sixteen, broke, alone—where could I have gone? Who would've believed me? The guilt is a tide drowning me, my chest heaving as I clutch her pillow to my face, her scent—strawberry and sunshine—a reminder of who I am, pulling me back from the edge. I see her at five, trusting me at that DNA test, her tiny voice asking questions I couldn't answer, and I hate myself—hate the girl I was, too scared to speak, hate the woman I'm becoming, a liar, a shell, a fighter with blood on her hands that no one else can see.

There really was a boy back then. Back in 2005. His name was Ethan—tall, wiry, with a smile that could charm the devil himself and a temper that flared like dry grass in a lightning storm. We'd met at a bonfire down by the bayou, the air thick with humidity and the sweet burn of roasting marshmallows, our laughter mingling with the crackle of flames. I'd been lost in him, in the way his calloused hands felt against my skin, in the promises he whispered under the stars—promises I clung to like driftwood in a flood. By the end of fall, I was pregnant, a secret I carried like a stone in my belly, too scared to tell anyone until the swell of it couldn't be hidden under oversized sweatshirts anymore. Ethan fell in with the wrong crowd. Started getting into trouble and has been incarcerated for quite some time now. Jada still sees his parents from time to time on holidays, or when I have to study or work an extra shift. Thankfully I'll be getting my degree soon in hopes of getting a real job outside of the diner. I'm going to have to tell them sooner rather than later that Ethan isn't really her father. I don't know how they will react. If they will abandon us in fury or be understanding of my plight.

I'm outside, the Louisiana night pressing in around me, cicadas screaming in the trees as I pace our sagging porch, my blonde hair glowing in the moonlight, my green eyes fierce with a mother's resolve. "This is war, Don," I think, my fists clenched so tight my nails bite into my palms, my voice a whisper in the dark, "and I'll burn it all down to keep her safe." I glance through the window at her sleeping form, my light, my reason, and I'm electrified—terrified, yes, but alive, a fire roaring in my soul that he can't quench. I've lost the lie, the shield I built to protect us, but I've gained something too—a fury, a boldness I didn't know I had, a mother's heart that'll fight until it stops beating. The bitter taste of his return chokes me, the betrayal of a system that doesn't care cuts deep, but the bold in me rises, a thunderclap against his shadow, vowing, "You won't take her—not her spirit, not her soul." I'm Crysta Byrd, fractured but fierce, a young woman forged in pain and love, and this battle's just begun—a war I'll wage with every breath, every tear, every ounce of my being, because she's worth it—she's everything.

CHAPTER 5

SHARKS IN THE COURTROOM

By Fall 2012, the war had forged me into something harder, each fight a scar from the summer I'd lost Jada half the time. I stood at the school gate, her six-year-old hand in mine, her warmth stoking the fire I'd wield to take her back. The drive home was suffocating, the silence heavier than the heat seeping through the cracked windows, pressing into me like a weight I couldn't shake. Every day without her was a slow burn, a resolve hardening in me to outlast the system that kept us apart.

When I got home, the house was too quiet—painfully so—her toys scattered across the living room floor, each one a stab of memory, a piece of her I couldn't hold onto. I walked to her room, her toys spread out like marks of a fight I was still in, and stood there, staring at them. "I'll get you back," I whispered into the empty air, my voice trembling but solid, a promise that held me together. "I swear I will." It was all I had left to give—the fight ahead, and the vow I'd never break.

Days later, I walked into Tom's office, my resolve a quiet ember ready to flare, needing his grit to turn it into a blaze. Tom waited in his smoke-filled office, grizzled and unyielding, my guide and sculptor in this war. His voice hit me first—a rough, guttural growl that landed like a fist to my stomach, knocking the air out of me before I could brace myself. Tom didn't mince words; he didn't have the patience for softness or the luxury of hesitation. He kept pushing me, that grizzled timbre a constant, unrelenting force grinding against my ears, sharpening me like a blade against a whetstone for the war I wasn't ready to wage. My heart was a wild thing in my chest, slamming against my ribs with a frantic, untamed rhythm that echoed in my skull, a drumbeat of terror I couldn't silence. I wasn't a shark—not then, not yet, not by a long shot. I was just me—Crysta—a trembling, fragile girl flung headfirst into a predator's jaws, my blonde hair scraped back into a tight ponytail that pulled at my scalp until it ached, a sharp little pain I clung to because it was something I could feel beyond the numbness. My green eyes, wide and raw, still burned from the tears I'd let spill in the shadowed corners of my bedroom the night before, tears I'd choked on until my throat was raw, my reflection in the mirror a stranger I didn't recognize anymore. Vulnerable didn't even begin to cover it—I was exposed, flayed open, a nerve laid bare to the world.

But Tom didn't care about that. He didn't see the quake in my hands, the way my fingers twitched and curled into themselves as if they could hold me together when everything else was falling apart. He didn't pause for the hitch in my breath, the way it caught in my throat like a sob I wouldn't let escape. To him, I wasn't a girl drowning in fear—I was a soldier, a raw recruit thrust onto a battlefield I hadn't enlisted for, untested and shaking in boots I didn't even own. He was the general, hardened and unyielding, and I was his conscript, dragged into this fight with no armor, no shield, just the ragged edges of my own desperation. "Say less, hide more, trust no one," he barked, his voice a whipcrack that lashed across the room, sharp and relentless, driving into me like nails hammered into soft, splintering wood. The words weren't advice—they were a command, a law etched into the marrow of this war I was losing before I'd even begun. "They'll twist anything—your words, your life, every damn piece of you—so shut it down, Crysta. Lock it tight, or they'll use it to gut you. Study the judgement and follow the rules. Don't step one tiny toe out of line or they'll hold it against you." The rules were many, and I had to learn to follow them, or I could lose Jada for good. They tell me how I can and cannot live my life. First right of refusal, which meant if I can't care for Jada during my time due to other obligations (work, school, etc.), then I had to ask him first if he can keep her. No company of the opposite sex, which meant I couldn't live with a man I'm not married to, not even a roommate. Consistent schedule, which means I have to be available to drop her off, pick her up and have good attendance when it's on my time—just to name a few.

Tom's eyes bored into mine as he said it, smoke curling from the cigarette dangling between his fingers, and I felt those words sink deep, rooting into the pit of my stomach where the fear already lived. My pulse raced faster, a staccato beat that drowned out the hum of the world beyond that stifling office, and I wanted to scream, to tell him I wasn't built for this—that I wasn't the warrior he needed me to be. But my lips stayed sealed, pressed into a thin, trembling line, because even then, I knew he was right. They—whoever "they" were, the faceless enemies lurking in the shadows of this nightmare—would take anything I gave them, every slip, every crack, and turn it into a weapon to tear me apart. So, I sat there, my hands clenched in my lap, nails digging into my palms until I felt the sting and let Tom's growl reshape me. I wasn't a shark yet—but God help me, I'd learn to bite back, because the alternative was losing everything, and that was a surrender I'd never survive.

I nodded, my throat burning as I swallowed the panic clawing its way up, and we sat there for hours—hours that stretched and bled into one another in that smoky den—rehearsing my testimony until my voice turned cold and steady, a steel blade forged in the heat of his relentless drills. I learned to choke back the sobs, to bury them deep behind a mask I was building with every word he hammered into me, my slim frame straightening under the weight of a resolve I didn't know I had until it was demanded. My hands stopped shaking as I spoke, my green eyes narrowing with a focus I'd never felt before, my heart still thundering but now with purpose. I wasn't just Jada's mom anymore—I was becoming something else, something fierce, something born in the fire of this endless fight. Tom watched me transform, his cigarette dangling from his lips, the smoke curling around us like a shroud, and I could see it in his eyes—a flicker of something like pride, or maybe just recognition that I wasn't going to break, not yet. I left that office late, the night pressing in around me, the air heavy with the promise of rain, and I stood on the sidewalk, my breath fogging in the damp chill, feeling the first stirrings of a strength I'd need to survive this war.

I found out soon after, that Don had another child by a woman he also took advantage of on a drunken night. He tried to take the boy away from his mom and she also had to fight the fight that I'm in now. He found out about him when he was almost two years old. He's done this before so he has a leg up on me. He already knows what to do and what to say. She spent her entire inheritance on making sure her child was out of reach of the clutches of his control. I spoke to her once, and she gave me the run down and how it was never enough for him. He always wanted more, more time, more everything. Her son was terrified of him and never wanted to go with him or be alone with him. This worried me to my core.

Fall 2012 bit hard, the air crisp as I stood at the school gate, Jada's six-year-old hand in mine, her warmth grounding me. I've started to set my alarm an hour earlier to make sure I had enough time to get her hair done neatly, iron her clothes, and make her look as presentable as possible. Jada fought me about it endlessly. She wasn't your typical "girl" child that Don wanted her to be. She didn't like dresses and ribbons and bows. She wanted to play in the dirt with her dog and wear big shirts with her hair a mess, but I couldn't let her be this wild, spirted child, especially on a school day, in case Don was there waiting for us, which he often was. On this morning, I slept through the first alarm due to a late night at the diner. I just graduated with a degree in business, but I could only take a part-time office job to keep my schedule open to get Jada back and forth to school because if I couldn't, they would take weekdays from me, and I would only get her every other weekend, so I had to keep some shifts at the diner to survive financially. Her ponytail was off-center as I was rushing, a flaw I'd brushed out, whispering, 'It'll have to do, I don't want you to be late.' She was perfect—every inch of her, my bright, shining light piercing through the shadows that clung to me like a second skin, my green eyes softening as I looked at her, my heart swelling with a love so fiercely it hurt. But then Don's truck was already there, and he stepped out, his massive frame casting a shadow that swallowed us whole. After looking at Jada for a second, "Her hair's a mess," he growled, his voice low and menacing, each syllable dripping with venom that sent a shiver racing down my spine. "Take her home, fix it, or she's late." The words hit me like a slap, igniting a fire in my chest, a hot, surging wave of defiance that clawed its way up my throat. "She's fine, Don! She's six years old; it'll get messed up on the playground anyway," I shot back, my voice trembling but fierce, desperation edging every word as I stepped between him and her. "School's starting—she doesn't need this!" But he stepped closer, his bulk an immovable wall, his presence suffocating, and hissed, "Do it, Crysta, or I'll tell the judge you can't manage her." That smirk of his curled across his lips, a glint of triumph flashing in his icy eyes, and I saw it—the sick satisfaction of a hunter who'd cornered his prey.

My chest tightened, my breath coming in shallow gasps as the world tilted beneath me, but I couldn't fight—not there, not with Jada's tiny hand still in mine, her blue-green eyes wide with confusion, her little brow furrowing as she looked between us. So, I turned away, my vision blurring with tears as I led her back to the car, my heart splintering with every step, my legs shaking under the weight of his threat. The drive home was tense, my grip tight on the wheel as I fought the ache in my chest, brushing her curls with a steady hand and she whispered, 'Why is he always so mad?' I replied, "He just likes things a certain way." Another rule of the court; we can't speak poorly of the other parent to or in front of the minor child. That's what my Jada was referred to as in the courtroom. Just another minor child. Nothing specific about her or her name or any other special identifying character. It drove me crazy. Oblivious to the storm raging inside me, I held her close, my heart pounding against her little back, my resolve hardening with every beat.

I delivered her late that day as well as a couple of other days the week before because of his insistence that I fix whatever was out of place. Mis-matched socks or a crease in her shirt. Her little backpack swaying as she walked into school, her teacher's glance a silent judgment that sank into my bones like a stone. I stood alone in the parking lot afterward, the autumn wind whipping my blonde hair across my face, my green eyes burning with a fury I couldn't release. It festered inside me, a wildfire trapped in a cage, scorching me from the inside out, my slim frame trembling as I clenched my fists, my nails biting into my palms until they bled. The next court date hit—a blazing fight where Don sneered, "She was late multiple times during Crysta's custody," his lawyers twisting it into proof I was unfit, handing over her attendance records. My devotion warped into chaos. They painted me as a mess, a mother unraveling at the seams, while I sat there, my hair pulled tight in a futile attempt to look composed, my fists clenched beneath the table until my knuckles ached. Inside, I was screaming—a primal roar that clawed at my throat—but Tom's grip on my arm, his sharp whisper, "Not now, Crysta, they won't believe you." He was right, why would they? I had no proof that Don was showing up at the carpool gate waiting in haste for us on my days to drop her off. It sounds insane.

I held it together—barely—my green eyes blazing with a fury I couldn't unleash, my heart pounding as I stared at Don across the room, his smirk a taunt that dared me to break. The gavel slammed down, 50/50 custody upheld, and I walked out into the daylight, my jaw set, my breath steadying as I steeled myself for the next round.

By 2013, my life had become an endless, suffocating siege—an unyielding war waged in the cramped, unforgiving confines of courtrooms that smelled of burnt coffee, faded hope, and the sharp tang of desperation. The trials rolled in like a relentless tide, crashing against me with a ferocity that left me breathless—two, three, sometimes six a year, a punishing cadence that hollowed me out, turning me into an emotionless drifter, floating through those cavernous halls one lifeless foot after another. My cheap, scuffed heels clicked against the cold, unforgiving tile floors, each step a metronome counting down the seconds of my disintegration, the sound reverberating off the walls like a dirge. My blonde hair, pulled back so taut it tugged at my scalp, throbbed with a dull, persistent ache—a pain I clung to like a reassurance that I was still human somewhere inside me, a pull towards reality amid the chaos threatening to swallow me whole. I'd sit there, rigid in those hard wooden chairs, my green eyes locked on Don across the room, his smug, lopsided grin cutting through me like a jagged shard of glass, daring me to break, to shatter under the weight of his disdain. His lawyers prowled the room like vultures, their polished shoes tapping out a rhythm of menace, their voices slicing through the air—sharp, calculated, venomous—picking apart every fragment of my life with surgical precision. They dragged my late shifts at the diner into the light, the grease that coated my hands and seeped into my pores like a badge of dishonor, the state of my crumbling little house, the threadbare edges of my resilience—all of it laid bare, dissected, and mocked.

I needed more money, so I got my massage therapy certificate. It was something I could do in my spare time for cash and could work around my schedule. They got warrants for my cell phone and saw the texts between myself and my clients. I finally had my own little place where I could do massages out of my home instead of paying booth rent. They accused me of running a prostitution business out of my home. I disputed these accusations of course. Then Don's attorney pulled out a sheet of paper he intended to present as evidence. It's a text between a female friend and I where she asks, 'I get a happy ending, right' and I give a 'haha, only for you' but Tom was right. They would say anything, even that the words deep tissue massage was slang for something inappropriate. It was a joke that I never intended anyone to see. "I have never done that nor would I ever. I'm a professional. In fact, I don't recall sending this. It was probably something fabricated by your client." I insist, and without me acknowledging that I wrote it, they aren't able to submit to evidence. To them, I wasn't a person, not a mother fighting tooth and nail for her child—just a target, a punching bag to pummel until nothing remained. That day, I learned that the truth doesn't really matter, the only thing that matters is how things are perceived, so I started to wipe every single thing from my cell phone no matter how innocent or meaningless I thought it was. Everything had to go.

And I saw him—Don, the man who'd carved out half my daughter's life as if it were his birthright, lounging there with his stern blue eyes glinting, a predator revelling in the kill, his satisfaction twisting my gut into knots. Before each hearing, I'd huddle with Tom, my weary attorney, in some dimly lit diner booth or cramped office, poring over notes, memorizing responses like a condemned woman pleading for mercy. My voice would come out flat, mechanical— "I work hard," I'd repeat, a mantra against their accusations—while inside, my heart pounded like a war drum, my mind shrieking Jada's name, her tear-streaked face on those wrenching drop-off nights burning behind my eyelids. The gavel would crash down, its echo a thunderclap sealing my fate—50/50 custody and now it's not just labelled as shared custody, but joint physical custody which gives him another inch. An iron chain I couldn't break—and I'd stumble out into the blinding daylight, my spirit unravelling, exhaustion seeping into my bones like a slow poison, heavy and unrelenting.

One sweltering afternoon in the thick of that brutal 2013 summer, I stood outside the courthouse after yet another soul-crushing session, my hands trembling so violently around a Styrofoam cup of water—You weren't allowed to drink or eat anything in the courtroom, and you wouldn't get a break for hours on end—I thought the tiny cup might crumple in my grip. The sun blazed overhead, merciless and unrelenting, scorching the asphalt until it shimmered, searing my skin until it felt like I might melt into the ground. But I barely registered the heat—all I could feel was the icy weight of Don's stare boring into me from across the parking lot, his light eyes gleaming with that sickening, triumphant glint that turned my blood to sludge. He sauntered over, his heavy boots thudding against the pavement, each step a deliberate taunt, and stopped just close enough that I could smell the sourness of his breath, feel the heat radiating off him like a furnace of malice. "She's mine half the time, Crysta, and soon it'll be more" he murmured, his voice low and dripping with venom, a serpent's hiss that coiled around my ears and squeezed. "And there's nothing you can do about it." My blood ignited, a wildfire roaring through my veins, a rage so raw and primal I nearly lunged at him then and there—my fists clenched at my sides, nails digging into my palms until they drew blood, crescent moons of red staining my skin.

But I didn't move—I couldn't—not with Jada's fragile future dangling by a thread so thin it seemed it might snap at the slightest gust, not with the courts hovering over me like vultures, their cold, unblinking eyes scrutinizing my every breath, every twitch of my hands, every faltering step, waiting for the inevitable stumble that would give them the excuse they craved to tear her away from me forever. My body felt rooted to the spot, heavy as stone, my feet sinking into the cracked pavement as if it might swallow me whole. Instead, I forced myself to turn away, my chest tightening with a suffocating dread, my legs trembling beneath me like brittle twigs ready to snap under the weight of it all. I staggered toward my car, each step a battle against the gravity of my own despair, his laughter chasing me like a relentless phantom—a cruel, jagged sound that clawed at my ears, a dark, mocking echo that reverberated through the empty street and into the hollows of my mind, a sound I couldn't outrun no matter how fast my heart pounded or how desperately I willed my feet to carry me forward.

That night, I collapsed onto my sagging couch, the worn fabric rough against my skin, the springs beneath me groaning in protest under my weight—a low, mournful sound that seemed to echo the creak of my breaking spirit, the slow fracturing of everything I'd fought to hold together. The room was dim, lit only by the faint, flickering glow of a streetlamp seeping through the blinds, casting long, skeletal shadows across the walls. In my hands, I clutched Jada's latest drawing—a lopsided heart scribbled in bold red crayon, its edges uneven but fierce with the innocence of her intent, the word "Mommy" scrawled inside in her wobbly, precious script, each letter a testament to her small, determined hands. She was with him that week, her absence a gaping wound carved into my soul, a hollow, throbbing ache that pulsed with every sluggish thud of my heart, every shallow, ragged breath I managed to drag into my lungs. The silence of the house pressed against me, thick and oppressive, broken only by the faint hum of the refrigerator and the distant wail of a train slicing through the night.

I traced her handwriting with a trembling finger, the paper crinkling under my touch, my skin brushing against the wax of the crayon as if I could somehow feel her presence through it. My tears came then, hot and fast, spilling over my lashes and down my cheeks, each drop a scalding testament to the grief I carried. They fell onto the drawing, smudging the red heart until it blurred into a chaotic smear of color and sorrow, the edges bleeding outward like the unravelling of my own resolve. I pressed the paper to my chest, clutching it as if it were her, as if I could hold her close through the thin barrier of this fragile keepsake. "I'll fight for you, baby," I whispered into the suffocating darkness, my voice cracking like brittle glass, barely audible over the relentless, piercing shriek of the cicadas outside my window. Their sound swelled and dipped, a wild, unrelenting chorus of anguish that seemed to rise from the earth itself, a roar that mirrored the scream I swallowed down, the cry I buried deep in my chest where it clawed and gnawed at my ribs.

The night stretched on, endless and unyielding, the air thick with the weight of my solitude. I curled into the couch, my knees drawn up to my chest, the drawing still pressed against me as if it could shield me from the cold emptiness that seeped into every corner of the room. My mind replayed every moment of that day—the sharp edge of his words, the smug curl of his lips, the way his eyes had glinted with a victory he hadn't yet won but believed was his by right. I saw Jada's face, her wide, trusting eyes, her gap-toothed smile, the way her laughter could light up even the darkest corners of my world. She was my anchor, my reason, the tether that kept me from drifting into the abyss—and now she was miles away, sleeping under his roof, her tiny frame lost in a bed that wasn't hers, surrounded by walls that didn't know her like I did.

And yet, in that moment, amid the wreckage of my life—amid the unpaid bills stacked on the coffee table, the chipped paint peeling from the walls, the dreams that had crumbled to dust beneath the weight of reality—I felt something stir. It was faint at first, a whisper of warmth in the frozen void of my despair, a spark igniting in the ashes of all I'd lost. It grew slowly, steadily, a bold, defiant ember flickering to life deep within me, its glow pushing back against the shadows that threatened to consume me whole. It spread through my core, a fire stoking itself with every memory of Jada's hand in mine, every promise I'd made to her in the quiet of her room as she drifted to sleep. It burned brighter, fiercer, refusing to be extinguished, fueled by a love so deep it defied the exhaustion, the fear, the hopelessness that had nearly claimed me. I sat up straighter, my grip tightening on the drawing, my jaw clenching as that fire roared into a blaze—a resolve so unshakable it felt like armor, a determination that whispered back to the darkness: I am not done. Not yet. Not ever.

The days bled into weeks, the weeks into months, and still the war raged on. Each court date was a fresh wound, a new scar etched into my soul—Don's presence a constant, gnawing torment, his voice a blade twisting deeper with every barbed word. I'd sit there, my hands folded tight in my lap, my green eyes burning with unshed tears as his lawyers painted me as unfit, unstable, unworthy. They'd sneer at my diner uniform, the faint stains of ketchup and coffee I could never quite scrub out, as if it were proof of my failure rather than my survival. They'd question my late hours, my exhaustion, the way I'd collapse into bed at dawn only to rise again for Jada, my body aching but my will unbroken. And Don—he'd watch it all, leaning back in his chair with that infuriating smirk, his fingers drumming lazily on the table, a king on his throne revelling in my torment. But Jada—she was my anchor, my reason, her laughter a melody that made my dreams better, her small arms around my neck a memory I clung to when the nights grew too dark. I'd see her on my weeks, her blonde curls bouncing as she ran to me, her eyes—so like mine—shining with a trust that broke my heart anew each time. "Mommy, why can't I stay?" she'd ask, her voice small and trembling, and I'd kneel before her, brushing her hair back, forcing a smile through the tears choking me. "I'm trying, baby," I'd say, my words a vow, a prayer, a plea to a universe that seemed deaf to my cries. "I'm trying so hard." And try I did—every shift I worked, every dollar I scraped together, every sleepless night I spent plotting, planning, fighting—was for her, for the chance to pull her from his grasp, to give her the life he'd never understand.

One weekend I got called in to the diner, Jada was seven now, and I told her that I had to call Don, which is also what she calls him. I don't think I've ever heard her refer to him as her father or Dad. She started to cry and begged me not to make her go over there any more than she had to, but this was a rule. I had to ask him first; I always had to follow the rules. She cried even harder and said, "Please, mom! He hurts me! He pinches my arms, twists my ears, and spanks me even when I'm not doing anything wrong." My heart aches for her, and I know he does these things to her, so I give in. My mom is already at my house visiting and offers for her to stay there. I rush through my shift as fast as I can, knowing this was a bad idea, cleaning tables like a maniac because I'm scared Don will call, and I won't be home yet to let him speak to Jada, but I make it home just in time, and I'm finally relieved after hours of panic like I was doing something illegal.

That summer stretched on, an endless furnace of heat and heartache, and with every passing day, the ember in me grew, fed by the pain, the fury, the love that refused to bow. I'd stand in my tiny kitchen, the floor cold beneath my feet, staring at the stack of legal bills I couldn't pay, the notices piling up like tombstones of my dwindling hope. But I'd grip the counter, my knuckles white, and whisper the hum of Somewhere Over the Rainbow—a litany that kept me upright when my legs begged to buckle. I'd see Don's face in my mind, that cruel glint in his eyes, and the fire would flare, a blaze of defiance that drowned out the despair. I wasn't just fighting him—I was fighting the system, the cold machinery of justice that saw me as a number, not a mother bleeding for her child. And so, I pressed on, my voice hoarse from shouting into the void, my body weary but unyielding, my heart a battlefield where love and rage clashed in a war without end. Because for Jada, I'd burn it all down—I'd fight until my last breath, until the world saw her worth, until she belonged to herself again, whole, and safe outside of his reach. The cicadas sang their mournful song, the night pressed in, and I stood there, a warrior forged in fire, my resolve a blade honed by every tear I'd shed, every wound I'd endured, every moment I'd lost. I was Crysta, her mother, her shield—and I would not break.

Late 2014 stretched into a blur of rain-soaked nights and sleepless dawns, and I remember that evening so clearly it burns—the night I broke open, then stitched myself back together. I was in my beat-up car after yet another defeat, the rain pounding the windshield like it wanted to shatter through and drown me. It was a deluge, a flood that matched the tempest tearing through my chest. Jada was with him that night—my little girl, my heartbeat, her blonde curls, and wide eyes haunting me like a ghost. I could still feel the echo of her arms around my neck from our last goodbye, hear the fading chime of her laugh, and something snapped inside me. I screamed—fists slamming the steering wheel, my voice ripping through the night, raw and primal: "You won't break us, Don! You hear me? You won't!" The sound shattered the silence of that empty parking lot, a howl from the depths of my soul, tears streaming hot and fast down my cheeks as I pictured her—safe, warm, pressed against me where she belonged. My blonde hair hung in wet, tangled strands, plastered to my face; my green eyes blazed wild with a fury only a mother could know. I pressed my forehead to the wheel, my breath fogging the glass, and I vowed it, fierce and unyielding: "I'll get you back, baby. I swear it."

It's another insufferable day of court, and I'm on the stand being questioned, "Ms. Byrd, where was Jada on the 16th of this passed month?" And I know exactly which day they were referring to, "She was spending time with my mother." "And why didn't you extend the first right of refusal of the minor child that day to the father?" I get tense, but I don't show it, "Because I didn't need a babysitter. My mom wanted to spend time with Jada, so I figured I'd run some errands while she was with her." Then his attorney pulls out a sheet of paper and presents it to me and the judge. It's a picture of my car parked outside of the diner with a time stamp on it. Then it hits me, I know Don has been following me, stalking me for only the Lord knows how long. Him or someone he's hired. She asks, "Is this your vehicle outside of the diner where you work?" Still, I don't let it shake me. I think I should tell the truth. Tell them that Don has been abusing her, but he's smart and doesn't leave lasting marks, so I have no proof, and it'll just be thrown out as hearsay. Plus, this could be it, this could be, not only a time I get held in contempt of court, but the smoking gun that takes my baby away from me, so, I lie on the spot, "Yes, that is my car. That is one of the errands I mentioned before. I had to pick up my check, so I could go deposit it at the bank." I see the look on Don's face. He thought he had me for sure. He may be a monster, but he's turned me into a monster as well; a bigger, better, more vicious one. I had to be smarter, more convincing, stronger, and craftier than him if I wanted to win.

I'd learned his game by then—every drop-off a test of his power, every trial a fresh scar—but I was still her mom, damn it, my love a roaring furnace no court could extinguish. The thunder rolled outside, a booming echo to my defiance, and I started the engine, driving home through the flood like a soldier marching to war, my slim frame trembling but unbroken, carved from the wreckage of every loss, every tear-soaked night. The rain washed the world clean, but it couldn't wash away the fire in me, the bold, unyielding strength that had taken root in my bones. I pulled into my driveway, the gravel slick beneath my tires, and I sat there, the engine idling, my hands gripping the wheel as I stared into the storm. I wasn't the same girl who'd stood outside that school three years ago, trembling and lost—I was something else now, something forged in the crucible of this endless fight, my heart a battlefield, my will a weapon.

This war wasn't over—it was just heating up, a blaze I'd stoke with every ounce of my being. I'd become a shark, just like Tom said—my teeth sharp, my will iron, swimming in waters Don thought he ruled. Every moment with Jada was a battle won, every night without her a wound I'd bear until I could bring her home for good. I'd sit on our porch some evenings, the air heavy with the scent of wet earth, my hands tracing the lines of her drawings, her absence a knife in my gut. I'd whisper into the dark, "You're my light, Jada," my voice breaking, "and I'll fight 'til I'm dust to keep you safe." The cicadas sang back, their shrill chorus a hymn to my vow, and I'd stand, my green eyes burning, my resolve a burst against the storm of his control. "I'm a shark now, Don," I'd think, the rain washing the earth clean as I steeled myself, "and I'll bite back harder than you can imagine." I was ready to bleed, to claw, to burn it all down if it meant saving her—my bold heart roaring against the bitter tide, a mother's love that would not, could not, be silenced, no matter how deep the waters rose.

The courtroom battles stretched on, each one a fresh wound, each one a test of the shark I'd become. I'd walk those halls, my heels clicking, my blonde hair pulled tight, my green eyes sharp and unyielding, meeting Don's gaze across the room with a defiance that made him flinch—just for a moment, but it was enough. His lawyers threw their barbs, their voices dripping with contempt, but I'd learned to parry, my answers cold and precise, my mask unbreakable even as my heart screamed beneath it. Tom would nod from beside me, his cigarette smoke curling around us, a silent signal that I was holding my own, that I was swimming with the predators now. The gavels fell, the rulings held, but I didn't break—not anymore. I'd drive home after each fight, my hands steady on the wheel, my mind replaying every word, every glance, thinking about what I could do better next time. I had to be quick, I had to think on my toes, and I had to be perfect. Jada depended on it, "I'm doing this for you, baby, and I won't ever stop." The walls echoed back my vow, and I'd feel it—the bold, unyielding strength of a mother who'd learned to bite back, who'd learned to swim in the deep, dark waters of this war.

Years passed, each one a chapter in this relentless saga, but I never stopped fighting—never stopped sharpening my teeth, never stopped stoking the fire in my chest. Don thought he'd won, thought he could break me with his taunts, his smirks, his endless assaults in those dreadful courtrooms, but he didn't know—couldn't know—the depths of a mother's love, the ferocity of a heart that beat for her child. I'd stand outside that school gate, later that schoolyard, watching Jada grow—six, seven, eight—her blonde curls lengthening, her blue-green eyes bright with a resilience I prayed came from me. Every drop-off was a battle, every pickup a victory, and I'd hold her close, her little arms around my neck, her giggle a balm to the wounds I carried. "I love you, Mommy," she'd say, and I'd choke back the tears, whispering, "I love you most. Always." The war raged on, the sharks circled, but I swam with them now, my slim frame unbowed, my green eyes blazing with a fire that wouldn't die. I was Crysta—Jada's mom, a fighter, a shark—and I'd keep swimming, keep biting, keep burning until she was safe again, until the waters stilled, and we were whole.

CHAPTER 6

A CRY FOR JUSTICE (2015)

July 2015 hit hard; at twenty-six, I sat in a Baton Rouge office, sweat-soaked and unravelling, ready to face a decade-old nightmare. Those eyes of mine darted around the room, frantic and restless, searching for an exit that wasn't there. They flickered from the peeling paint curling off the walls like old scars to the grey-haired woman sitting across from me, her presence both a tether and a torment. Dr. Evelyn Marsh—that was her name, I think, though my mind was too fractured to hold onto it with any certainty. It swirled instead in a hurricane of noise: the slight hum of the yellow lights overhead, the thudding pulse in my ears, the echoes of a past I'd tried so hard to bury.

She was older, her face lined with a quiet strength, her voice a soft but unyielding thread that sliced through the noise with a calming vibration. "Crysta," she said, and my name in her mouth felt like a plea and a command all at once. She leaned forward, her chair scraping faintly against the worn hardwood, her eyes locking onto mine with an intensity that pierced through the fog of my despair. There was kindness there, a gentleness that stung like a fresh wound and soothed like a long-lost embrace, a duality that left me reeling. "You can still report it." Her words hung in the air, heavy and electric, a live wire in the suffocating silence of that tiny room. Report it. Two simple syllables that unravelled me, that ripped open the fragile stitches I'd sewn over a decade of pain and flung me back into the abyss I'd fought so hard to escape

My hands trembled in my lap, fingers twisting together until my knuckles turned white, as if I could hold myself together through sheer force of will. But I couldn't—not then, not there, not with her looking at me like she could see every jagged piece of me, every secret I'd buried beneath layers of silence and shame. That moment, that sweltering July day in 2015, wasn't just a memory—it was the breaking point, the instant when the weight of my past became too much to carry alone, and the first fragile spark of something like hope flickered to life in the wreckage of my soul. Those words—simple, steady, seismic—hit me like a bolt of lightning that split the hollow cavern of my chest wide open and sent a decade of buried screams clawing up my throat, raw and ragged and unstoppable. For a moment, I couldn't move, couldn't blink, couldn't even draw a breath—my body froze, a statue carved from pain and panic, while my mind reeled, spinning back through the years to that night, that couch, that shadow that had haunted me since I was sixteen. I'd been spilling my guts to Dr. Marsh for weeks, maybe months—time was a blur back then—laying bare the nightmares that dragged me kicking and screaming back to December 15, 2005, to his house in Ponchatoula, to that grimy, threadbare couch where he'd pinned me down, his hands like iron shackles, my screams swallowed by the suffocating dark.

I told her about the panic attacks that ambushed me out of nowhere, I told her how his name on a court notice last week stopped me cold, my hands shaking as I gripped Jada's latest drawing. I told her how I'd wake up in the dead of night, choking on his shadow, my sweat-soaked sheets twisted around me like a straitjacket, my green eyes wide and wild as I clawed my way back to reality, whispering Jada's name like a prayer to keep me sane. Jada. My daughter. My light. She was nine years old then, a beautiful, wild miracle with blonde curls that danced in the sunlight and blue-green eyes that held the best parts of me—the parts he hadn't managed to destroy. She was the reason I kept going, the love that tethered me to this earth when all I wanted was to disappear, to dissolve into the wind and never feel again. But she was also the wound that never healed, because he—Don, that monster, that predator—had her half the time, thanks to a cursed 50/50 custody ruling handed down when she was just a baby, when I was twenty-two and still too broken to fight hard enough in that stuffy courtroom. Now, in 2015, knowing he'd raped me made every moment Jada spent with him a fresh terror I couldn't ignore.

I was unravelling, thread by fragile, fraying thread, my mind a battlefield of memories I couldn't outrun, my body a vessel for a pain I couldn't name. And now here was Dr. Marsh, her grey hair pulled back in a neat bun, her notepad resting on her lap, looking at me like I wasn't just a ghost, like I still had a pulse, like I could still do something about it. "Thirty years after eighteen," she added, her voice steady as a rock in a storm, "Louisiana gives you time." Time. That word—small, sharp, infinite—pierced me like a blade, slicing through the fog of my despair and sparking something in the pits of my soul, something alive in the ashes that remained there. A flicker of hope, an ember of rage, a tiny, trembling flame that I grabbed with both hands, my breath hitching in my throat as I whispered, "Okay." It wasn't just a word—it was a vow, a battle cry, a hope I clung to as my chest exploded with a fire I hadn't felt since Jada's first kick against my womb all those years ago, when I was seventeen and terrified and still somehow dreaming of a future. That fire roared through me, a resolve that screamed, I'm not just a victim anymore—I can fight back. I sat there, fingers gripping the chair arms until my knuckles whitened, and I felt it—the shift, the awakening, the moment I stopped being the girl who'd floated away from that night and started being the woman who'd make him pay. It was days later—how many, I couldn't tell you, not with any certainty. Three? Five? Time back then was a slippery, treacherous thing, sliding through my fingers like the muddy waters of the Tangipahoa River after a hard rain. All I know is that it was July, and the Louisiana heat clung to me like a second skin, a suffocating, humid shroud that pressed down on my shoulders as I pushed open the heavy glass door of the Tangipahoa Parish Sheriff's Office.

The air outside was thick, heavy with the sour tang of swamp water and the faint, desperate rot of something dying in the distance. It followed me in, that smell, mixing with the stale cigarette smoke and the sharp bite of industrial cleaner inside the station. My cheap dollar-store flip-flops—flimsy, faded pink things I'd worn down to nothing—slapped against the cracked, yellowed tile floor, each step a sharp, echoing beat that matched the wild thumping of my heart. Sweat stung as I faced the deputy, breath sharp. And my eyes—they were alive that day, lit with a fire I hadn't felt since I was a girl, a fury that had been smoldering deep in my bones for a decade, waiting for this moment to erupt. I stood there, all five-foot-three of me, trembling like a leaf caught in a storm, but fierce—fierce in a way I hadn't been since I was sixteen, before the world broke me open and left me bleeding. My slim frame, wiry from years of carrying more than my share of burdens, vibrated with something primal—rage, yes, but also shame, and love, and a grief so deep it felt like it might swallow me whole. I faced that deputy behind his scratched-up wooden desk, his notepad splayed open like some sacred book, his pen hovering in the air as if he could write me a new ending. He looked up at me, his face weathered and tired, and I didn't care—I didn't care that he'd probably heard a hundred stories like mine, didn't care that the fluorescent lights buzzed overhead like a swarm of angry wasps, didn't care that my voice cracked as I opened my mouth. I let it all pour out of me, a flood I'd held back for ten long years, a torrent of jagged, ugly truth that I couldn't stopper up even if

I'd tried. "December 15, 2005," I said, and my voice—God, it shook, but it was strong, slicing through the dead air of that station like a knife through flesh. "His house in Ponchatoula, on that damn couch—I was sixteen, and he raped me." The words ripped out of me, each one a splintered piece of glass I'd carried lodged in my throat since that night, cutting me every time I swallowed, every time I tried to breathe. I named him—Don.

Don, the monster whose shadow still slithered into my nightmares, whose crooked smirk still twisted my guts into knots, whose rough, greedy hands still ghosted over my skin every time I shut my eyes. His name tasted like bile on my tongue, but I spat it out anyway, let it hang there in the air between me and that deputy, heavy and real and undeniable. Ten years I'd carried that name, ten years I'd let it fester inside me, a wound that never healed, a poison that seeped into every corner of my life. And now, here I was, spilling it all out, my voice rising, breaking, raw as an open wound. I didn't stop there. I couldn't. The words kept coming, tumbling over each other like they'd been waiting all this time to be free. I listed witnesses—friends from that night at the bar, the night that started with laughter and cheap beer and ended in a hell I couldn't escape. Candace, with her loud, brassy laugh that could fill a room, her cloud of cheap perfume that clung to everything she touched—I could still hear her voice, still smell that sickly-sweet scent if I tried hard enough.

Cami, who'd wrapped her arms around me that night, hugged me tight before she left, never knowing what was coming after she walked out that door. They were there, they saw me before it happened, before Don turned that night into something dark and twisted and wrong. Their names fell from my lips like ghosts clawing their way out of a grave, rising up to stand beside me in that sheriff's office. They'd drifted away over the years, those girls—scattered like smoke on the wind, lost to time and distance—but I threw their names out anyway, desperate for anything that might tether my story to something solid, might make it real to this stranger scratching notes on his pad. My heart was a war drum in my chest, pounding so hard I thought it might break through my ribs and spill onto the floor. Sweat trickled down my spine, soaking the back of my thin tank top, and my hands—God, they wouldn't stop shaking, clenched into fists at my sides as I sat there, pouring out a decade's worth of pain. The deputy nodded, his face unreadable, and let out a low grunt, a sound that might've been sympathy or just habit. "We'll look into it, ma'am, and don't tell anyone that you've made the report. We don't want him getting tipped off; but we'll handle it, don't worry," he said, his voice flat but steady, like a rock I could cling to in the middle of this storm. And I believed him—Lord help me, I did. I had to. After ten years of silence, ten years of carrying this alone, I needed to believe that someone, somewhere, would finally hear me. That this wasn't just another scream into the void. That maybe, just maybe, this was the beginning of something—justice, or healing, or at least a chance to breathe without feeling his shadow on my back.

I stood there, chest heaving, eyes burning, and for the first time in a decade, I felt like Crysta again—not the broken girl he'd left behind, but the woman who'd walked through fire to tell her truth. I left that station lighter than I'd felt in years, my shoulders lifting as if I'd shed a decade of shame right there on that cracked tile floor, my green eyes blazing with a hope I hadn't dared to feel since Jada came screaming into the world nine years before. I walked out into the oppressive heat, the sun searing my skin, and I let myself dream—oh, how I let myself dream! I imagined Don in handcuffs, his smug grin wiped clean off his face, his power stripped away as they hauled him off to rot where he belonged. I pictured Jada safe in my arms, safe to be who she wanted to be, her blonde curls tickling my chin, her blue-green eyes free of his shadow forever. That dream carried me home on wings of fire, a soaring, reckless hope that burned so bright it blinded me to the storm that was coming, the silence that would snuff it out. But the days stretched into weeks, and that fire—God, that beautiful, blazing fire—began to flicker, smothered by a silence that grew heavier with every unanswered call, every empty promise, every moment I realized they weren't coming for him. I'd pace my tiny kitchen in Hammond, Jada at school, the linoleum cold under my bare feet, the phone pressed so hard to my ear it left a red mark on my cheek. My voice was tight with desperation, cracking with every plea—"Any updates? Please, he's got my daughter, don't you get that?"—but all I got were grunts, "It's in process," or worse, the cold, hollow click of a dial tone that felt like a slap across my face. My nails were bitten down to bloody stubs, jagged and raw, my blonde hair falling in my face as I dialed daily, obsessively, begging detectives who never called back, my pleas echoing into a void that swallowed my hope whole.

August bled into September, the Louisiana heat relentless, a mirror to the torment churning in my soul, and I'd stand at my sink, staring out at the backyard where Jada should've been running around or playing volleyball with her friends over the net I'd hung for her last spring. "They'll help," I'd whisper to myself, my voice small and trembling, "they have to," but the silence mocked me, a cruel, sneering reminder that I was alone—always alone—in this fight. By October, I was a live wire, my patience snapped clean in two, my heart a furnace of rage and despair that burned hotter with every passing day they let him walk free. I couldn't take it anymore—the waiting, the wondering, the not knowing if Jada was safe when she was with him, if he was biding his time, if he'd hurt her like he'd hurt me.

I stormed back to that sheriff's station, my blonde hair a wild, sweaty tangle, my voice hoarse from crying myself to sleep every night, demanding answers like a mother possessed, a woman unhinged. "What's happening with my report?" I shouted, slamming my hands down on the counter so hard the pens rattled, my green eyes flashing with a fury that scared even me, a wildfire that could've burned that whole damn building to the ground. The deputy—this one younger, with a blank, bored stare—shrugged, his words a knife plunged straight into my gut: "Never assigned, ma'am. Slipped through." Slipped through. Slipped through? Ten years of pain, a predator loose in the world, my child at risk—and it was a clerical error? I leaned forward, voice low and steady. "Ten years, and it slipped through? My daughter's with him now—fix this." Tears streamed down my face, hot and unstoppable, a flood I couldn't dam even if I'd tried, as my voice broke, splintered, shattered into a thousand pieces right there in front of strangers who didn't care. They ushered me out, hands gentle but firm, treating me like a nuisance, a hysteric, not a victim, not a mother bleeding for justice, not a woman who'd just had her last shred of hope ripped away. I collapsed in my Toyota, rain streaking the windows, sobs racking me as the betrayal sank in—a file lost, a name ignored. And then, as if the universe hadn't taken enough, another blow landed. Papers arrived, served cold and official, from Ethan's parents—not Jada's blood.

They were demanding grandparents' rights, claiming one weekend a month with my daughter, despite having no biological tie to her. Another party carving out a piece of my child's life, another claim on her time, her heart, her freedom. I stood in my kitchen, the papers trembling in my hands, my vision blurring with tears and rage. Ethan's parents—good people, I'd thought, with their warm smiles and Sunday dinners—had gone to court behind my back, petitioning Judge Coyne for a share of Jada. And he granted it, slicing away one of my precious weekends a month, handing it to them like it was nothing, like my time with my daughter was a commodity to be bartered. More time with her, lost. Another wound, another theft, another piece of my heart ripped away by a system that seemed hell-bent on breaking me. I wanted to scream, to tear the papers to shreds, to storm into that courtroom and demand to know why everyone—Don, the sheriff, now Ethan's parents—thought they could take from me without consequence. But after the trial, Ethan's parents approached me, their faces soft with something like regret. "Crysta," they said, their voices low, "we did this to have something legally binding.

If something happens to you, we don't want Don to keep her from us. We're not trying to take her—we're trying to protect her." Their words landed heavy, a mix of comfort and salt in the wound. They were good people, I knew that, and their reasoning made a kind of sense, but it didn't ease the ache of losing those hours with Jada, didn't dull the sting of yet another loss in a war I was fighting alone. It was another reminder that even those who meant well could hurt me, could chip away at the fragile life I was trying to build for my daughter. That night, I curled up on the couch in our little house in Hammond, the spot where Jada should've been sprawled out with her journal, her laughter filling the air like music, her blonde curls bouncing as she chattered about her day. Instead, it was empty, silent, a void that mirrored the gaping hole in my chest where my heart used to be. I clutched her photo—God, that photo, the one from her eighth birthday, her blue-green eyes sparkling, her smile so wide it lit up the world—and whispered, "I'll find a way, baby," my voice cracking, my tears soaking the frame as they fell, relentless, a river of grief and love and fury I couldn't hold back. My hair hung damp, my frame taut with exhaustion and resolve, because the system had failed me—turned its back and left me to drown—but I wouldn't fail her. I remembered Candace's laugh, Cami's hug—maybe they'd speak for me yet.

The sheriff's neglect stung, a bitter pill, but the fire in me roared louder, a scream rising from my soul's wreckage, shaking the foundations of who I'd been. I'd filed that report with every ounce of courage I had left, laid my shame bare for strangers who didn't give a damn, stripped myself raw and bleeding in front of that deputy's scratched-up desk, and though it hadn't moved the needle—not yet, not an inch—it had moved me. I was done being silent, done being the ghost who'd floated away from that night on that couch, done being the girl who let him win. My cry for justice had been met with nothing, a scream into a void that didn't scream back, but it wasn't the end—it was the spark, the ember that would grow into a blaze I'd wield like a weapon. I sat there in the dark, the cicadas outside shrieking their endless, mournful song, my green eyes staring into the shadows, fierce and unyielding, unblinking as I saw his face—Don's face, that smirk I'd never forget, that smug, predatory grin that had haunted me for a decade. "You can't silence me forever," I vowed, my voice a low, guttural growl that rumbled from the depths of my chest, a promise carved in blood and bone. The bitterness of their abandonment chokes me, a thick, sour taste that lodges in my throat and threatens to drag me under. It's a weight, heavy and relentless, pressing down on my chest until I can barely breathe, until I feel like I might crumple, fold in on myself like a house of cards caught in a hurricane. But something's rising in me now, something bold and fierce, a tide of fury and love so powerful I can't hold it back—I won't hold it back. I've screamed for justice before, my voice raw and ragged, and all I got was silence, a cold, hollow nothing that rang in my ears like a death knell tolling for every hope I'd ever clung to. But that silence? It's not the end of me. It's the beginning. It's the spark that feeds the inferno in my veins, the fuel that keeps me moving when my legs shake and my soul aches.

I wipe the tears from my cheeks, my slim fingers—still trembling, but stronger now—tracing the edges of Jada's face in that worn-out photo I keep tucked against my heart. Her smile, so innocent, so pure, cuts me like a dagger, slicing through the numbness to remind me of what's at stake. But it's more than pain—it's a beacon, a light in the endless dark, a promise that I can't stop, won't stop, not ever. "I'll scream louder than you know," I whisper into the stillness of the night, my voice steady now, a vow carved in steel and tempered by a decade of agony. It's a promise to Don, that bastard who thought he could break me and walk away. It's a promise to the sheriff who failed me, who looked at my tears and saw nothing worth his time. It's a promise to every single soul who's turned their back, who's let Jada slip through the cracks like she doesn't matter. They don't know what I'm capable of, not yet. They don't know the love that fuels me, a love so fierce it could burn cities to the ground, a love that's kept me alive when I wanted to give up. Ten years of pain have forged me into something new, something unbreakable, and I'll use every ounce of it to bring her back to me. This isn't just a fight—it's my life, my soul, my redemption, and I'll be damned if I let them take that from me too. Love doesn't quit, you see, and neither would I. Not then, not now, not ever.

I'd march through walls of fire, my bare feet blistering on the coals, my voice tearing through the howling storms until it was hoarse and ragged. I'd claw my way through the thick, suffocating mud, nails splitting, hands bleeding, if it meant Jada would be safe. If it meant Don, that shadow of a man who'd haunted me for a decade, would finally face the reckoning he'd slipped away from for ten unbearable years. Ten years of his smirk, his evasion, his victory over a system that let him dance just out of reach. I could still feel the weight of that deputy's blank stare, those cold, hollow words—"slipped through"—sinking into my chest like a blade, twisting until I couldn't breathe. But I didn't let it bury me. No, I let it fuel me. I let it pile kindling on the fire inside me, stoking the flames until they roared, wild and untamed, licking the sky with a fury that could've set the heavens ablaze. I sat there that night in Hammond, the darkness pressing in, thick with memories. My hair hung wild, framing a face that had seen too much. My eyes burned through the shadows, refusing to dim. I stood firm, a warrior forged in loss and love, tempered by a pain carved into my bones. The cicadas wailed outside, echoing my ache, while the rain hammered down, each drop a drumbeat to the war I was waging within myself. "I'm not done," I whispered into that night, my voice soft but fierce, a vow to the universe, to God, to anyone who might still be listening. And I meant it—down to the marrow of my being, I meant it.

I wasn't done, not by a long shot, not while there was breath in my lungs and a heartbeat thudding defiantly in my chest. A few weeks after October had nearly broken me, we faced off again in court. Don was furious—Jada had learned the truth about how she was conceived, spilled by a neighbor who knew the story. He accused me of telling her he raped me, claiming it broke the court's rule against badmouthing him. I was out of money and out of time—Tom refused to help—so I stood alone. With no one to hold me back, I unleashed my rage. When Don took the stand, I asked, "Do you know Louisiana's statutory rape law?" He said, "yes." "Cite it," I demanded. His lawyer objected—relevance—but the judge allowed it. I pressed again, and I saw fear flicker in his eyes. He knew what I was after—the truth, loud and clear for all to hear. It'd been hinted at before, but never this direct, and Tom wasn't here to stop me. Then he hid behind his Fifth Amendment right, refusing to answer. Coward. I asked, "How do you know I told her?" He blamed the neighbor, but that got tossed as hearsay. Still, by the end, they named him domiciliary parent—handing him control over Jada's school, her health, her life. Another blow, but it didn't kill my fire—it fueled it. I thought of Dr. Marsh, her steady voice cutting through the chaos of my mind like a lighthouse beam piercing the fog. "You can still report it," she'd said, her words simple but solid, a lifeline tossed to a woman drowning in her own despair. I clung to them, gripped them tight like a raft in a flood that threatened to sweep me away. She'd seen me—really seen me—when I'd forgotten how to see myself, when I'd become a ghost in my own life, drifting through the wreckage of what Don had left behind.

I don't know how and I don't know when, but I believe others will see me too one day. Her belief in me, her quiet strength, it stitched something back together inside me, something I thought had been torn beyond repair. And then there was Jada—my heart, my soul, my reason for every step I took, every tear I shed, every scream I let loose into the void. I pictured her, my beautiful girl, running toward me, her arms outstretched, her face alight with freedom, whole and unbroken and herself again. That image—God, that impossible, breathtaking image—it was the thread that kept me tethered when the weight of it all pressed down so hard, I thought I'd crumble beneath it. It was the spark that kept my fire burning, the dream that kept my legs moving when all I wanted was to collapse. I left the courtroom, the weight of his victory crushing me, but my fire still flickered, refusing to die. I'd filed that report, you know. I'd sat in that suffocating sheriff's office, my hands shaking as I poured out my truth, every word a shard of glass I'd pulled from my own heart. I'd screamed it, sobbed it, laid my soul bare on that cold, unforgiving table, hoping—praying—someone would hear me. But the deputy's eyes stayed empty, the system's wheels stayed still, and Don stayed free. It gutted me, that silence, that indifference. It felt like a betrayal so deep it could've swallowed me whole. But even then, even when it seemed like my cries had fallen on deaf ears, something shifted inside me.

Speaking it, naming it, letting it spill out into the world—it changed me. It woke me up. It armed me. That report might not have brought justice yet, but it lit a fuse, turned me into something new, something fierce, something Don could never silence again. He might've thought he'd won, you see. He might've sat there, smug and untouchable, believing he'd crushed me for good all those years ago. But he didn't know—he couldn't know—the fire he'd ignited in me, the beast he'd unleashed with every lie, every dodge, every moment he thought he'd gotten away with it. That fire was mine now, and it burned hotter than he could ever imagine, a blaze that would consume him if I had anything to say about it. The sheriff's office might've failed me, the system might've turned its back with a shrug, but I wasn't finished. I'd find another way, another door to kick down, another battleground to claim. I'd keep fighting, keep clawing, keep screaming until the world couldn't ignore me anymore. Because this wasn't just a cry for justice now—it was a declaration of war. A war I'd wage with every ounce of my being, for Jada, for me, for the pieces of myself I was still piecing back together. I'm Crysta, and I'm not done—not by a long shot. And I'd fight it with everything I had—every tear, every scream, every ounce of love in my battered, beating heart—until Jada was safe, until Don was dust, until the sixteen-year-old me could finally rest. The night closed in, the rain a curtain around my resolve, and I sat there, a mother on fire, a survivor rising, ready to tear the world apart and build it anew. Because I was Crysta Byrd, and I was done running, done hiding, done losing. The fight was mine now. Tomorrow, I'd call Tom—find a way to make them listen, or I'd do it myself.

CHAPTER 7
ISOLATION AND THREATS

It's August 2016, and I'm twenty-seven, teetering on the edge of a crumbling abyss as I stand on the fractured asphalt outside Don's house in Ponchatoula. The Louisiana dusk unfurls above me, a wild canvas of orange and purple bleeding across a sky so vast it feels like it's mocking me—mocking the chaos clawing at my chest, the storm of love and fear and helpless rage that's been brewing inside me for days. Just six nights ago, on August 29th, Jada turned ten. I can still feel the weight of that evening, the way I hunched over our chipped kitchen counter, my hands trembling like fragile leaves in a gale as I stirred the chocolate batter for her birthday cake. The oven's faint warmth had kissed my skin, a fleeting whisper of comfort against the icy dread that had already begun to seep into my bones, chilling me to the marrow. I'd frosted that cake with shaky fingers, each swirl of icing a desperate act of devotion, while Jada's laugh—bright, fleeting, a melody I'd cling to forever—danced through the air. She'd smeared a dollop of chocolate on my nose, her blue-green eyes locking with mine, sparkling like the only stars I'd ever need. She was my lifeline, my anchor, my entire world wrapped in a small, fierce soul. But now, here I am, buckling her into the sagging, rust-eaten sedan that's carried us through so much, and the air hangs heavy—humid, oppressive, laced with a darkness I can't name but feel in every fiber of my being. Her blonde hair falls limp, framing a face that's lost its radiant glow, her eyes dulled as though a storm has swallowed the sun within her. "How was it, baby?" I ask, my voice a fragile, quivering thread threatening to snap, my hands fumbling with the seatbelt, aching to pull her into my arms, to wrap her in a shield of love and safety and everything I'd die to give her. She shrugs—a small, broken twitch of her shoulders, a gesture so defeated it rips through me—and stares out the grimy window, her silence a blade sinking deeper into my gut with every breath she doesn't take to answer me.

Don looms behind her, a towering figure in the doorway, arms crossed over his chest like some unyielding sentinel guarding a treasure he has no right to claim. His broad frame casts a shadow that feels like it's swallowing us whole, and when he speaks—"She's fine"—his voice is a low, cold slash, a jagged edge cutting through the stillness of the evening. But I know she's not fine. Oh, God, I *know* she's not, and the certainty of it grips my chest like a vice, squeezing until I can barely breathe. I slide behind the wheel, my hands trembling on the keys, Don's shadow clinging to us like a dark, oily stain I can't wash away, and I drive off, leaving him standing there, his presence a specter that haunts the edges of my vision.

The drive home is a slow, torturous descent into a private hell, the road unfurling endlessly before me like a ribbon of despair. Headlights carve weak paths through the gathering dark, illuminating nothing but the void that's swallowing my daughter whole. Jada sits beside me, mute, her small hands folded in her lap as though she's afraid to move, afraid to exist too loudly in this moment. I steal glances at her, my green eyes burning with tears I refuse to let fall, my blonde hair clinging to my sweat-damp neck like a shroud. I'm drowning—drowning in a flood of questions I can't bring myself to voice: *What did he do to you? What's he saying when I'm not there? Why won't you talk to me, baby?* Each unspoken word is a stone piling onto my chest, crushing the air from my lungs, leaving me gasping in the wreckage of my own fear. We pull into our gravel driveway, the tires crunching against the stones in a harsh, grating rhythm that jars against the suffocating silence between us. I carry her inside, her backpack slung over my shoulder like a burden I'd bear a thousand times over if it meant I could carry her pain instead. Her steps are slow, heavy, as though she's dragging invisible chains behind her, and I feel them too—phantom weights pulling at my heart, my soul, my every desperate hope.

That night, I tuck her into bed, her room a fragile sanctuary of faded stuffed animals and crayon drawings pinned haphazardly to the walls—little pieces of her spirit captured in brighter days. I linger there, my fingers brushing back her soft hair, my voice a trembling whisper as I murmur, "You can tell me anything, baby. Anything at all." But her eyes flutter shut, sealing me out, locking away whatever truth she's buried deep inside. I'm left standing there, alone in the dim glow of her nightlight, my heart pounding a frantic, erratic beat against my ribs, my mind spiraling into a whirlwind of terror I can't name but can't escape. It's a fear that claws at me, raw and relentless, whispering that something's wrong—terribly, irrevocably wrong—and I'm powerless to stop it, to save her, to pull her back from the edge of whatever abyss she's teetering on. All I have left is this moment, this fragile thread of love stretched taut between us, and the sinking dread that it might not be enough.

November descended upon Hammond like a heavy, suffocating veil, its grey tendrils wrapping around my soul, tightening with every passing day. The air grew thick, oppressive, as if the town itself conspired to mirror the turmoil festering within me. I was coming apart at the seams, my nights a relentless storm of restless pacing and haunting nightmares—his face, etched with that cold, unyielding stare, his hands, possessive and inescapable, and that cursed couch from 2005, a scene replaying in my mind with such vivid, sickening clarity that I could still feel the fabric beneath my trembling fingers. Sleep eluded me, a cruel phantom slipping through my grasp, leaving me raw, exposed, and drowning in memories I'd fought so hard to bury.

It was the 19th, a Saturday cloaked in the dull hum of routine, when the fragile threads holding me together began to snap. I stood in the living room, folding laundry with mechanical precision, the dryer's low roar a constant companion to my spiraling thoughts. The pile of clothes grew—socks, towels, Jada's tiny shirts—each fold a desperate attempt to anchor myself in the present. Then she appeared, my little girl, shuffling in with the weight of a thousand unspoken burdens. Jada, my heart's light, clad in faded pajamas that hung loose on her small frame, climbed into my lap as though she were still five, seeking the safety of a time long lost. Her warmth pressed against me, a fleeting comfort, and I wrapped my arms around her instinctively, the scent of her strawberry shampoo a bittersweet reminder to the child she once was.

The television flickered in the background, a kaleidoscope of bright colors and cheerful cartoon voices dancing across the screen, but her eyes didn't follow the motion. Her head rested heavy against my chest, her breaths shallow and uneven, as if each one carried a secret too heavy to release. I felt it before she spoke—the tremor in her stillness, the quiet storm brewing beneath her silence. "He won't let me see my friends," she whispered, her voice so fragile, so small, it nearly dissolved into the dryer's drone. My world screeched to a halt. My hands, mid-fold, froze, a worn T-shirt slipping from my grasp to crumple on the floor like a discarded piece of my sanity. "What?" The word clawed its way out of my throat, ragged and choked, as dread coiled tight around my heart. She burrowed deeper into me, her face pressed against my shirt, her muffled confession slicing through the air like a blade—"No sleepovers, no calls, nothing. I ask him why, and he just yells at me."

The room spun. My arms tightened around her, a mother's desperate shield, as my pulse thundered in my ears, a war drum echoing the fury igniting within me. I could see it—her, my vibrant, giggling Jada, trapped in his house, her laughter snuffed out, her spirit locked behind invisible bars. Rage surged through my veins, hot and unrelenting, warring with the icy terror that gripped my soul. She was ten, just ten, and already he was stealing her—piece by precious piece—caging the girl who once ran through our home with boundless joy, her voice a melody that could chase away even my darkest days.

The next morning arrived like a thief, silent and uninvited, the weight of her words still pressing against my chest. I waited until the house grew still, until her soft snores floated down the hall like a fragile lullaby, a sound that both soothed and shattered me. Barefoot, I crept into her room, the hardwood cold against my skin, each step a quiet rebellion against the fear clawing at my insides. Her backpack sat by her desk, a pink canvas relic of a happier era, its faded patches and frayed straps a testament to the innocence we'd lost. My hands trembled as I reached for it, my breath catching in my throat, a jagged hitch that betrayed the storm raging within. I unzipped it slowly, as if the sound might wake the ghosts lurking in the shadows, and there it was—her diary, glitter-crusted and dog-eared, a gift I'd given her years ago with a smile that now felt like a cruel mockery of the past.

I sank to the floor, the diary cradled in my lap, and flipped through its pages with a frantic urgency, my heart pounding so fiercely it drowned out the cicadas' relentless shrieking beyond the window. Then I saw it—pages torn out, their ragged edges like open wounds, a violent scar across her story. And there, scrawled in his jagged, angry handwriting, were the words that broke me: "No secrets." The air fled my lungs. My knees gave way entirely, and I collapsed fully, clutching that diary to my chest as if it could hold the pieces of my fracturing world together. Tears came then, hot and unstoppable, soaking the carpet beneath me as the truth crashed over me like a tidal wave—he was isolating her, stripping away her friends, her freedom, her very essence, locking my bright, laughing girl in a prison forged by his control.

I saw her then, in my mind's eye, at six years old, hosting tea parties with Ellie and Mia, their chatter a symphony of life that once filled our home with warmth. She'd been a whirlwind of joy, her tiny hands pouring imaginary tea, her laughter a light that could pierce any darkness. Now, at ten, she was a shadow of that girl, her diary a chilling testament to his dominion, his insatiable need to own her every thought, every breath, every spark of who she was. My chest heaved with silent sobs, the weight of my failure as a mother pressing down until I could barely breathe. He was taking her from me, from herself, and I was left grasping at the remnants of the child I'd sworn to protect, vowing in that tear-soaked moment to fight for her with every ounce of strength I had left.

The kitchen feels like a battlefield tonight, the linoleum beneath my bare feet an icy wasteland that bites into my soles as I stumble forward, my trembling fingers fumbling for the phone. My breaths come in jagged gasps, each one a plea, a scream trapped in my chest as I dial Tom—my lawyer, the only remnants I have left to sanity. The line crackles to life, and his name spills from my lips like a prayer, "Tom, Tom, please—" My voice shakes, a fragile thing teetering on the edge of collapse, as I pace the tiny room, my eyes darting to the chaos of Jada's crayons strewn across the table. Those bright, defiant streaks of color—reds, blues, yellows—lie scattered like shards of a life he's hell-bent on shattering, a life I've fought tooth and nail to protect. "Can he do this?" I beg, the words tumbling out in a rush, raw and unfiltered, dripping with the desperation that's clawing at my insides. "He's cutting her off, Tom—her friends, her laughter, every scrap of joy she clings to—can he really do this to her? He won't even let her speak to me on the phone when he has her without him listening." My voice breaks, a sob threatening to swallow me whole, and I grip the edge of the counter, my knuckles whitening as I wait for his answer.

Tom's voice rumbles through the receiver, gruff and worn, heavy with the weight of a man who's seen too many broken mothers like me. "He's got rights, Crysta," he says, each syllable landing like a hammer on my fragile hope. "Unless she's hurt—physically hurt, bruises or blood the courts can see—it's his call. That's the law." Physically hurt? The words ignite a fire in my gut, a rage so fierce it blinds me.

Physically hurt? She's fading before my eyes, my little girl, her spirit withering under his suffocating grip, her light dimming with every day he tightens the chains around her soul. That's not hurt? That's not a wound? I slam the phone down, the clatter echoing through the empty house like a gunshot, and my fists crash against the counter, over and over, the pain exploding through my hands as my knuckles split open, blood smearing the chipped wood in crimson streaks. A howl rips from my throat, primal and guttural—"He's killing her soul, Tom! He's killing her, and I can't stop it!"—and I collapse into a chair, my blonde hair falling like a tangled curtain over my face, hiding the tears streaming down my cheeks. My green eyes burn, blazing with a fury that has no outlet, no release, and I'm drowning, a mother lost in a nightmare where love is powerless, where the law turns a blind eye and hands my daughter to a monster, calling it justice. I sit there, chest heaving, blood dripping onto the floor, and wonder how it came to this—how I became a warrior with no weapons, a mother whose heart bleeds for a child I can't save.

That was now, but the memory of April 2017 haunts me still, a humid beast of a month that sank its claws into my life and never let go. It was the 23rd, and I was outside our little house, the air thick and sticky, the sun a relentless tyrant beating down on me as I unloaded groceries from the trunk of my battered sedan. Sweat trickled between my shoulder blades, soaking my shirt, and I could hear Jada inside, her soft humming drifting through the open window as she was eating at our rickety kitchen table. Those smiles that returned when she's been back home for a few days—her tiny rebellion against the greyness he'd cast over her world—were my anchor, a reminder of the light I swore to protect. I juggled the bags in my arms—milk sloshing in its jug, bread squashed under my elbow, a dented can of soup that screamed our budget's limits—when the growl of his truck tore through the quiet. My heart lurched into my throat, a trapped bird flapping against my ribs, and I froze, the bags slipping in my sweaty grip as his tires crunched the gravel, each sound a threat, a promise of something dark and unstoppable.

He stepped out, his boots hitting the ground like thunder, his bulk looming over me like a storm cloud swollen with menace. I was sixteen again in that moment, pinned to that couch, his weight crushing the air from my lungs, his breath hot and victorious against my skin as I froze with fear. Time collapsed, and there he was—older, broader, but the same predator, his piercing blue eyes glinting with the same cruel hunger. He leaned in close, too close, his voice a hiss that slithered into my ears and coiled around my spine. "I've got connections, Crysta," he said, his lips curling into a smirk that chilled my blood. "Cops, judges—I can take her anytime I want. Be careful." The bags slipped from my hands, apples tumbling into the dirt, rolling away like my world unravelling thread by thread. I couldn't move, couldn't breathe, my green eyes locked on his, wide and unblinking, as his words sank in—cops, judges, his power a noose tightening around my neck, a guillotine poised above my daughter's life. He smirked again, a flash of teeth that was more snarl than smile, and then he was gone, climbing back into his truck, the engine roaring as he peeled away, dust rising in a choking cloud that stung my eyes and clogged my throat. No one around to see his display of strength. He must have been watching for the right time to approach.

I filed the paperwork this time. For the first time, I was taking HIM to court, with a motion that exhibited physical abuse on her, and he didn't like that I had that power. He wasn't in control in that moment, and it was killing him. He must have been served with the papers that day. I was asking for full custody because he caught Jada with a secret cell phone that she was using to talk to her friends. He was furious and kept yelling and pushing her down and hitting her in the back of the head. Terrified, she ran to the neighbor's house bare foot, through the mud and used their phone to call me to come and pick her up. We called the cops and told them what happened, but after getting a statement from Don, they refused to let us press charges against him. I don't know what he told the officer to make him do this, but it wasn't fair, and I wanted the judge to know about it although the he wouldn't do anything about it. The officer in question would testify that we tried to file a false report.

I stood there, trembling, my blonde hair plastered to my sweat-soaked neck, my hands shaking as I bent to gather the spilled groceries—milk pooling in the dirt, bread crushed beyond saving, those damned apples bruised and broken like my spirit. His threat echoed in my skull—"Anytime, anytime," a ghost that wouldn't leave, a shadow that followed me back into the house." I dropped the bags on the counter, my knees buckling as I sank to the floor, Jada's humming a faint sound pulling me back from the edge. I looked at her then, her small hands clutching a chicken nugget, her face lit with a peace I hadn't felt in years, and I swore—silently, fiercely—that I'd fight him. I'd fight the cops, the judges, the whole damned system if I had to. Because he could take her body, drag her away in his truck, but I'd be damned if I let him take her soul. I wiped the sweat from my brow, the tears from my cheeks, and stood up, a mother reborn in the ashes of her fear, ready to wage a war I didn't know how to win—but one I'd never stop fighting.

The door slams shut behind me, a hollow echo in the dim kitchen, and I stumble forward, my arms trembling as I drop the grocery bags onto the counter. Plastic crinkles, cans clatter, but it's all drowned out by the storm inside me. I collapse against the wall, my back sliding down the chipped paint, my knees buckling as sobs tear through my chest—raw, jagged, unstoppable. My mind spins, a chaotic whirlwind of his wealth, his connections, his empire: Geaux Digital Branding, a gleaming shield I can't scratch, let alone shatter. The Ponchatoula Police bow to his whispers, judges tilt their heads at the mere mention of his name, and I'm nothing—just a broke, battered mom, my body bruised from years of fighting, my soul frayed to threads. I've got no armor but the love that burns in my veins, no weapon but the stubborn will that keeps me breathing. He's a god in this swamp, his power a towering fortress of shadows and secrets, and I'm a speck of dust clawing at its gates, desperate to break through. Jada's soft footsteps patter closer, and I look up through blurry tears to see her peeking from the living room, her blue-green eyes wide with a child's confusion, her voice a fragile thread—"Mommy, what's wrong?" I force a smile, my lips trembling as I lie through the ache—"Just tired, baby"—and pull her into my arms. Her small frame quivers against me, her warmth a comfort, and I bury my face in her blonde curls, swearing an oath that shakes me to my core—"I'll protect you; I'll find a way." But the fear is alive, a serpent coiling tight around my heart, hissing that I'm powerless, that he'll win, that I'll lose her. I fight it, my nails dig into my palms until they bleed, my resolve a flickering ember in a suffocating dark, refusing to die.

May 2018 unfurls like a fever dream, the air thick and sticky, the Louisiana heat pressing down on me as if it's his hand on my throat. It's the 9th, a Wednesday, and I'm rushing Jada to school, her blonde curls tangled from a morning that slipped through my fingers. I overslept, haunted by nightmares—his face looming over me, his voice a venomous taunt, "I can take her whenever I want." She's twelve now, clutching her backpack in the passenger seat, her shirt wrinkled, her blue-green eyes darting nervously as we pull up to the curb. And there he is—Don—waiting like a vulture circling a dying thing, his ritual of control a blade he's sharpened to perfection. He steps out of his gleaming truck, his dark eyes raking over her—hair, shoes, shirt—narrowing into slits as he snarls, "Unacceptable." His hand clamps around her arm, a grip that makes her flinch, and her small gasp slices through me like a shard of glass. "Take her home, fix it, or I'll report you," he snaps, his voice a whip cracking through the humid morning air, each word a lash against my skin. I argue, my voice rising, cracking with desperation—"She's twelve Don, not six, she does her own hair now. If that's how she wants it, then that's how it will be." but he's a monolith, unyielding, towering over us with his broad shoulders and cold stare. His threat lands like a guillotine—"Do it, Crysta, or it's court again." My blood surges, a molten rage boiling in my veins, my fists clenching until my knuckles whiten, muttering curses under my breath—"Damn you, Don, damn you, No! I'm not cowering down to you this time! I've had enough," my heart pounding with fury and helplessness; I push past him and send Jada on her way to class. I see the look of surprise and delight on her face as she walks past him. I can tell his blood is boiling, and I know that there will be a price to pay for this, but I don't care right now. Right now, I'm proud of myself for standing up to him. The school bell tolls in the distance—a death knell for my pride. He'll twist this, I know it—another mark against me, another piece of evidence to paint me as "unfit." It's his game, his battlefield, and every move is a victory for him, every tear I shed a trophy in his war of domination. But, it isn't me that has the consequence this time. He takes it out on Jada. He punishes her by not letting her go to the school dance and she has to clean his entire house from top to bottom instead, and he makes sure I know that I did this to her by not doing what he said. I feel horrible for her, and the guilt is so painful that I know I'll never stand up to him like again in the future. He knows she's my weakness. I don't care what he does to me anymore, but I'd do anything for that girl, and he knows it. We're trapped, Jada and I, in his reign. The fight we have left, being suppressed by the weight of him.

June creeps in, a sweltering haze that clings to my skin, and it's the 15th when I steal a rare day with Jada at the park—a fragile gift I hold with white-knuckled hands. I sit on a weathered bench, watching her swing, her blonde hair flying like a banner of light, her laughter a faint echo of the girl she used to be before he started caging her spirit. My green eyes trace her every arc, my water bottle trembling in my grip, my heart swollen with a love so fierce it's a physical ache, a wound that never heals. A woman settles beside me—short, greying, a stranger with eyes that crinkle with kindness—and her voice breaks the silence, "She yours?" I nod, my throat tight, my "Yeah" barely a whisper, and she smiles, soft and warm, "She's beautiful." The words pierce me, and I want to spill it all—the rape that birthed her, the custody battles that bleed me dry, the way he's strangling her joy—but the words choke me, my throat closing like a fist, my mind screaming *Don't trust, don't tell*. I've been burned too many times, my faith in people torched to ash by his war. I nod again, my smile a brittle mask as she rises and walks away, leaving me alone once more. My world is shrinking, mirroring Jada's, my trust a ghost that haunts me, and I'm trembling, my fingers, my blonde hair a wild tangle as I watch her swing higher. Her joy is a fleeting spark, a flame I'd claw through hell to keep alive, and I will—I'll fight until my last breath, until my bones break, until the swamp itself swallows me whole.

July 4th explodes with fireworks, the town alive with celebration, but I'm alone on our porch, the booms echoing like gunshots in my skull. Jada's with him, her absence a void that swallows me, and I'm rocking in a chair, my hands gripping the armrests, my green eyes staring into the dark as his threats replay—"I can take her anytime"—a mantra of terror that won't let me rest. I see her at nine, chasing sparklers in our yard, her laughter a symphony, and now at twelve, she's a prisoner, her diary a cry I can't answer. I stumble inside, grab a beer from the fridge, and chug it in the bathroom where there aren't any windows, the cold a fleeting balm against the fire in my chest, my mind racing. I should probably be on anxiety medication at this point, but I'm too scared to have a prescription in my name. They'll use it against me, call me crazy. Maybe I am crazy, reduced to this—drinking in the bathroom where no one can see me; trying to take the edge off as I stare at myself in the mirror thinking of his words. One time, I drank too much. My mom found me passed out on the floor, and I had to go to the hospital. I told them it was an accident, but really I don't think it was. I'm under too much pressure to be perfect maybe I wanted a way out. I don't know. . The thought scares me—not because I wanted to die, but because I didn't know how to live. I pressed my hands against the sink, my reflection blurring through tears, and whispered, "What's left of me?" The answer was a void, a hollow space where the girl I'd been used to be. Cops, judges, his power a wall I can't climb. I'm nothing, a speck against his empire, but I'm hers, her mom, her shield, and I'm swearing it again, my voice a growl— "I'll save you, Jada"—as the fireworks fade, the night swallowing my vow.

It was August 2018, and with it came her thirteenth birthday, a milestone that loomed like a beacon in the darkness of my days. I was in the kitchen, baking again, my hands steady for the first time in months as I smoothed vanilla frosting over a cake, I'd poured my heart into. My green eyes blazed with determination, a fierce light cutting through the shadows that had claimed me. This was for her, something pure and untouchable, something he couldn't rip away. That weekend, by some rare twist of mercy, she was with me, and we stood side by side in the kitchen, her laughter a fragile, precious gift that pierced the silence. She licked the spoon, her blue-green eyes sparkling for a moment, and I clung to it, my blonde hair falling into my face as I brushed it back with trembling fingers. My heart swelled until it threatened to burst—"Glad you're having fun, baby"—and I vowed it again. My voice soft but forged in steel—"This is the girl I know her to be." When she's with me she's free to be herself without having to be perfect and looking over her shoulders for Don's shadow. The same way I do. For those fleeting hours, I was her mother again, not just a someone just peeking in on the edges of her life. But Monday dawned, cruel and inevitable, and she was back with him, her silence descending once more like a shroud. His control was a dark cloud I couldn't outrun, and I shattered, my fists clenched so tight my nails drew blood, my drink I just knocked over soaking the counter as I pressed my forehead against the cool surface. "I'll find a way," I whispered, my voice breaking, my soul battered but unbroken. Each moment with her was a blessing, each loss a wound, and yet I fought on, driven by a love so deep it defied the chains he'd bound me with, a mother's promise etched into the very marrow of my being.

September 2018 arrived, a crisp morning on the 20th, and I found myself stepping into the shadowed auditorium of Jada's school, my heart thundering in my chest like a war drum. It was a rare chance, a stolen moment to see her, my little girl, and I slipped into the back row, my blonde hair pulled taut in a ponytail, my green eyes scanning the crowd with a mix of hope and dread. There she was, on stage, dancing, her eyes—mirrors of my own—catching mine for a fleeting, electric second. A smile flickered across her face, fragile and fleeting, before it vanished, snuffed out by the weight of our reality. And then I saw him—Don—sitting in the front row, his broad shoulders a wall, his presence a suffocating force that pressed down on me even from across the room. I shrank into my seat, my hands twisting in my lap until my knuckles whitened, my mind a whirlwind of panic—*He's watching. He's waiting.* The play ended, and I surged forward, my arms aching to wrap around her, to feel her warmth against me, to reclaim even a sliver of being a normal, proud parent. But he was there, stepping between us, his voice a low growl—"Time to go, Jada"—and she was torn from me, her small frame pulled into his orbit. Her eyes avoided mine, her silence and a piercing scream I couldn't answer, and I stood there, frozen, as the auditorium emptied around me. Tears threatened to come, but I wouldn't let them, my chest heaving with the effort to breathe, and I whispered into the void, "I'm still here, baby." My love for her was a wildfire, fierce and unyielding, a flame he could never extinguish, no matter how hard he tried to smother it. He treated me like a pariah, just some inconvenience until the time came where he could shut me out for good.

October 2018 crept closer, a Sunday, the 12th, when the weight of my world pressed down so hard, I could barely breathe. I stood in the fluorescent-lit aisle of the grocery store, my cart a pitiful collection of ramen packets and dented cans of vegetables, each item a testament to the life I'd been reduced to. My blonde hair, once a cascade of light I'd worn with pride, was shoved haphazardly under a worn baseball cap, hiding me from a world I no longer trusted. My green eyes—those windows to a soul I barely recognized anymore—darted nervously, like a deer caught in the crosshairs, every sound a potential threat. The cashier, a young girl with freckles dusting her nose, looked at me with innocent curiosity and asked, "How's your weekend?" Her voice was light, carefree, a stark contrast to the storm raging inside me. My chest tightened, a vise squeezing my ribs until I thought they'd crack. My breath hitched, caught in my throat like a trapped bird, and I forced out a single word—"Good"—but it was a lie, a hollow, brittle sound that echoed in the cavern of my emptiness. I grabbed my bags, plastic handles cutting into my palms, and bolted, my legs trembling as I fled to my car, the groceries banging against my thighs like accusations. I was a liar now, a ghost drifting through a life I couldn't claim, my isolation a fortress he'd forced me to erect brick by suffocating brick. I didn't even use my real name anymore. If someone asked me, I said, "Veronica" my alter ego. A name I now hid behind, so I could become someone else. Behind the wheel, I collapsed, I wanted to cry but I don't allow myself to do that anymore, my hands shaking uncontrollably as I gripped the steering wheel—*Why can't I stop? Why can't I break free?* His threats reverberated in my skull, a relentless drumbeat of fear, his control a chain wrapped tight around my soul, choking the life from me. I drove home, the road a blur as I'm on autopilot, and in that moment, I swore it again, my voice a ragged whisper—"I'll break free, for her." My resolve was a fragile thread, dangling in the abyss, but it was all I had left to cling to.

November 2018, a cold snap hit, and I'm at the library on the 17th, researching custody laws, my blonde hair a mess, my eyes burning with a desperate hope. The librarian—old, spectacled—asks, "Need help?"

and I freeze, my throat closing— "No, I'm fine"—my voice a lie as I flee, my books abandoned, my heart pounding—Don't trust, don't tell. He's always watching me. I'm isolated, a prisoner in my own skin, his threats a wall I can't breach, but I'm clawing at it, my resolve a spark in the dark, my love a fire he can't extinguish.

December 2018, Christmas Eve, and I'm alone, Jada with him, the tree unlit, the house silent. I'm on the couch, clutching her photo, my blonde hair wild, my green eyes blazing— "I'll save you"—my voice a roar in the stillness, my chest heaving as his threats echo, his control a noose I can't slip. He's isolating us both—her in his rules, me in his fear—but I'm still here, still hers, my love a wildfire he can't tame. I stumble to bed, my hands balled into fists, my tears soaking the pillow, and I'm vowing it again— "You can't have her soul"—my heart a dull ache, my will a blade sharpened in the dark. The cage tightens, the threats loom, but I'm alive, I'm hers, and I'll burn it all down to set us free, a mother's unbreakable vow against his bitter reign.

CHAPTER 8
LOSING JADA (2022)

It was the middle of March in 2022, and I had reached the age of thirty-two, standing on the precipice of a life that felt increasingly like a fragile thread stretched taut across a gaping hole of ruin. The Louisiana spring air hung heavy around me, deceptive in its warmth, its gentle breeze brushing against my skin like a false promise of peace. It didn't match the tempest roiling within me, a storm of dread and fury that churned relentlessly in my chest, rattling my bones with every breath. I was still reeling, unsteady on my feet, from the phone call that had shattered my world five days earlier—a call from the hospital, Jada's voice trembling through the receiver like a ghost reaching out from some shadowed place. "Mama, I need you," she'd said, her words fragile and thin, but I knew. I knew what he had done to her, with her arms a brutal tapestry of purple and black from Don's fists, a rape kit shoved into some far away drawer at Our Lady of the Lake, untested, abandoned by a world that shrugs at broken girls.

She was fifteen, my little girl, my heart walking outside my body, and she'd run from Don's house—fled from the man who was supposed to protect her—after two nights of terror, his hands leaving marks on her soul as much as her skin. When she called me, her voice breaking through the static, I'd thrown myself into my beat-up Toyota, tearing down the highway from Ponchatoula to New Orleans, the longest drive of my life with my pulse hammering in my ears and her name spilling from my lips in a desperate chant against the windshield. I sat with her in the hospital, brought her home, held her close as she cried violently every night after, thinking maybe, just maybe, we could stitch ourselves back together, and finally start to heal from the havoc he caused. But the courts didn't see it that way. They sent her back to him—court-ordered, like some cruel joke—because that's how this warped, unforgiving machine operates, grinding up the innocent and spitting them out broken. Now, I was pacing the creaky floors of my shotgun house in Ponchatoula, barefoot, the warped wood cool against my soles, my mind a frantic loop of fear and helplessness, waiting for the next inevitable blow I could feel gathering strength in the distance.

The phone rang at precisely 3:47 p.m. that Tuesday, slicing through the thick silence of the afternoon, and I stopped dead in my tracks, one foot hovering above the floor as if movement might summon worse news. My chipped coffee mug—Jada's favorite, the one she'd always pick out of the cupboard, its daisies faded to faint yellow ghosts—slipped from my hand and hit the counter with a dull clatter, coffee sloshing over the rim. I didn't care. My eyes locked on the phone, its shrill ring echoing in my skull, and I knew, with a certainty that sank into my marrow, that whatever waited on the other end would unravel me further. I answered, my fingers trembling as I pressed the receiver to my ear, and it was Tom, my lawyer, his voice rough and low, like he'd spent the morning gargling shards of glass. "Crysta," he said, and then there was a pause—a heavy, deliberate silence, the kind that carries the weight of ruin in its stillness. My breath caught, snagged on the edge of that pause, and I braced myself, knowing instinctively that I was about to lose something I couldn't bear to let go.

"Don's filed for sole custody," Tom continued, each word landing like a hammer blow. "Emergency hearing. He's claiming you can't control her—says she ran off, got herself hurt, and he's twisting it all around to make you look like the danger here. Says she made it all up." My knees gave way, buckling beneath me as if the ground itself had turned traitor, and I lurched forward, catching myself on the edge of the kitchen sink. The cold metal bit into my palms, grounding me just enough to keep me from collapsing entirely. "What?" I choked out, my voice ragged, barely audible, but it wasn't really a question—it was a plea to the universe, a prayer flung into the void, a scream clawing its way up from the depths of sixteen years ago when Don had first shattered me, leaving me to pick up the pieces alone. My vision blurred with rage, and I forced out another word. "When?"

Tom's sigh came through the line, heavy and final, a sound that tolled like a shot to the heart in the quiet of my kitchen. "March 15," he said. "He filed yesterday. Hearing's set for six days from now—March 21. "Six days? How can I prepare for a trial in just six days?" I asked him. "It's ex parte, Crysta. Judge Coyne signed off on it." The names and dates spun in my head, a dizzying whirl of legal jargon and timelines that meant nothing and everything all at once. Ex parte—secret, one-sided, Don's voice whispering lies to a judge without me there to fight back. And Judge Coyne, a name that tightened the knot in my gut, a man known for rulings as unyielding as stone. I gripped the sink harder, my knuckles whitening, my breath coming in shallow gasps as the walls of my little house seemed to close in, trapping me in a nightmare I couldn't wake from. Jada was slipping through my fingers, and I was powerless, pacing a worn-out floor, waiting for a system that had already failed us to deliver its final, crushing verdict.

Ex parte. Two syllables that gut me, rip the air from my chest, leaving me gasping like I'm drowning in tar. It's Don's ace—secret, one-sided, his lies slithering into Coyne's chambers, his oily smile greasing the gears before I can even draw breath to scream. Jada's slipping away, her blue-green eyes— my everything—fading like a photograph left in the rain, colors bleeding out. The phone slips from my hand, clatters to the floor with a hollow thud, Tom's voice a faint buzz—"Crysta, you there?"—but I'm not here, not anymore. I'm sixteen, belly swollen, Don strolling free while I retched into a sink; I'm thirty, pen trembling as I begged the system, trusting justice that laughed in my face, leaving my report to yellow in a drawer. Now he's burying me alive, stealing my daughter with the same hands that broke me, his wealth and ties a sledgehammer smashing what's left of my world, and I'm powerless, a moth pinned under his glass dome, wings tearing with every futile flap.

I have a lot to do and very little time to do it. The six days that follow unfold like a relentless, feverish nightmare, a chaotic whirlwind of desperation and creeping dread that gnaws at my every waking moment. I find myself dialing Tom's number incessantly, almost ritualistically, every hour on the hour, my footsteps wearing deep, frantic grooves into the faded wood of my home. My voice, raw and ragged from endless pleading, cracks with every word I hurl into the receiver. "He hit her, Tom! She didn't just run away for no reason—he raped her! There's a kit, there's proof, damn it!" But Tom, on the other end of the line, remains maddeningly composed, his voice a steady, measured hum that grates against my unravelling nerves. "We need hard evidence, Crysta," he says, as if explaining something simple to a child. "The rape kit's still untested—sitting in some evidence locker, gathering dust. The hospital report's too vague to hold up; all it says is 'bruising, possible forced entry. Doesn't name him as the attacker.' Meanwhile, Don's spinning his story like a pro. He's calling Jada rebellious, a troubled kid acting out, and he's pinning neglect on you. He's got affidavits lined up—neighbors swearing she's wild, his employees vouching for his character. We're not just up against him; we're fighting a ghost, a shadow with no edges." His words ignite a fury in me, and I slam the phone down so hard the cheap plastic casing splinters, a jagged fracture mirroring the state of my heart. I'm not battling some intangible being—I'm locked in a war with a flesh-and-blood monster, a man who's twisted my daughter's suffering into a sharpened blade aimed straight at us both.

"Not her," I whisper, my voice cracking, barely audible over the storm inside me. "Not my baby." The words are a plea, a prayer, a desperate chant as I rock harder, my fingers digging into the pillow until my knuckles ache. She's my light, my reason, the piece of me that survived all his wreckage—and now he's taking her, too, twisting the law into a weapon to finish what he started. I can still see her face, those eyes wide with trust, the way she'd curl into me on this very bed when nightmares woke her from what he'd done, her small voice whispering, "Mama, I won't have to go back to him right? Please don't make me go back!" And I'd promised her—every time, I'd promised. But I didn't. I couldn't. And now the air is thick with my failure, the room closing in, and all I can do is hold this pillow and pray for the daughter I'm losing, for the mother I couldn't be.

It was March 18th when the stillness of my restless afternoon was shattered once more by the piercing ring of the telephone, a sound so shrill it halted my endless pacing in an instant, as if the world itself had paused to catch its breath. I froze mid-step, my worn-out slippers scuffing against the scratched hardwood, before lunging for the cracked cell phone. On the other end was Miss Ellie, the sweet but nosy widow who lived just two doors down the street, her voice trembling with a mixture of nervous excitement and the kind of hesitant compassion that only comes from years of surviving a small town's tangled web of loyalties. "Crysta, oh honey," she began, her words spilling out in a rush, "I've been hearin' things—whispers 'round town that Don's been workin' his magic again, pullin' strings with the cops, them slick lawyers, and even that old Judge down at the courthouse. But listen, sugar, I saw somethin'—I saw Jada myself, not more'n a month ago, comin' back from his place. He was pushing her and yelling at her. She looked wore out, Crysta, them pretty hazel eyes of hers all shadowed and heavy, like she was draggin' somethin' awful behind her, somethin' she couldn't put down. I'll testify if you need me to, I swear it—I'd put my hand on my mama's grave and tell 'em everything I seen."

My heart surged in my chest, a wild, desperate flare of hope igniting like a spark in a pile of dry leaves. Someone had seen her—someone believed me. My grip tightened around the phone, knuckles whitening as my breath caught in my throat, ragged and uneven. "You'd do that, Ellie? You'd really go up there and tell 'em what you saw?" I asked, my voice cracking with the weight of needing her to say yes, needing her to be the anchor I'd been grasping for in this storm. There was a pause on the line, a soft intake of breath, and then her tone softened, laced with a pity that stung as much as it soothed. "I'd try, sugar. Lord knows I'd try for you. But you know how it is 'round here—Don's word might as well be carved in gold and hung above the altar, while ours ain't nothin' but dirt kicked up in the wind." The silence that followed was deafening, her words sinking into me like rain into parched earth, only to drown what little optimism I'd managed to nurture. The hope I'd felt flickered and died, snuffed out as swiftly as a match dropped into a puddle during a downpour. I slid down the wall, my back scraping against the peeling paint, and landed in a heap, the phone still dangling from my hand. Ellie's promise echoed in my mind, a fragile testimony fraying thread by thread as I replayed her words over and over, willing them to hold more weight than they could bear. I resumed my pacing moments later, my steps heavier now, the floorboards groaning beneath me as if they, too, were exhausted by the weight of it all. Her offer lingered like a ghost in the room—help that wouldn't come, a shimmering mirage in this endless desert of betrayal and broken trust.

The next day, March 19th, found me back in the cramped kitchen, my eyes fixed on my old phone resting on the counter, its cracked plastic casing staring back at me like a fractured reflection of my own unravelling spirit. The splintered edges caught the dim light filtering through the curtains, a jagged reminder of how close everything was to falling apart completely. I snatched it up again, my fingers trembling as I dialed Tom's number for what felt like the hundredth time that week, my voice emerging as a low, guttural growl born of frustration and sleepless nights. "What about Ellie, Tom? She saw Jada with her own eyes—she said she'll talk! That's gotta mean somethin', right?" His response came slow and heavy, a sigh that carried the weariness of a man who'd seen this story play out too many times before. "We can call her up, Crysta, sure. We can put her on the stand if it comes to it. But you gotta understand—she's just one voice, and a shaky one at that. She's no match for what Don's got lined up: a whole stack of sworn statements, typed up neat, notarized, and signed by folks who'd sell their souls for a pat on the back from him. It's her word against a damn machine. Useless. We need hard evidence. I'm worried to say too much over the phone. You never know who's listening. From now on, you come to the office to talk in person, okay."

The phone hit the counter with a force, not quite shattering the already-broken thing but making me wish it would—just so I could feel something break that wasn't inside me. My fist hovered in the air, trembling, as Don's smug face flashed in my mind, that crooked smirk of his presiding over an empire that swallowed every shred of truth, every glimmer of light I tried to hold onto. My knees buckled, and I sank to the floor, the cold wood floors pressing against my thighs like a slap of reality I couldn't escape. My gaze drifted to a coffee stain, spilled days ago and left to dry into a crusty, stubborn ring—a mark I hadn't bothered to clean, just like the invisible bruises I knew Jada carried, the ones no one else would see or believe. I sat there, staring at that stain, my hands limp in my lap, as the weight of it all settled deeper into my bones, another layer of despair I couldn't scrub away.

On March 20, There's an ambulance in front of my house. Poor Miss Ellie was found dead in her home by her daughter. Ruled as natural causes. I think maybe it was them, or maybe I'm just being paranoid, but it's odd that I just spoke to her yesterday about testifying and now she can't speak. I feel like I have to do something to take my mind off of it. I need that rape kit tested, and I can't just sit here anymore, so I slide into the worn driver's seat of my aging Toyota, its engine coughing to life with a reluctant sputter, and begin the trek to New Orleans. The hour-long drive stretches before me like an eternity, the silence inside the car so dense it presses against my chest, suffocating me with its weight. I leave the radio off, unwilling to shatter the stillness with anything but the mournful hum of tires rolling over the fractured, weathered highway. The dashboard trembles with every bump, a loose screw rattling incessantly, its erratic tapping mirroring the unsteady rhythm of my pulse. My hands tighten around the steering wheel, gripping it with such force that my knuckles turn pale, drained of color, as if the blood has fled elsewhere. Each mile unfurls like a desperate, whispered prayer—I'll make them test that damn kit myself if I have to. When I got there, I asked to speak to the person in charge of testing evidence. The lab tech approached me and said the detective already instructed them to dismiss it. "She said nothing happened, that it's just a custody battle and the daughter made it up." Damn it, I'm too late. The detective got here first. Another one of Don's goons. "Well, doesn't the victim get a say in this?" "Are you the victim, ma'am?" He asked. “No, she isn’t here…” He looks sorry, “Then there’s nothing we can do.”

I climb into my rattling old sedan and make the drive back and head straight to Tom’s office, a grueling hour-long drive steeped in suffocating silence. The radio stays off; every station seems to blare hollow, mocking tunes that clash with the storm raging inside me. When I arrive, Tom’s cramped office smells of stale coffee and musty paper. He’s hunched over his desk, surrounded by a chaotic spread of documents, their yellowed edges curling like dying leaves. At fifty-two, he looks a decade older, his face etched with deep lines that seem to carry the weight of too many lost fights. “They’re hitting you with backdated child support now,” he says, sliding a crisp, official-looking paper across the desk toward me. “$117 a month, retroactive to 2015. And that’s not all—they want you to cover his legal fees, too. Another thousand bucks on top.” The absurdity of it rips a laugh from my chest, a harsh, brittle sound that scrapes my throat raw. I’m a part-time office assistant, scraping by on $12 an hour, my hands stained with the grime of penny-pinching survival, while Don lounges in his sprawling mansion, his construction business raking in cash, his connections greasing palms all the way up to the courthouse. “I can’t pay that. He knows I can’t pay that. They’re trying to bleed me dry, so I can’t fight back.” I choke out, my voice trembling with equal parts rage and despair. Tom nods, his expression weary but resolute, as if he’d already calculated the odds and found them dismal before I even stepped through the door. "We'll fight it, Crysta," he says, leaning back in his chair. "But Judge Coyne… he's thick as thieves with Don's crowd. We've got one shot at this, and it's riding on your testimony. Make it count."

Sleep eludes me that night, slipping through my grasp like smoke. Everything is happening so fast, and I don't know what to do next. I sit alone at my scarred kitchen table, the single bulb overhead buzzing and flickering, casting erratic shadows across the room. A notebook lies open before me, and I pour my soul onto its pages, my hand trembling as I write. Every punch Don ever landed, every venomous threat he spat, every suffocating moment his shadow loomed over Jada and me—it all spills out in a torrent of ink and anguish. Ten pages, scrawled in a shaky hand, the words smeared where tears have fallen and dried. I grip the notebook like it's a lifeline, a fragile tether to hope, convincing myself that if I can just get these words in front of Judge Coyne, he'll have to see the truth etched into every line. In my mind's eye, I see Jada standing in that courtroom tomorrow, her blonde hair falling like a curtain across her face, shielding her from the stares. I hear her voice—small, fragile, but unyielding—saying, "He hurt me, Mama," and I cling to the image, repeating it like a prayer. We'll win, I tell myself, my heart pounding against the lie. We have to win, because the alternative—a yawning, endless void where my daughter's safety should be—is a darkness I cannot fathom, a loss I know I wouldn't survive.

A few minutes later, I hear a knock on my front door. I don't know who it could be this late of an hour. I peeked through the window and see that it's the detective on Jada's case. I open the door hoping for news of a breakthrough in the case. Maybe there was other evidence found. "Good evening ma'am. I have a warrant for your cell phone on the grounds of conspiracy. We need it for evidence." I shouted back, "This is insane! There's nothing on my phone. I need it to talk to my daughter." "Well, we have a warrant and the right to take it from you if you don't comply." "That won't be necessary, here, just take it!" I shoved it into their awaiting hands. I added, "Now, if there's nothing else you need from me, please leave." She told me to have a good night and that they would call me when I could come and pick it up. That tipped me right over the edge. How could they call me when they had my phone? How can I contact people and gather information without my phone? I rushed to the store to buy a burner I could use in the meantime.

It was the morning of March 21st, the clock ticking precisely to 8:47 a.m., when I found myself standing within the hallowed yet stifling walls of the Tangipahoa Parish Courthouse. The air was oppressively thick, saturated with a cloying humidity that seemed to cling to my skin, mingling with an even heavier sense of injustice that weighed down my every breath. I had taken great care to present myself as best I could, donning my finest navy-blue dress—a garment I had painstakingly ironed not once, but twice, in a futile attempt to feel in control. Yet, despite my efforts, the fabric draped awkwardly over my frame, hanging too loosely, a silent testament to the weeks I'd spent unable to stomach food, my appetite stolen by grief and dread. My hands, trembling uncontrollably, clutched a sheaf of papers—documents that held my truth, my fight, my last fragile hope—as though they were a floatation device in a storm I feared I'd never weather.

Beside me stood Tom, my attorney, his presence a small comfort amidst the chaos swirling in my chest. His suit was rumpled, creased from too many hours spent hunched over case files, but his voice was a steady whisper in my ear: "Stay calm, Crysta. We've got this." But how could I stay calm? Across the courtroom, there he was—Don, my adversary, my tormentor—standing tall and immaculate in a crisp grey suit that screamed money and power. His hair was slicked back with meticulous precision, and a smirk played across his lips, a smug curl that radiated confidence, as if he'd already orchestrated the outcome of this day. That smirk was a blade, slicing through what little composure I'd managed to muster. And then there was the absence that cut even deeper: Jada, my daughter, my heart, wasn't here. Don had kept her from me, no doubt sequestered behind the towering gates of his sprawling estate, a prisoner in a gilded cage. The realization twisted in my gut like a jagged knife. "Where's my daughter?" I hissed to Tom, my voice a raw, desperate rasp, but he only shook his head, his expression grim. "Ex parte, Crysta. He didn't have to bring her." The words landed like a blow, stealing the air from my lungs.

At precisely 9:02 a.m., the heavy oak doors swung open, and Judge Coyne entered, his black robes billowing behind him like the wings of some dark monarch ascending his throne. He settled into his seat with an air of detached authority, his gaze sweeping the room—yet never once did it land on me. Not a glance, not a flicker of acknowledgment. It was as though I were invisible, a ghost in my own story. Don's lawyer rose first, a man named Brent who carried himself like a predator—a shark in a tailored suit, all gleaming teeth and polished leather shoes. His voice, when he spoke, was smooth as oil, gliding over the room with a practiced ease that made my stomach churn. "Your Honor," he began, his tone dripping with deference, "my client, Mr. Don, seeks sole custody of his daughter, Jada, due to Mrs. Abelseth's (I go by my married name now) gross neglect and inability to provide a safe environment. On March 7th, Jada ran away from Mrs. Abelseth's care, only to be found injured and requiring hospitalization—a clear and undeniable sign of an unstable, chaotic home. We have affidavits to substantiate this: neighbors who witnessed the child wandering the streets, unkempt and unsupervised; staff from Mr. Don's household who attest to her defiance and distress while under Mrs. Abelseth's so-called supervision. Since 2011, Mr. Don has been the rock of stability in Jada's life, offering financial security and emotional support where Mrs. Abelseth has consistently failed. We respectfully request sole custody be granted to Mr. Don, with supervised visitation for Mrs. Abelseth, as well as child support retroactive to 2015 in the amount of

$117 per month, plus all associated legal fees." With a flourish, Brent slid a thick stack of meticulously prepared documents across the bench to Judge Coyne, who accepted them with a curt nod, his fingers flipping through the pages as though following a script he'd memorized long ago.

By the time Tom rose to speak, I was trembling so violently I could scarcely breathe, my nerves frayed to threads. It was my turn—our turn—to fight back, to claw some semblance of justice from this nightmare. I shoved my testimony into Tom's hands, my voice a frantic whisper as I pleaded, "Read it, Tom. Please, read all of it. Don't leave anything out." He nodded, clearing his throat, and when he spoke, his voice was steady but thin, a fragile thread of defiance against the polished onslaught we faced. "Your Honor," he began, addressing the bench with quiet resolve, "Mrs. Abelseth contests every aspect of this filing. The truth is this: Jada didn't run from her mother's home—she fled from Mr. Don's residence after suffering an assault. The evidence is documented—bruises photographed at Our Lady of the Lake Children's Hospital, a rape kit administered, though, shamefully, it remains untested by the authorities. Crysta Abelseth has been Jada's primary caregiver, her fierce protector, since 2005, when Mr. Don raped her—a crime she reported in 2015, only to see it ignored by a system that failed her then and threatens to fail her now. This isn't neglect, Your Honor; this is survival, a mother's desperate struggle to shield her child from harm. We ask that this filing be dismissed outright, that Mr. Don's actions be investigated thoroughly, and that Jada be protected from further trauma." Tom handed my pages—my story, my pain—to the clerk, and I held my breath, my eyes locked on Judge Coyne's impassive face. I searched for something, anything—a flicker of doubt, a spark of compassion, a hint of the humanity I so desperately needed him to show. My heart pounded in my chest as I waited, suspended in that agonizing moment, praying for a sign that the truth might finally be heard.

The courtroom was suffocatingly silent for a fleeting moment, the air thick with tension that seemed to cling to every surface—the polished wooden benches, the high ceiling, the stern portraits of past judges staring down in mute judgment. Nothing stirred, save for the faint rustle of papers and the distant hum of a vent somewhere overhead. Judge Coyne reclined in his towering chair, the leather creaking faintly under his weight, his pen tapping rhythmically against the desk like a metronome counting down to some inevitable doom. The sound was maddening, a tiny percussion underscoring the chaos brewing beneath the surface. Then Brent, the attorney for Don, rose to his feet once more, his polished shoes clicking faintly against the floor as he adjusted his tie with a practiced flourish. His voice slithered through the room, oily and sharp, each word laced with a venom that made my skin crawl.

Silence coils, tight and suffocating, the air humming with tension, Coyne's pen tapping a dirge—tap, tap, tap—each strike a nail driven deeper into my coffin. Brent stands again, voice a serpent's hiss, sharp and venomous. "Baseless, Your Honor—unproven, incendiary lies spun from desperation. Mrs. Abelseth's unstable—married to three different men in a short period of time, scraping by, no evidence beyond her trembling word. Mr. Blackwell's a cornerstone—businessman, community pillar, a man of means and merit. The child's safer with him, shielded from her mother's chaos." His words ignite me, and I surge up, chair screeching across the floor, voice a volcano erupting. "He raped us both! Look at her bruises—look at me! See what he's done!" My arm jabs the air, pointing at scars they refuse to see, at Jada's ghost hovering between us, her bruised arms a silent scream. Tom grabs me, his grip tight, hissing, "Sit down," but I'm trembling, a live wire sparking, the room a blur of faces—clerks, bailiffs, spectators—blind or bought, staring through me.

The gavel crashed down, a thunderous crack that reverberated through the courtroom, splintering the blunt of my outburst. Judge Coyne's voice followed, cold and unyielding, cutting through the air like a blade forged from ice. "Mrs. Abelseth, you will control yourself, or you will be removed from my courtroom and held in contempt." His eyes, hard and dispassionate, flicked toward me for only a moment before returning to the papers before him. He shuffled them with deliberate care, the rustle loud in the sudden hush, then scratched something onto the top sheet with a pen that moved too quickly, too decisively. When he looked up again, his gaze settled not on me—never on me—but on Don, seated smugly across the aisle. "Motion granted," Coyne declared, his voice flat, final.

"Sole custody awarded to Mr. Blackwell, effective immediately. Mrs. Abelseth is restricted to supervised visitation only, limited to four hours every other Saturday from 12pm-4pm. Child support is set at $117 per month, retroactive to 2015, totalling $16,848, to be paid in instalments. Additionally, Mrs. Abelseth will cover $1,000 of Mr. Blackwell's legal fees. I'm setting another hearing for July 25th to reassess at that time."

The gavel descended once more, its fall a violent punctuation—a gunshot ringing in my ears, a guillotine slicing through the fragile thread that still linked me to my daughter. The sound echoed, amplifying the hollow ache that swallowed me whole. I screamed then, a primal, animalistic wail that tore from my core and bounced off the wood-paneled walls, filling the space with the weight of my despair. Across the room, Don's lips curled into that familiar smirk—the same one he'd worn in 2005, the same one that had haunted every courtroom battle since. It was a look of triumph, of ownership, of a predator who knew he'd won again.

Tom was at my side, his hands pulling me back, his voice a low, urgent whisper in my ear. "We'll appeal, we'll fight this," he promised, but the words felt empty, drowned out by the roar of my grief. My arms flailed, fingers grasping at the air, at the table, at the stack of papers I'd painstakingly prepared—my pleas, my evidence, my truth—now scattered and crumpled on the floor like so much trash. "Jada!" I roar, a cry to pierce forty miles, to shatter his gates, to pull her from his grasp, but it's swallowed by the shuffle of the room emptying—Brent packing his briefcase with a snap, Coyne vanishing through a side door, Don strutting out,-shoulders square, untouchable, king of my ruin.

The drive home is a fevered haze, hands quaking on the wheel, tires swerving as rage blinds me, a low moan seeping out—soft, fractured, a dirge weaving through the engine's growl. The road blurs, headlights smearing into streaks, and I nearly clip a guardrail, metal screeching a warning as I wrench the wheel, my reflection in the side mirror a stranger—hollow eyes, wild hair, a woman unmade. I stumble through my door at 11:43 a.m., legs giving way, and collapse in Jada's room—not on the bed, but the floor, knees buckling, fingers tracing her magnolia sketch, its lines blurring through a flood of saltwater. Numbers haunt me—$16,848, $1,000, $117—shackles I'll never break, a debt chaining me to his victory while he chuckles in his marble palace, king of my wreckage. Her face burns behind my lids—fifteen, eyes shadowed, blonde hair veiling a whisper, "He did this," a lash across my soul. I failed her, failed us, failed that sixteen-year-old me who thought love could outrun his shadow, who believed grit and heart could rewrite this cursed script.

The hours stretch and bleed into one another, time losing all meaning as the light shifts from the harsh glare of midday to the muted hues of dusk. I remain there, curled into a tight, protective ball on Jada's bed, my body folding in on itself as though I could shield my heart from the wreckage of my reality. The room grows dim, shadows stretching across the walls like fingers reaching for me, and still, I don't move. Then, a sudden buzz jolts me—a vibration from my burner phone, insistent and sharp. I fumble for it with shaking hands, the screen illuminating the gloom. It's Tom, his message flashing across the display: "We'll fight, Crysta. I'm doing research on a motion we can file— Hold on." His words don't mean anything to me, tossed into the abyss, a flicker of something that might resemble hope, but I can't grasp it. I don't answer, don't type a reply, don't even let my thumb hover over the keys, because I'm numb—it feels like holding on is just another way of letting go. Nothing matters. Jada's gone, my bright, beautiful light extinguished by a system that didn't just fail her—it crowned her rapist king, draped him in power and impunity while we were left to shatter.

The silence presses in, thick and suffocating, and I find myself whispering her name into the gathering dark— "This can't be it. This can't be over." It's a chant, a prayer, a mantra that spills from my lips unbidden, each syllable a thread tying me to her, to keep me from drifting entirely into the void. It's a vow, too, forged in the crucible of this endless day—this isn't the end. It can't be. Not while her name still burns on my tongue, not while the memory of her face fuels the ember of rage beneath my grief. I'll claw my way out of this darkness, for her, for us, for the sixteen-year-old girl I owe a reckoning to. This isn't over—not yet.

CHAPTER 9
REWIRED FOR PROTECTION

It's late November 2022, and I'm thirty-three, perched on the sagging edge of my best friend, Cami's couch in her Lake View living room, a sanctuary that smells of vanilla candles and cedarwood, a fleeting refuge from the storm that's been my life since 2005. The Louisiana night presses against the windows, thick with humidity that clings to my skin like regret, and the soft hum of her air conditioner fights a losing battle against the damp heat seeping through the cracks. My blonde hair, once a bright cascade I'd toss with teenage gusto, now hangs in tangled strands, a veil over my face, hiding the green eyes that have seen too much—too much pain, too much betrayal, too much of a world that turned its back on me. My hands twist in my lap, fingers knotted like the thoughts I can't untangle, and my heart—oh, my heart—beats a frantic rhythm, a drumroll of dread that never quiets. She's sitting across from me, my best friend, her sandy hair catching the lamplight, her hazel eyes soft but piercing, a lighthouse in the fog of my chaos. "Crysta," she says, her voice gentle as a summer breeze but sharp enough to cut through my defenses, "what's your favorite memory?"

The question lands like a thump, a grenade lobbed into the fragile quiet of my soul. It's so simple, so innocent—a query anyone else might answer with a laugh, a nostalgic tilt of the head: a childhood Christmas, a first dance, a moment unscarred by darkness. But for me, it's a bomb, a spark igniting a fuse I've spent years trying to smother. My chest tightens, a vise squeezing my ribs until I can't breathe, and my pulse roars in my ears, drowning out the cicadas screaming outside. I'm not here anymore—not in this warm room, not safe with her. I'm back in the Tangipahoa Parish courthouse, the air stale with old coffee and older lies, Don's lawyers circling like sharks, their voices cold and cutting: "Tell us, Mrs. Abelseth, what did you do that night? What did you say? Who were you with?" Every word I ever spoke, every scrap of my life—my texts, my tears, my truths—twisted into a noose to choke me, to steal Jada, to paint me as the unfit mother, the unstable girl, the liar who deserved to lose everything. My vision blurs, my hands tremble, and I stammer, "Uh, I don't know," my voice a fractured whisper, barely audible over the storm in my head. I lurch to my feet, my legs unsteady as a newborn colt's, and bolt for the bathroom, the door slamming shut behind me like a guillotine falling.

I'm alone now, the ambient light buzzing overhead, a cruel spotlight on the wreck I've become. I grip the sink, my knuckles white, and splash cold water on my face, gasping as it drips down my chin, mixing with the salty sweat on my brow. My reflection stares back—a stranger, a ghost. My green eyes, once bright with teenage dreams, are hollow, haunted, ringed with shadows that no concealer can hide. My blonde hair, matted and wild, frames a face I don't recognize, a woman carved hollow by trauma, her edges jagged from years of fighting a war she didn't start. I sink to the tiled floor, the cold biting through my jeans, and pull my knees to my chest, raw and ragged, I want to cry and wail, but I don't. Tears don't come anymore; they haven't for a long time, they just hide behind my eyes the way I hide from the world. PTSD's got me in its jaws again, shaking me like a rag doll, and I'm drowning—drowning in the memories, the fear, the relentless truth that I'm not the Crysta I was supposed to be. I'm rewired, reprogrammed by pain, and I hate it—hate the paranoia, the panic, the way a simple question can unravel me like a spool of thread yanked loose. I bury my face in my hands, my palms still wet, and whisper, "Why can't I just be me?"

This isn't living. It's surviving, and even that feels like a lie I'm too tired to keep telling. My mind's a battlefield, scarred and smoking, littered with the wreckage of every moment I've been stripped bare. It started in 2013, when Don's lawyers subpoenaed my phone, tore it open like a vulture gutting prey. A stupid text I'd sent a friend—some dumb joke about a bad date, the kind of thing you laugh over with coffee—was plucked out, held up in court like a smoking gun: "See, Your Honor, she's reckless, unfit, a danger to her child." I'd laughed once, free and careless, before that moment taught me nothing's safe—not my words, not my thoughts, not the smallest piece of my heart. Now, it's a ritual, a compulsion that haunts my nights. Picture me at midnight, alone in my cramped bedroom, the world outside silent except for the distant wail of a train, my only comfort.

I sit hunched over the worn wooden surface of my desk, the faint, ghostly light from my phone casting long, jagged shadows that stretch across the room, pooling over Jada's empty bed. The sight of it—her pillow still indented from where her head last rested, her favorite stuffed bear abandoned in a corner—slices through me, a relentless blade twisting deeper into the raw wound of her absence. My hands shake, unsteady as they clutch the phone, my fingers hovering over the screen before plunging into the task I've set for myself. I'm deleting everything, purging every trace of our life as if it could somehow shield us. There's a text from my mom, her words soft and familiar—"Call me, honey, I'm worried about you"—and I erase it with a swipe, my throat tightening. Next, a grocery list I'd jotted down in a hurried moment, mundane and achingly normal: milk, bread, eggs, a jar of peanut butter for Jada's sandwiches. Gone. Then come Jada's selfies, each one a dagger to my soul—her blue-green eyes catching the sunlight, alive with mischief, her wide, toothy grin as she sticks out her tongue in a grainy video, her voice warbling through an off-key rendition of some fleeting TikTok tune. My chest heaves as I press delete, muttering to myself, "They can't use it. They can't take her again." The words are a fervent, desperate prayer, spilling from lips that tremble with fear and defiance.

Each tap on the screen feels like raising a barricade, each swipe a brick in a wall I'm frantically building to protect what little I have left. But it's a hollow triumph, a bitter illusion of control. With every memory I erase, I'm not just hiding Jada from the world—I'm erasing her, my light, my reason for waking each morning. I'm erasing myself, too, scrubbing away the fragments of a life we'd stitched together through years of pain and small joys. My pulse races, a frantic drumbeat echoing in my ears, and my breath comes in shallow, uneven gasps. I'm terrified—terrified that one stray word, one careless moment captured in a text or a photo, could summon Don's lawyers back into our lives like vultures circling a wounded animal. They'd swoop in, wielding their polished briefs and cold calculations, ready to tear Jada from me again, to rip open the scars of a loss I've already endured once, a loss that still bleeds fresh every day. My face is hot and red, and I choke on the silence of the room. The phone slips from my trembling hands, clattering onto the desk, and I bury my face in my palms. This isn't protection—it's a prison, a suffocating cage I've constructed with my own fear, and I'm trapped inside it, gasping for air that won't come.

I wasn't always like this. God, I wasn't. There was a time, a lifetime ago, when I was a different Crysta—a sixteen-year-old girl with a laugh that rang like wind chimes on a summer breeze, bright and unburdened. Back then, I'd sprawl across my bed in our little Ponchatoula house, a spiral notebook balanced on my knees, my pen racing to capture dreams too vast for our sleepy Louisiana town. I'd write about a future in a city that pulsed with life, where skyscrapers touched the stars and I'd craft stories—novels, maybe, or screenplays—that would reach into people's hearts and remind them they weren't alone. At the diner down the street, I'd sit across from my best friend, sipping milkshakes that tasted like strawberries and freedom, my green eyes alight as we traded secrets about crushes, or the new song we couldn't stop humming, or the way fireflies danced in the dusk, flickering like stars you could scoop into your hands. That Crysta trusted without hesitation—trusted her friends, trusted the world, trusted the quiet strength blooming inside her own heart.

But that girl was stolen from me, piece by piece, starting with that night in 2005. Don's hands, heavy and unyielding, pinned me to that couch, and though I broke free, the damage was done—not just to my body, but to the very wiring of my soul. The system took what was left, grinding me down in courtrooms that felt like battlegrounds. Judges peered over their benches, their questions sharp as knives, slicing through my story as if I were the one on trial. Lawyers twisted my words, and the sheriff—God, the sheriff—let my rape report sit untouched, gathering dust in some forgotten file for seven years, as if my pain were an inconvenience, a footnote not worth reading. They didn't just fail me; they rewrote me, turning every question into a threat, every connection into a potential betrayal. I see it now, with a clarity that cuts deeper than any blade: those courtrooms didn't just take Jada from me, didn't just rip my daughter from my arms. They took the girl I used to be—the one who loved fiercely, who laughed without looking over her shoulder, who believed kindness was a gift, not a trap. They left me as this hollowed-out shell, a woman who flinches at a stranger's smile, who guards every word as if it could be weaponized. I'm still here, still breathing, but the Crysta who dreamed of fireflies and stories—she's gone, buried under the weight of a system that broke me and a fear that won't let me go.

I fought with everything I had to hold onto her, to keep her close, to not let the tides of my own fear and pain sweep her away from me. It was last spring, in the tender bloom of 2023, when I dared to let a flicker of hope ignite within me. I found myself seated across from a man in a cozy Baton Rouge coffee shop, one of those places with mismatched ceramic mugs and the gentle strum of folk music weaving through the air like a soft exhale. He was kind, his brown eyes crinkling at the corners with a warmth that seemed to invite trust, his voice rich and steady as he leaned forward, his elbows resting on the worn wooden table, and asked, "What was your childhood like?"

The question was simple, earnest, a bridge extended toward connection. I wanted to cross it. I wanted to open the floodgates and let the memories spill out—vivid, sunlit summers with my mother, the two of us wading into the creek behind our house, our hands darting through the cool water to catch crawfish, her laughter ringing out like a melody that promised the world was safe, that I was safe. Riding horses with my dad on the farm, wrangling cattle and chasing chickens. I could almost feel the damp earth under my bare feet, smell the wild honeysuckle that clung to the air, hear their voices calling my name with a love so fierce it could hold back any storm. But as I reached for those words, something inside me seized. My throat tightened, my pulse quickened, and a voice in my head screamed, *Trap!*

It wasn't just a word—it was a warning, sharp and jagged, slicing through the fragile moment. My mind conjured Don's lawyers, their faces cold and calculating, their pens hovering over legal pads, ready to dissect my every word, to twist my memories into a narrative that branded me as broken, unfit, unworthy of Jada. The weight of their imagined scrutiny crushed me, and before I could stop it, my hand trembled, knocking over my latte. The hot liquid splashed across the table, scalding my skin, a sharp sting that yanked me back to reality. I didn't apologize, didn't pause to clean up the mess. I bolted, my sneakers slamming against the hardwood floor, then the pavement outside, my breath coming in ragged gasps as I ran—ran from him, from the kindness in his eyes, from the version of myself who might have answered, who might have trusted.

I fled all the way home, my heart pounding louder than my footsteps, and locked myself inside. The world stayed out, but the pain came with me. I collapsed onto my couch, curling into myself, my arms wrapped so tightly around my body it was as though I could hold the pieces of me together by sheer force. The doubts came hard, wrenching, each one tearing something loose inside me. "I can't, I can't, I can't," I whispered, over and over, the words a desperate prayer to a god I wasn't sure was listening. My green eyes burned with tears, my blonde hair clung to my damp cheeks, and in that moment, I hated myself—hated the fragility that let something so small, so human, unravel me. I hated how trust had become a landmine, buried beneath every interaction, waiting to detonate with the lightest touch.

It's not just strangers who set off those explosions. It's everyone, even the people I hold closest to my heart. My best friend, that fierce, hazel-eyed woman who's been my anchor through every storm, tries so hard to reach me. Her voice is soft, careful, as she asks about my day, my dreams, anything to coax me out of the fortress I've built around myself. But I'm locked inside, my responses short, my walls towering higher with every question. I dodge her invitations—backyard barbecues where kids chase fireflies under a twilight sky, movie nights with bowls of popcorn and cheesy rom-coms that used to leave us gasping with laughter, quick coffee runs where we'd talk until the baristas shooed us out at closing. I make excuses—work's too much, I've got a headache, Jada needs me—and they're flimsy, transparent, but I can't stop myself.

I hear the whispers, the quiet speculations from others who notice the change. "Why's she so weird now? What's wrong with Crysta?" The words cut deeper than I'll ever let on, each one a fresh wound slicing through the scar tissue that's grown over my heart. But how can I explain? How can I tell them that every conversation feels like stepping into a courtroom, every question a subpoena poised to tear me open, to lay bare the parts of me I've fought so hard to protect? I can't find the words to make them understand that I'm not cold, not distant by choice, but terrified—terrified that letting anyone in means giving them the power to hurt me, to use my truths against me, to prove I'm not enough.

Some nights, I sit on my porch, the Louisiana air thick with the scent of jasmine and the weight of my own sorrow. The cicadas scream into the darkness, their song raw and relentless, like they're grieving the girl I used to be, the one who laughed freely, who trusted without hesitation. Across the street, my neighbors gather on their porch, their voices mingling with the clink of glasses, their laughter spilling into the night like light from their glowing windows. They're living a life that feels so close, yet impossibly far—a life of easy connection, of shared stories and unguarded moments. I want to cross the road, want to step into their circle, to let their warmth wrap around me like a blanket. I want to belong to their chatter, to their joy, to the simple beauty of being known without fear.

But I'm frozen, my body rooted to the porch, my phone silent in my pocket, my heart whispering a mantra that's been carved into my soul by years of trials, of betrayals, of losses too heavy to name: *"If they know you, they'll hurt you."* It's a truth I've learned the hard way, etched into me deeper than the secret I carried at sixteen, heavier than the $117 checks I wrote to my rapist, more crushing than the gavel that fell like a guillotine, stealing my daughter from me. I'm safe behind my walls, but the safety is a lie, because the loneliness is a weight I can't bear—a weight that presses down harder than all the pain I've fought to survive. And so, I sit, night after night, watching the world move on without me, aching for the courage to step back into it, to trust again, to believe that I could be enough.

This rewiring—it's not just fear; it's survival, and it's cost me everything. I think of Jada, my light, my reason, and how even with her, I'm guarded, a mother afraid to love too openly. Last month, she called from her dorm, her voice soft, tentative, asking, "Hey Mom, what are you doing?" I wanted to tell her that I just woke up from a nap—having a dream God sent just for me of us together at the beach with pina coldas in our hand—but I froze, picturing her words slipping to Don, to a judge, to someone who'd use them to chain her again. Useless, napping when she should be taking care of her daughter. Even though she's eighteen and can take care of herself, that's how my brain works now. "Nothing," I said, my voice flat, hating the distance it built between us, hating how I couldn't even share a scrap of beauty with my own daughter. She's a woman now, with her life and her own friends, her blonde hair glowing like it did when she was five, her blue-green eyes holding a strength I pray I helped forge. But I'm terrified to open up, terrified to let her see the wreckage of her mom, terrified that my brokenness will hold her back. I don't want her to worry about me, as I write this, my blonde hair falling across the page, ink smudging under my trembling fingers, because I'm not just protecting her—I'm protecting the ghost of us, the mother and daughter we were before Don's war rewrote our story, before the system turned love into leverage and trust into a weapon.

Oh, the ache—it's a relentless, marrow-deep yearning that gnaws at the very core of me, a soul-splitting longing to reclaim the pieces of myself that time and pain have stolen. I want to be Crysta again, the woman who could laugh with abandon, her joy spilling freely without the instinct to scan the shadows for threats. I crave the version of myself who loved with an open heart, unguarded, unafraid, not this guarded figure who's built a fortress of stone and steel around her emotions. I want to live—truly live—not merely endure, not just survive the days as they stack into years, each one heavier than the last. This longing hits me like a tidal wave at dawn, when the world is hushed, and the absence of my daughter, Jada, carves itself into my chest like a blade—cold, sharp, unyielding, cutting deeper with every breath.

I find myself drawn, as if by some invisible tether, to her room—a sanctuary frozen in time, untouched since the courts ripped her from my arms. The air feels heavy with her absence, yet it's here, in this quiet space, that I feel her most. I sink onto her bed, my fingers trembling as I clutch her pillow, pressing it to my face. Her scent lingers—lavender and the faint edge of teenage rebellion, a fragrance that clings to the fabric like a ghost of the life we once shared. It's a memory I can't release, a link to the girl who is my heart's center. "I want to feel again," I whisper, my voice fracturing under the weight of my grief. Tears spill, hot and unrelenting, soaking the pillowcase as my slim frame hunches over as I'm about to unravel entirely, leaving only raw sorrow and the stubborn grit that's kept me standing. I have to claw my way back—not just for myself, but for her, for the daughter who deserves a mother who is whole, not fractured, not diminished by the weight of a decade's worth of wounds.

I rise from her bed, my legs unsteady but my resolve fierce, like an ember refusing to die in the wind. My blonde hair catches the first rays of dawn as they slip through the blinds, painting faint streaks of gold across the room. My green eyes, reflecting the soft light, glint with something new—defiance, perhaps, or the fragile, flickering spark of hope, delicate as a moth's wing yet fierce enough to withstand a storm. I think of Jada, of the trust she placed in me even when my own faith wavered, of her voice, steady and sure, saying, "Mom, I'm okay." That memory becomes my vow—to her, to myself, to the sixteen-year-old girl I once was, the one who didn't know she'd rise from that couch, from that night, from a decade of battles that tried to bury her beneath their weight.

"I'll unlearn this, I have to," I whisper, my voice trembling but laced with steel, addressing the shadow that's haunted my mind for too long. "You won't own me forever." My heart thunders in my chest, a wild, untamed rhythm that feels like rebellion, like freedom, like the pulse of a life I'm ready to seize with both hands. Fear claws at me—terrified of stumbling, of slipping back into the cage I've fought so hard to escape, of the whispers that still linger, insisting I'll never be free. But there's something else too, something electric coursing through my veins, a thrill born of possibility. This is my chance to rewire myself—not for mere survival, not for dodging the next blow, but for living, for loving, for unearthing the bold, unbroken woman I know still exists within me.

She's there, buried beneath layers of scar tissue and instinct, but she's fighting her way out, clawing through the wreckage with a ferocity that leaves me breathless. I stand taller now, my breath steadying as the dawn light grows stronger, illuminating the room and the resolve within me. This is not just a moment—it's a turning point, a declaration that I will not let the past define me forever. For Jada, for the woman I was, for the woman I still can be, I will keep fighting, keep rising, keep chasing the life that's been waiting for me all along.

I step outside, the dawn air heavy with dew and promise, and I feel it—a shift, a crack in the armor I've worn too long. The cicadas are quiet now, the world holding its breath, and I'm standing tall, my blonde hair a banner in the breeze, my green eyes blazing with a fire I thought I'd lost. I see Jada in my mind—free, laughing, her sketches covering the walls of a life she's building—and I see me, not the shark, not the ghost, but Crysta Byrd, survivor, mother, warrior, a woman who's been shattered a thousand times and still rises, still fights, still loves with a fierceness that no court, no predator, no system can snuff out. The bitter's deep, a scar that'll never fade, but the bold's stirring, a flame I'll stoke until it burns bright enough to light my way home—to Jada, to myself, to a future I'm ready to claim, one trembling, triumphant step at a time. This isn't the end—it's a reckoning, a rebellion, a heart screaming to be free, and I'm ready to run toward it, no matter how hard, no matter how far, no matter the cost. Watch me rise, Don—watch me burn.

CHAPTER 10
A CHURCHYARD BATTLE

It's mid-summer 2022, and I'm thirty-three, parked in the gravel lot of a small Ponchatoula church, the kind with weathered clapboard walls and a cross atop its steeple that tilts slightly, like it's bowing under the weight of too many prayers. The Louisiana heat is a living thing, thick and oppressive, pressing against my skin until my T-shirt clings damply to my back. My blonde hair hangs in limp strands, tucked behind my ears, and my green eyes dart nervously, searching for her—my Jada, sixteen, my heart, my reason for every breath. The air buzzes with cicadas, their relentless drone a jagged soundtrack to the dread coiling in my gut, a knot that tightens with every second I wait. My hands grip the steering wheel of my old sedan, knuckles white, fingers trembling, as if holding on can keep me from unravelling. This is a custody exchange, one of dozens I've endured since the court split Jada's life in half, but it feels like stepping into a trap, every moment watched, every word weighed. Don's truck is here already, a hulking black shadow parked carelessly across two spaces, its chrome bumper glinting like a warning. I feel him—his presence a ghost that's haunted me since 2005, a weight I carry in my bones, a fear I can't outrun.

I step out, my sneakers crunching on the gravel, kicking up dust that swirls and settles on my jeans. The churchyard is quiet, save for the bugs chirping and the faint creak of a wooden sign swinging in the breeze, its faded letters proclaiming *Peace Be With You*. The irony stings, a bitter twist in my chest, because peace is a stranger to me, stolen long ago on a couch I'll never forget. I'm here for Jada, bound by a court order that cares nothing for the tears we've shed, the nights I've lain awake, or the love that's kept me fighting. My heart hammers, a frantic rhythm that echoes every exchange before this—stolen glances, whispered *I love you*s, the ache of watching her walk away. Four hours. Four hours are all I get. I'm scared to talk to her, terrified of the eyes that watch us, the ears that listen, ready to twist my words into ammunition. There's always someone—Don, a supervisor, a stranger—hovering like a vulture, waiting for me to slip, to give them a reason to take her from me again. My green eyes scan the lot, catching the glint of a car window, the shadow of a figure near the church steps, and I flinch, my breath hitching, my body wired for danger.

The heavy wooden doors of the church creak as they swing wide, and there, framed in the morning light, stands Jada—my daughter, my heart, my reason for enduring. Her blonde curls, once wild and free, are now tamed into a tight ponytail, accentuating the pallor of her delicate face. Those blue-green eyes, so like my own yet burdened beyond her sixteen years, flicker with a guardedness that pierces me to my core, a silent wound that never heals. She's grown tall, her lanky frame teetering on the precipice between childhood's innocence and womanhood's uncertainties, but her movements are cautious, deliberate, as though each step risks triggering an unseen explosion. Her shoulders slump beneath a weight I cannot see but know all too well—a weight forged by control, by rules, by a life shaped in the iron grip of another's will. My chest tightens, a raw, searing ache that threatens to unravel me, because I recognize that burden. It's his shadow, cast long and unyielding over her fragile light.

I stand rooted to the gravel path, my feet unwilling to move, my arms aching to reach for her. The urge to run to Jada, to enfold her in an embrace and whisper promises of safety and freedom, surges within me, but fear holds me fast. My voice lodges in my throat, each unspoken word heavy with the risk of consequence. To speak to her, to even meet her gaze for too long, feels like tempting fate—a betrayal that could sever the fragile thread connecting us. Because he's here, too. Don strides beside her, his heavy boots grinding the stones beneath them, each step a declaration of dominance. At forty-seven, his frame has thickened, his once-lean build now carrying the weight of years and power. His jaw is set, unyielding, and his eyes—those cold, calculating eyes—gleam with the same merciless intensity I remember from the night he tore my world apart.

Don's shadow looms over Jada, dimming the radiance that should be hers, and I feel the familiar sting of helplessness. Geaux Digital Branding, his empire built on police contracts and whispered deals, cloaks him in untouchable authority. The system bends to his will, offering him protection while it leaves me voiceless, my truths buried under layers of silence. I am merely Crysta—Jada's mother, yes, but also the woman who pays him $117 a month, a paltry sum that feels like a ransom for the privilege of staying in her life. I am the survivor who dared to report a rape and received only echoes of indifference in return, the woman who has learned to swallow her anger, to bite her tongue until it bleeds, all to preserve the fleeting moments I'm allowed with my daughter. Each glance at Jada reignites my resolve, but it also deepens my despair, for I know that every step she takes beside him is a step further from the freedom I dream of giving her.

"Crysta," he snaps, his voice cutting through the air, sharp and impatient. "Let's make this quick." Jada's a step behind, her eyes flicking to mine, a silent plea I feel in my soul, but I can't speak, not yet, not with him so close. A supervisor—a court-appointed woman with a clipboard and a bored expression—stands near the church steps, her gaze flitting between us, her pen poised like a judge's gavel. I nod, my throat tight, and move toward them, my steps slow, deliberate, each one a battle against the fear that screams *Be careful, Crysta, they're listening*. Jada's close now, close enough to see the freckles dusting her nose, the way her lips twitch like she wants to smile but doesn't dare. "Hey, baby," I whisper, soft as a breath, meant only for her, but the supervisor's head tilts, her eyes narrowing, and I clamp my mouth shut, my heart racing. Don's watching, his smirk a familiar blade, and I hate how small I feel, how my love for Jada feels like a secret I'm not allowed to speak.

The supervisor extends a form toward me, just another routine check-in for the exchange, her expression neutral, almost bored. My fingers, unsteady and slick with sweat, fumble with the pen as I scrawl my signature across the page, the ink smudging slightly under my grip. The weight of the moment presses against my chest, and I clear my throat, keeping my voice low but firm, a quiet rebellion stitched into my words. "I need a copy of this for my attorney," I say, the statement landing like a stone in still water. Don's head jerks up from where he's been leaning against the wall, his eyes narrowing into slits, and the air around us thickens, charged with something raw and menacing. His presence looms, a shadow that seems to swallow the light, and I feel the familiar prickle of unease crawl up my spine.

"What for?" he snaps, his voice a low growl, each syllable laced with suspicion and threat. He steps closer, his boots scuffing the gravel, his frame casting a darkness over me that feels like it could smother me whole. My knuckles whiten as I clutch the form tighter, my pulse hammering in my ears, but I lift my chin, forcing myself to meet his gaze. My green eyes blaze, defiant, even as fear claws at the edges of my resolve, threatening to unravel me. "It's my right," I reply, the words sharper than I intended, cutting through the tension like a blade. Beside me, Jada's breath hitches, her wide eyes darting between us, her body tensing as if she's waiting for the storm to break. The supervisor, oblivious or choosing to be, scribbles something on her clipboard, the scratch of her pen deafening in the heavy silence that follows. I feel the weight of every gaze in the churchyard—curious, judgmental, expectant—each one pinning me in place, waiting for me to falter, to cross some invisible line.

Don moves suddenly, his motion a blur, his hand shooting out to seize the form from my grasp. "Give it here," he snarls, his voice rough with barely restrained anger. Instinct surges through me, primal and fierce, and I jerk the paper back, my body screaming its refusal to yield, not this time, not again. His fingers brush the edge of the form, and then—before I can react—his fist grazes my chest, a sharp, intentional strike. It's not enough to send me sprawling, but the impact steals my breath, pain blooming hot and bright across my ribs. I stumble backward, the gravel crunching beneath my sneakers, my hands flying up instinctively to protect myself. My green eyes widen, shock and fury warring within me as the world shrinks to this moment, every insect hums, swelling into a deafening roar.

In an instant, I'm no longer here, no longer standing in this churchyard. I'm flung back to 2005, to that night—his couch, his hands, the suffocating darkness that swallowed my screams. The memory crashes over me, vivid and merciless, my chest heaving as tears sting my eyes, hot and unbidden. But I blink them back, refusing to let them fall, not here, not in front of him. Jada's voice cuts through the haze, soft and trembling— "Mom"—and it's like a recollection, yanking me back to the present, grounding me in this fight, this moment. I steady myself, my breath ragged but resolute, and I square my shoulders, the form still crumpled in my grip, a small but unshakable symbol of my defiance.

"Don't you touch me!" I shout, my voice raw, trembling, but fierce, a mother's fury unleashed. I stare him in shock, my palms sweating, he takes a step away from as he realizes what he has just done, his boots slipping in the gravel. His smirk falters, just for a second, and it's everything—a crack in his armor, a glimpse of the man who's not invincible, not untouchable. Jada's frozen, her hands clasped tight, her eyes darting between us, and I want to tell her I'm okay, that I'm fighting for her, but Don recovers, his face twisting with rage. He steps forward, his fist raised, and I brace, my heart thundering, my body screaming *Not today, Don, not ever*. The supervisor gasps, her clipboard clattering to the ground, but she's useless, a bystander in my war, her pen no match for his fists.

"Stop it!" The voice is sharp, commanding, slicing through the chaos like a blade. It's Stacie Triche, a woman from the church, her dark hair pulled back, her brown eyes blazing with a fire that matches mine. She's on the steps, her phone in hand, her posture steady, a warrior stepping into my fight. "I saw that, Don," she says, her voice clear, unwavering, each word a hammer striking his shield. "You hit her.

Back off—now." My chest heaves, my tears falling now, hot and unashamed, streaking my cheeks as I cling to her words, to the power of being *seen*. Don freezes, his fist still raised, his jaw tight, but Stacie's gaze holds him, unyielding, and the weight of her witness is too much. He curses, a low, guttural sound, and spits into the gravel, the wet splat loud in the silence. "This ain't over," he mutters, his eyes burning into me, a promise of worse to come, but I don't flinch—not with Jada here, not with Stacie's courage bolstering mine.

In a heartbeat, Stacie is beside me, her presence a steady anchor in the storm raging within. Her hand rests lightly on my arm, warm and grounding, her voice threading through the chaos with a quiet urgency that feels like a lifeline. "Crysta, are you okay?" she asks, her words soft but piercing, cutting through the haze of my pain. It's the first time today—maybe in longer than I can remember—that someone has truly seen me. Not the mother shouldering an unbearable burden, not the case file in a broken system, but me, the woman trembling beneath the weight of years of grief and fear. My green eyes, raw and brimming with unshed tears, lift to meet hers, and I shake my head, the motion small but heavy. "No," I manage, my voice fracturing under the truth, "but I don't have a choice. I have to keep going."

Before I can catch my breath, Jada is there, her small body crashing into mine with a desperate kind of love. Her arms encircle me entirely, clinging tightly, her sobs muffled as she presses her face against my chest. I wrap her in my embrace, holding her as if she's the only thing keeping me standing straight, tethering me to the ground when everything else feels like it's slipping away. "Mom," she whispers, her voice trembling, her soft curls brushing against my chin, her warmth seeping into the aching cold that's taken root inside me. My hand finds her hair, stroking gently, though my fingers shake with the effort. "I've got you, baby," I murmur, the words barely audible, a fragile promise I'm not sure I believe myself. Am I reassuring her, or am I pleading with my own heart to hold on just a little longer?

Stacie moves with purpose, her phone already in hand, pressed to her ear as she speaks with a clarity I can't muster. "Yes, it's the church on Oak Street," she says, her voice crisp and unwavering as she addresses the police. "Domestic violence—he struck her. I saw it happen." Her words are a shield, a decisive step toward justice I'm too shattered to take myself. I pull Jada closer, my arms tightening around her small frame, my green eyes fixed on Stacie as a wave of gratitude surges through me, overwhelming and fierce, like a tide washing away some of the despair. When she lowers the phone, her gaze softens, her eyes searching mine with a tenderness that unravels me further. "Crysta, tell me what's going on," she says, her voice gentle now, an invitation to unburden the weight I've carried alone for so long.

And so, it pours out of me—a torrent of pain and truth I've held back for years. I tell her about the rape in 2005, a wound that never healed, a violation that reshaped my world. I speak of Jada's birth, how she became my light in the darkness, and the brutal custody battles that followed, each one a fresh cut to my soul. I recount Don's suffocating control, his shadow looming over every step I took, and how Geaux Digital Branding is what he's using as a cover, it's the link to all this somehow. I confess the system's betrayal—how it failed me, how it failed Jada, how it left us to fight battles we shouldn't have had to face alone. My voice breaks, raw and jagged, each word a shard of glass, but I can't stop. Stacie is listening—really listening—and it's a relief I didn't know I was starving for.

Jada remains silent beside me, her hand soft and warm in mine, her presence a quiet, unshakable strength that keeps me grounded. I tell Stacie everything—how fear has stolen the ease of talking to my own daughter, how every word I speak to Jada feels like it could be twisted into a trap, how I'm waging a war I'm not sure I have the strength to win. The weight of it all spills into the space between us, heavy and unyielding, but Stacie doesn't flinch. Her steady gaze holds mine, and for the first time in what feels like forever, I don't feel so alone in the fight.

The police arrive, two officers in blue, their cruiser kicking up dust as it pulls into the lot. The older one, his badge reading *Carter*, has a calm, steady gaze, his notepad open as he takes my statement. I'm shaking, my words tumbling out—Don's blow, his threats, Stacie's witness—

and he nods, his pen moving quickly, capturing truth I've screamed into voids for years. Stacie corroborates, her voice firm, her details precise—the form, the fist, the moment she stepped in—and I want to hug her, to sob my thanks, but I'm too raw, too exposed. Jada clings to my side, her eyes on the ground, and I squeeze her hand, whispering, "It's okay, baby," though I'm not sure it is. Carter looks at me, his eyes kind but tired, and says, "We'll take him in. Domestic violence, given your shared child—he'll be charged, and we'll push for a restraining order." My heart leaps, a fragile hope, and I nod, my tears falling faster now, relief and fear warring in my chest.

That evening, the world shifts under my feet when Stacie's call comes through, her voice taut but certain: Don's been arrested. I can almost see it—the sharp click of handcuffs locking around his wrists, his eyes blazing with that cold fury as the officers guide him into the patrol car, the dusky light fading around him. Relief floods me, a wave so strong it nearly knocks me over, and soon after, Jada is allowed to come home. My daughter, my heart—she steps through the door of my home, her duffel bag slung carelessly over one shoulder, her steps lighter than I've seen in weeks. There's a quiet strength in her, a spark that hasn't been snuffed out, and as we cross the threshold together, it feels like we're reclaiming something stolen.

We sink into the couch, the familiar creak of the springs grounding us. Jada curls into me, her head resting against my chest, her light curls fanning out across my shirt like a soft, living tapestry. My arms wrap around her, holding her close, as if I could shield her from the world forever. My fingers trace gentle patterns on her shoulder, each touch a vow, a promise to keep her safe. I'm memorizing every detail of this moment—the warmth of her against me, the faint scent of her strawberry shampoo, the way her breathing slows as she relaxes. "You're safe now, baby," I whisper, my voice catching, raw with emotion. I press a kiss to her forehead, lingering there, letting the moment anchor us both.

We turn to simple comforts—popcorn spilling over the edges of a shared bowl, an old movie flickering on the screen, its dialogue a soft hum beneath our laughter. Jada's giggle is a melody I've ached to hear, a sound that fills the hollow spaces in my chest. For these precious hours, it's just us—Crysta and Jada, mother and daughter, wrapped in a fragile bubble of freedom. The weight of fear lifts, if only for a while, and I let myself believe we're untouchable, that we've carved out this pocket of peace and made it ours.

Later, I tuck her into bed, her room exactly as she left it—posters curling at the edges, a stuffed bear slumped against the pillow. The indent of her head still lingers in the fabric, a quiet testament to her presence. I pull the blanket up to her chin, smoothing it with care, and stand there, watching her sleep. Her face is soft, unguarded, her breath a steady rhythm that soothes my jagged edges. "I love you most," I murmur, the words barely audible. My heart swells, daring to hope that we've won this time, that we've outrun the shadows chasing us.

But then, at 11 p.m., everything fractures. A knock pounds against the door—heavy, deliberate, reverberating through the house like a gunshot. Jada stirs in the bed, her eyelids fluttering, a small frown creasing her brow. My heart lurches, but I force a smile, crossing to her side. "Go back to sleep, baby," I say, my voice a fragile thread, trembling despite my efforts to keep it steady. She settles, her breathing evening out, and I pad to the door, my bare feet icy against the stained concrete. Dread coils in my stomach, tightening with every step. I lean toward the peephole, my breath catching as I peer through.

A deputy stands on the other side, his badge catching the dim hallway light, his expression carved from stone. My pulse hammers, but I open the door just a crack, my body instinctively positioning itself as a barrier between him and Jada. "Mrs. Abelseth," he says, his voice flat, devoid of warmth, "there's no restraining order in place. The Sheriff dropped the charges. Jada needs to return to her father—immediately." The words land like blows, each one shattering the fragile hope I'd built, threatening to tear my daughter from my arms once again.

The words are a fist, knocking the air from my lungs, splintering the hope I'd dared to hold. "No," I choke, my voice breaking, my hands gripping the doorframe. "He hit me—you can't! The police said—" But he cuts me off, his eyes cold, unyielding. "Court's orders stand. Don's custody holds. Don't make me force this." Jada's behind me, her duffel clutched tight, her blue-green eyes wide with fear, her voice a whisper— "Mom, please." It's a blade, carving me open, spilling every failure, every moment I couldn't save her. I turn to her, my green eyes burning, my blonde hair wild, and pull her close, my lips against her forehead, memorizing her warmth, her scent—strawberry and defiance. "I'll fix this," I whisper, my breath in her hair, my voice a vow I'll die to keep. "I love you, most." She nods, her courage shattering me, and I release her, my arms empty, my soul screaming as she follows the deputy to his cruiser, her silhouette fading into the night.

I collapse onto the cold ground of the car port, thinking and thinking as I watch him drive away with her. Why did they release him? The officer assured me that he wouldn't be able to have Jada back even if he bailed himself out. My fists slam against the rough concrete, over and over, the sharp sting of hard rock biting into my skin until my knuckles split, blood welling up, warm and slick, mingling with the gritty ground beneath me. It's a mess of red and on grey, a testament to the fury and grief that consume me. "You won't win, Don," I choke out, my voice hoarse but resonant, a resolve in the quiet night, a vow etched into the air. It's a promise to Jada, to the stars glittering coldly above, to the girl I've clawed and fought to remain despite everything—but I'm broken by betrayal, by a system that's turned its back on us.

Yet in the darkness, there's a flicker of hope, fragile but fierce. Stacie's call to WBRZ—a reporter, a voice, a chance—glows like a lone ember in the ashes of our despair. It's small, but I'll nurture it, fan it with every ounce of my will until it roars into a fire, a blazing beacon that will cast our truth into the open, exposing the lies and the pain for the world to see. My green eyes burn with determination, catching the faint glow of the moonlight as it weaves through my blonde hair, tangled and wild from sleep, a halo of defiance. Trembling, I push myself to my feet, my legs unsteady but my spirit unyielding. The fight isn't over—it's only just begun, and I stand ready, heart pounding, to face whatever comes next.

CHAPTER 11
THE MEDIA FIRESTORM

It's the waning breath of summer 2022, and I'm thirty-three, sprawled across the worn-out couch in my house in Hammond, its frayed cushions exhaling the ghosts of spilled coffee and years gone by. The Louisiana air is a living thing, heavy and unyielding, slinking through the cracked windows to press against my skin until my tank top fuses to my shoulders, damp with sweat and sorrow. My blonde hair, a wild tangle of neglect, is wrestled into a haphazard bun, strands escaping like memories I can't hold. My throat burns, raw and swollen from the pollen. The churchyard brawl with Don lingers like a storm cloud, his fist's glancing blow blooming into a bruise across my chest—a cruel signature of his rage, his dominion, the shadow he's cast over me since I was sixteen in 2005. Jada, my daughter, my pulse, my everything, was torn from me again last night. Her blue-green eyes, wide with terror, haunted me as the deputy's cruiser devoured her into the night, leaving me hollow, my soul a keening wail trapped in my ribs. Yet, somewhere in the wreckage of my despair, a spark flickers—an ember, fragile but defiant, refusing to die.

This morning, Stacie Triche, the church witness with a voice steady as gospel, called me. Her words were a rope thrown into the abyss: she's connected me to WBRZ, to a reporter named Chris Nakamoto. It's more than a lead—it's a saving grace, a trembling chance to scream my truth to someone who might finally listen. I cling to it with the desperation of a mother whose child is slipping through her fingers, with the ferocity of a woman who's been silenced too long. The phone rests in my lap, its cracked screen a mirror of my splintered life, Stacie is calling now. My fingers hover over it, trembling, caught in a war between fear and resolve. What if this call is another dead end, another door slammed shut like the Sheriff's office, the courts, every institution that's turned my pleas to dust? My breath hitches, a sob clawing at my throat, but I choke it back, the burn in my chest a reminder that I'm still here, still fighting.

Jada's face surges into my mind, vivid and piercing—her blonde curls, once wild and free, now dulled under Don's iron rules; her freckles stark against skin grown too pale; her voice, small and breaking, whispering "Mom, please" as she was pulled away. The memory is a knife, twisting deep, but it's also fuel, igniting that ember into something fierce. I can't let her vanish into the life he's forged for her, a prison of threats and lies, walled off by his empire. Geaux Digital Branding, with its police contracts and whispered deals, has armored him for years, turning my cries into rumors that dissolve in the humid air. But I'm done being a rumor. I'm done being a shadow.

My heart thunders, each beat a drumroll of dread and daring. The phone feels like it weighs a thousand pounds, but I lift it, my fingers unsteady as they grip the small device, and Stacie's voice is sure, confident on the other line, "I emailed Chris and he wants to speak to you in person, and he's already started an investigation into yours claims." I want to do this. I want to do it for every night Jada's spent under his control, for every door that's shut in my face—but I'm scared. What if they aren't really on my side, and they give me a bad edit and make things worse than they already are? I'm terrified to put my story out there, but I have to choose to trust in this moment, and it's taking everything in me to do so, but I hesitantly agree. "Okay, I'll speak to him."

A few days later, I'm sitting across from Chris, my heart a raw, pulsing wound, and as the mic is hooked to me under my clothing and the lights hit my face, I freeze. I open my mouth, but I can't say a word. "I thought I would just be speaking to him today; I'm not prepared to an actual interview. I don't know if I can do this." Stacie is sitting next to me and grabs my hand gently, "It's okay, Crysta. We're here to help, I swear it. You can do this. Think of Jada." I close my eyes, take a deep breath, and when I open them, I'm ready. I start out slow with my answers then as I become more comfortable, my words flood out of me, unstoppable, spilling from a place so deep it feels like they've been carved into my bones. I don't just tell him my story—I relive it, every jagged edge, every suffocating shadow, every fleeting spark of hope that kept me clawing forward. It's 2005 again, and I'm sixteen, curled up on Don's couch, my body trembling, my soul fractured after the rape that stole my voice, my light, my everything. The memory is a blade, slicing through the years, and my voice quakes as I speak it aloud, the pain as fresh as if it happened yesterday. But I don't stop. I can't. This is my truth, and I've carried it alone for too long.

I tell him about Jada, my daughter, my life. Her birth was a miracle born from ashes—those tiny, grasping hands, her soft cries that tethered me to life when I wanted to let go. I was seventeen, barely more than a child myself, and I wove a lie about her father to shield us both from the monster who'd already taken so much. I painted a fragile world for us, one where we could be safe, but the truth has a way of breaking free. In 2011, a DNA test chained us to Don, his shadow looming like a storm that would never pass. The custody battles that followed were a war I wasn't ready for—courtrooms that smelled of stale coffee and broken promises, lawyers who saw me as a case number, not a mother fighting for her child. I learned to fight like a shark, circling, bleeding, never stopping, even when my heart was shredded with every loss, every moment Jada was pulled from my arms.

The years blur, but 2015 stands sharp in my mind, a wound that never scabbed over. I was twenty-six, storming into the Sheriff's office, my blonde hair wild, my green eyes blazing with a fury that could've burned the building down. I reported the rape, laid my pain bare, demanded justice. But the Sheriff just shrugged, his desk a fortress of excuses, his indifference a weight that crushed what little hope I'd carried. My voice shakes as I tell Chris this, my hands trembling in my lap, but I push on, because this isn't just a story—it's my life, my fight, my refusal to be silenced.

I tell him about Don's reign of terror, his threats that slithered into every corner of our lives, his control that tightened like a noose. He tore Jada's diary, her private thoughts scattered like confetti, banned her friends, made her small in ways that broke me more than any fist ever could. I tell Chris about Geaux Digital Branding, a name that sounds harmless but casts a shadow long and dark, stretching over judges, cops, records sealed tighter than a vault. It's a machine I've been running from, fighting against, a force that makes you question if truth even matters when power pulls the strings.

And then, a few days ago—the memory so raw it burns. The church, a place that should've been sanctuary, turned battlefield. I see it all again: the form in my hand, Don's fist crashing into me, the pain blooming in my chest like a wildfire. Jada's soft "Mom" anchors me, her voice a calm through the chaos. Stacie's voice cuts through, fierce and unwavering, demanding someone stop him. The police arrive, their promises of justice glinting like fool's gold. But by 11 p.m., they send Jada back to him, no restraining order, no mercy, just the cold slap of a system that's failed us again. My voice cracks as I tell Chris this, sweating through my tank top, my body shaking with the weight of it all.

Through it all, Chris listens, his silence a sacred space where my pain can breathe. His questions come gently, like a cartographer mapping a battlefield littered with my scars. "When did the Sheriff first fail you?" he asks, and I'm back in that office, my younger self raging against a world that wouldn't listen. "What did Don say when he hit you?" he probes, and I'm in the churchyard again, my chest throbbing, Jada's presence the only thing keeping me from shattering. Each question unlocks another piece of me, and though my voice is raw, jagged with grief, I keep going. Seventeen years of fear, defiance, and love pour out, a torrent I can't hold back.

I'm trembling now, sweat dripping down my back, but there's a fire in me, growing with every word. It's a blaze that's been smoldering since I was sixteen, fed by every injustice, every betrayal, every moment I refused to break. I look at Chris, my eyes burning with a truth I won't let anyone bury. This is my story—my blood, my bones, my heart laid bare. And as I speak, I feel it: the weight lifting, the silence shattering, the fire roaring loud enough to drown out the darkness. I am still here, still fighting, and no one can take that from me.

The moment I stop speaking, my voice cracks like brittle glass, raw and ragged from the truths I've spilled. My throat burns, hoarse from the weight of every word, and my eyes—swollen, stinging—betray the tears I've fought to keep inside. Yet, there's a strange lightness in my chest, as if I've peeled away a suffocating layer of shame, I hadn't even realized was smothering me. It's exhilarating and terrifying all at once, like standing on the edge of a cliff, the wind daring me to leap. Across from me, Chris lets out a breath—a long, deliberate exhale that seems to carry the weight of what I've just confessed. His voice, steady but laced with urgency, cuts through the haze. "Crysta, this is massive. Monumental. I need to dig into some things—Stacie's contacts with the government officials, court records, Sheriff's reports—to make sure we've got it airtight. But I want to run this story. I believe you. Do we have your consent to air this?"

My heart surges, a wild, untamed thing, pounding with a reckless kind of hope I haven't felt in years. It's a spark, a flame threatening to catch, but just as quickly, fear slithers in, cold and venomous, coiling around that fragile light. *He'll come for you, Crysta.* Don's face flashes in my mind—his cruel smirk, the glint in his eyes when his fist clenched, the low growl of his voice promising worse than I'd already endured. It's a memory that claws at my resolve, threatening to drag me back into the shadows. But I grit my teeth, shoving it down, burying it deep where it can't touch me. Not now. Not anymore. "Yes," I say, my voice trembling at first but growing stronger, a vow forged in fire. "I consent."

I stand up from my chair, my hands shaking so violently I can't stop it. I rush to my car and leave swiftly, scared I'll change my mind. When I get home, I stare up at the ceiling fan, its blades slicing lazy circles through the stale air. Its soft hum is a faint echo of the storm raging inside me—a whirlwind of dread, defiance, and something dangerously close to freedom. The room feels too small to hold it all, and I'm left wondering if I've just set something unstoppable in motion.

I think about the last question he asked me. "Why keep fighting?" he asks, and I choke, my hands gripping the chair, my answer raw: "Because she's my daughter. Because I love her. Because I have to advocate for her when no one else will because you see all of this really isn't about me, it's about her. I would have let this go a long time ago if she wasn't still suffering." I'm drained, my body heavy, but there's a spark in Chris's eyes, a promise that this isn't the end. "This airs in two days after we've had time to edit it," he says. "Brace yourself, Crysta. It's going to hit hard."

It's a Friday night and the evening news is scheduled to come on at 6pm, as I'm sitting on my worn couch, the world outside fading into a blur as the TV cast its cold, flickering light across the room. The emptiness of Jada's absence clawed at my chest, a relentless ache that no amount of time could dull. My heart was a tangled knot of grief and defiance, each beat a reminder of the fight I'd vowed to wage for her. The WBRZ logo flared on the screen, a beacon in the darkness, and then—there I was. My blonde hair pulled back with frayed strands locked behind my ears, my green eyes glistened with unshed tears, and my voice, though trembling, carried the weight of a truth I'd carried for too long. I looked like a woman haunted, broken, baring my soul to the world. "Crysta Abelseth says she was raped at sixteen by Don, the father of her child, a claim the Sheriff's office never pursued," Chris Nakamoto's voice sliced through the air, sharp and unyielding, like a blade cutting through years of silence. "Now, she's fighting for her daughter, alleging years of abuse and a system that's failed them both."

The broadcast unspooled like a fever dream—clips of me in the studio, my hands clasped tightly to steady their shaking; Stacie's statement, her words sure and unwavering; and then a blurred photo of Don, his face a spectral shadow I could never outrun. Each frame was a wound reopened, each word a spark igniting the fury and fear that had simmered in me for years. The story crescendoed with Chris standing outside the Sheriff's office, his voice a whipcrack of accusation: "They declined to comment, but questions are mounting about why this case was buried." I clutched a pillow to my chest, Jada's faint scent—strawberry and innocence—still woven into its fibers. My pulse thundered, a storm of hope and terror colliding within me. I was exposed, raw, my truth laid bare for all to see, and yet, in that vulnerability, there was a flicker of something new—something fierce.

By midnight, my phone had become a living thing, wild and untamed, erupting with a deluge of texts, calls, and notifications that poured in faster than I could grasp. My hands shook as I held it, my green eyes scanning the glowing screen through a haze of sleepiness. Friends I hadn't spoken to in years reached out, their words like anchors pulling me from the depths: "Crysta, I saw you on TV—you're so brave." Strangers, too, their messages raw and urgent: "I went through this too. Thank you for speaking out." Survivors, their voices trembling with shared pain, wrote, "How can I help?" Each message was a surge of confidence that I wasn't going through alone anymore, a brick in a fortress I hadn't known I could build. I smiled, a smile so broad, so simple. Something that everyone does, yet I hadn't truly done it in so long I wasn't sure I still could. I was overwhelmed by the tidal wave of support crashing over me. My story—our story—was no longer just mine. It was a beacon, a rallying cry, a spark that had ignited something unstoppable.

I stumbled to my laptop, my fingers clumsy with adrenaline, and what I saw stole my breath. WBRZ's website had crashed, overwhelmed by a flood of visitors hungry for the truth. On *X (Twitter)*, posts about Jada and me were spreading like wildfire, thousands of shares rippling across Baton Rouge, Louisiana, and far beyond—across the country, maybe the world. Hashtags like #JusticeForJada pulsed with life, trending in a digital roar that no one could silence. My heart pounded as I scrolled, each retweet, each comment, a testament to the power of a truth finally spoken. I was no longer just a mother fighting in the shadows; I was a voice, a force, a woman who had dared to stand against a system that had tried to bury us. The fire I'd sparked was blazing now, fierce and untamed, and no one—not Don, not the Sheriff, not the weight of years of silence—could smother it. In that moment, alone in the glow of my screen, I felt Jada's spirit beside me, and I knew: this was only the beginning.

The next morning, I'm bleary-eyed, coffee cold in my mug, when my phone rings—Stacie, her voice urgent, alive. "Crysta, turn on the TV. Now." I fumble with the remote, and there's the Sheriff, his face tight, standing at a podium, cameras flashing. "We acknowledge mistakes were made in Mrs. Abelseth's case," he says, his voice clipped, forced. "The 2005 report wasn't properly followed up. We're reviewing procedures to ensure this doesn't happen again." My jaw drops, my heart pounding, tears spilling as I grip the couch, my nails digging into the fabric. It's not enough—not justice, not yet—but it's something, a crack in the shield that's protected Don for years. I'm shaking, my blonde hair falling loose, my green eyes burning with a fire I haven't felt in too long.

But it's not over. By noon, another call—Chris, his voice taut with excitement. "Crysta, Nancy Grace is on this. She's tearing into Judge Coyne on her show tonight." I'm stunned, my breath catching, my mind racing to catch up. Nancy Grace, the woman who takes no prisoners, who's made predators tremble—she's heard me, seen Jada. That night, I watch, curled on the couch, my heart in my throat. Nancy's face fills the screen, her eyes blazing, her voice a thunderclap: "Judge Coyne, what were you thinking? A mother reports a rape, her daughter's trapped with an abuser, and you do nothing? I'm calling for your disbarment!" She holds up my interview clip, my tear-streaked face, and says, "Crysta Abelseth is a hero, fighting for her child against a system that's failed her. Shame on you, Louisiana!" I'm sobbing, my hands pressed to my mouth, my green eyes wide, disbelief and gratitude crashing through me like a wave.

The weight of the world presses down on me, a suffocating storm swirling with chaos and hope, a tempest no one can turn away from. By the next morning, the air crackles with reckoning. Judge Coyne, once untouchable behind his bench, is staggering under the deluge—his office drowning in a torrent of phone calls, each ring a cry for justice, while outside the courthouse, a sea of voices surges, their signs held high like battle standards: #JusticeForJada, #FireCoyne. The world is watching, and it's roaring.

I'm behind the wheel, driving to the grocery store, but my hands tremble so violently I can barely grip the steering wheel. My heart thunders in my chest, a drumbeat of dread and defiance. My phone buzzes, and it's Tom, his voice slicing through the haze. "Crysta," he says, urgent, alive with something I haven't dared to hope for. "It's happening. Coyne just caved—he's issued an order. Jada's being placed with a third party, effective immediately. You and Don get alternating supervised visits until a new hearing. Crysta, you did this."

The words hit me like a lightning bolt, and I swerve to the side of the road, my vision dissolving into a blur of tears. My sobs erupt, raw and uncontainable, tearing through me as my blonde hair clings to my tear-soaked cheeks, a tangled curtain framing my breaking heart. "She's out?" I whisper, my voice a fragile thread, trembling on the edge of collapse. "She's out, Crysta," Tom says, steady and sure. "She's safe for now."

I lose myself then, a wild, untamed thing—screaming, laughing, crying all at once, my fists pounding the dashboard in a rhythm of release. My green eyes burn, blazing with a joy so fierce it feels like it might consume me, a fire born of pain and triumph intertwined. Jada, my Jada, is free from that shadow, if only for this moment, and it's enough to make my soul sing.

I race home, the world a blur beyond my windshield, my apartment a sanctuary I stumble into like a pilgrim reaching holy ground. My fingers shake as I dial Stacie, my voice quivering with a gratitude so deep it feels like it might swallow me whole. "You saved us," I choke out, tears streaming anew, and her laugh comes through, soft yet fierce, a warrior's laugh. "No, Crysta," she says, "you did. I just made a call." But I know better—her call was a spark, and now the fire is spreading.

I'm pacing now, my heart a soaring bird, when my phone hums again—a text from a number I don't recognize. A friend of a friend, someone who saw the story unfold. "Keep fighting, Crysta. We're with you." Before I can catch my breath, another message lands, then another, a cascade of voices pouring in—survivors with scars like mine, mothers with hearts as fierce as my own, strangers who've become kin through this shared battle. It's a chorus, a symphony of solidarity I never dared imagine, each word a note that lifts me higher.

I sink to the floor, overwhelmed, my green eyes scanning every message as tears carve rivers down my face. My blonde hair falls wild around me, a halo of chaos and hope, and I feel it—really feel it—for the first time in so long: I'm not alone. The weight of their words wraps around me like armor, like wings, and I'm alive, trembling with the thrill of this moment, this fight, this fragile, beautiful victory. Jada's safe, and the world is with us, and for now, that's everything.

The days bleed into one another, a relentless storm of interviews, phone calls, and plans that stretch my soul thin. Each moment feels like a battle, yet I'm fueled by a fire that refuses to flicker. Today, I met a new lawyer—a woman with eyes that cut like steel and a spirit that roars with the same unyielding resolve I've carried for Jada. She leaned across the table, her voice steady as stone, and said, "Crysta, we're bringing her home—all the way." Those words landed like a gift, pulling me from the depths of despair into a surge of hope so fierce it stole my breath. I've spoken to reporters again, my voice no longer trembling but sharp, honed by truth. My story—Jada's story—is no longer just mine to bear; it's a blade I wield, cutting through the lies that have held us captive.

The world is shifting, and I feel it deep in my bones. The Sheriff's office is under scrutiny, whispers of Don's name echoing in shadowed corners. His empire, once a towering fortress, sways on unsteady ground. Geaux Digital Branding's contracts—those tangled threads of power woven through police ties—are unraveling, exposed to the light. Each crack in his untouchable armor feels like a victory, a promise that justice isn't just a dream but a tide turning in our favor. I'm at my kitchen table now, papers strewn like battle plans, my coffee long cold. My hands tremble, not from fear but from the weight of what's coming. Then the phone rings, and the voice on the other end delivers a blow of joy so raw it nearly breaks me: Jada's first visit is tomorrow. My heart surges, a wild, leaping thing, and I clutch the receiver as tears spill down my cheeks—tears of hope, not anguish, for the first time in too long.

That night, I stand on my porch, the Louisiana sky sprawling above, heavy with stars that seem to pulse with secrets. The cicadas hum their ancient song, a soft chorus to my racing thoughts. My blonde hair dances in the warm breeze, and my green eyes lift to the heavens, tracing constellations as if they might spell out a sign, a vow that Jada will be in my arms again. She's not home yet—not fully—but she's closer than she's been in years, and I'm stronger, forged anew by a world that's finally listening. I think of Nancy, Stacie, Chris—friends and strangers alike who've lifted my story like a banner, carrying it into places I could never reach alone. My lips part, and I whisper to the night, "Thank you," my voice breaking under the weight of gratitude and grit.

Tears fall, carving warm paths down my face, but they're not the same tears I've cried before. These aren't born of grief alone—they're defiance, love, a mother's fire that burns hotter with every step toward truth. Don's still out there, his threats lurking like a shadow at the edge of my vision, but I'm no longer the woman who cowered in silence. I'm Crysta Abelseth—survivor, fighter, mother—and I'm not alone anymore. This firestorm is mine, blazing fierce and unyielding for Jada, for us, for every buried truth clawing its way to the surface. The stars above bear witness, and I stand taller, ready for whatever comes next, my heart a beacon calling my daughter home.

CHAPTER 12
THE FINAL BATTLE

July 25, 2022, breaks over Baton Rouge like a fever dream, the Louisiana sky swollen with bruised, grey clouds that seem to carry the weight of a thousand unspoken prayers. The air is thick, humid, pressing against my skin as if the heavens themselves are holding their breath, waiting for judgment. I'm thirty-three, but I feel ancient, my bones heavy with the ghosts of battles fought and scars earned. My blonde hair is curled to perfection, strands clinging to my sweat-damp neck, my green eyes darting across the stone facade of the 19th Judicial District Courthouse. The building looms like a sentinel, its cold, unyielding presence daring me to step inside, to face the reckoning I've clawed toward for fourteen years. There are crowds of people on every corner holding signs of support for Jada: Where is the rape kit?, Justice for Jada!, and other outcries scribbled across posterboard. My hands tremble, clutching a worn folder—its edges frayed, pages creased from countless nights spent poring over medical reports, Jada's testimony drafts, a subpoenaed doctor's affidavit. These are my weapons, forged in the fire of sleepless nights, each document a piece of my soul, a map of my fight to save my daughter, Jada, the pulse of my heart since I was seventeen.

The air tastes of rain and retribution, sharp and electric, as if the storm brewing above mirrors the one raging inside me. Today is no ordinary hearing. It's a trial, a 14-hour crucible that could sever the chains binding Jada to Don, the man whose shadow has haunted us both for too long. My daughter, my fierce, radiant girl, deserves a life free from his grip, and I've poured every ounce of my being into making that possible. I'm not ready—how could anyone be?—but I've never been more prepared. Every scar on my heart, every tear shed in the dark, every moment of doubt swallowed like bitter medicine has led me here. This is my war, and I will fight it with the ferocity of a mother who knows no surrender.

The courthouse doors stand before me, cold steel and glass, a portal to a battlefield I've crossed too many times to count. Each step up the stone stairs feels like a pilgrimage, my sneakers scuffing against the worn surface, each scrape a whispered prayer—not only to God but to Jada. For her to be brave during this time, in front all these people. To the wide-eyed toddler who clung to my hand, to the brave teenager who faced horrors no child should know, to the woman she's becoming, her spirit braking because of it all. I see her face in my mind's eye—those eyes, so like mine, brimming with dreams she's fought to keep alive. For her, I would storm a thousand courthouses, face a thousand Dons. For her, I am unstoppable.

Inside, the air is stale, heavy with the scent of wood polish and despair, the kind that seeps into the panelled walls and hums beneath the flicker of fluorescent lights. The courthouse is a labyrinth of echoes—murmured conversations, the shuffle of papers, the distant wail of someone's heartbreak. My chest tightens, but I force myself to breathe, to anchor myself in this moment. Claire, my attorney, waits by the entrance, a beacon in the chaos. Her dark hair is sleek, pulled back to reveal brown eyes that gleam with the sharpness of a hawk's, unyielding and fierce. She's new to my story, hired after the media storm that turned our private pain into public spectacle, but she's proven herself a warrior in her own right, a woman who doesn't flinch at power or cower before intimidation. "You've got this, Crysta," she says, her voice low and steady, a raft tossed across turbulent waters. I nod, my throat too tight for words, my fingers brushing the folder like it's a sacred relic, a talisman to carry me through the fire.

The hallway stretches before us, a gauntlet lined with strangers—clerks, lawyers, spectators whose eyes linger a moment too long, as if they can sense the weight of what I carry. My heart pounds, a drumbeat of fear and resolve, as memories flood unbidden. The night Jada was born, her tiny cries filling the hospital room, a promise I made to protect her forever. The years of running, of hiding, of building a fragile peace only to have it shattered again and again. The countless courtrooms, the judges' gavels falling like guillotines, the endless fight to prove what I've always known: that Jada's safety, her future, rests on my shoulders alone. Each memory is a wound, but also a spark, fuelling the fire that burns in my chest as I step toward the courtroom doors.

This is no mere trial; it's a reckoning, a collision of past and present, of truth and lies. Don sits somewhere beyond those doors, his presence a nightmare that has haunted us for too long. I can almost feel him, his arrogance, his cruelty, the way he's twisted our lives to suit his own narrative. But today, I am not the frightened girl I once was, cowering under his shadow. I am Crysta, mother, survivor, warrior. I am the storm, and I will not be silenced. The folder in my hands is more than paper—it's evidence of his wrongs, a chronicle of Jada's courage, a testament to my refusal to break. As Claire pushes open the courtroom doors, a rush of cold air hits me, and I step forward, my heart a blazing ember, ready to face whatever lies ahead.

For Jada, I will fight until my last breath. For Jada, I will win.

We pass through security, my heart hammering as the guard's wand hovers over me, as if it might detect the storm inside. The courtroom is down a long hall, its double doors shut, a murmur of voices seeping through. Claire pushes them open, and the room unfolds—pews packed with faces I don't recognize, reporters with notebooks, a sketch artist's pencil already moving. The judge's bench towers, empty for now, a throne of judgment. Don sits at the defense table, his suit crisp, his dark hair slicked back, his eyes avoiding mine but sharp with calculation.

He's not the man who loomed over me at sixteen, but he's no less dangerous, his presence a shadow that's choked me for decades. Jada isn't here yet—she's with her guardians, protected until her moment to speak. My chest aches at her absence, but it's a fire, too, fuelling me to stand taller.

I take my seat, the wooden chair hard against my spine, Claire beside me sorting papers with calm precision. The bailiff calls order, and Judge Evelyn Harper enters, her robe a black cascade, her silver hair pulled back, her face unreadable but not unkind. She's not Coyne, thank God—his bias exposed by the firestorm forced a recusal. Harper's reputation is steel: fair, unflinching, a woman who cuts through lies. My pulse steadies, just a fraction, as she settles, her gavel a quiet thunder. "We begin," she says, her voice clear, slicing the tension. "This is a custody and abuse hearing for Jada Blackwell. Let's proceed."

I wake to the weight of the world pressing down on my chest, my heart pounding like a war drum in the pre-dawn silence. Today is the day I've dreaded and dreamed of—the day I stand in a courtroom, my daughter Jada's fate hanging in the balance, her truth pitted against the man who tried to break her. The air feels thick, electric, as if the universe itself is holding its breath. I'm no stranger to battles, but this one? This one is for her soul, for every tear she's shed, for every scar she carries—some visible, most hidden deep where only a mother's love can find them. I'm Claire's mother, and this is my story, raw and unfiltered, a tale of rage, redemption, and a fight I'll wage until my last breath.

The courtroom is a coliseum, cold and unforgiving, its wooden pews filled with strangers who will decide if my daughter's pain is real. I sit, spine rigid, my hands trembling as I clasp them in my lap, nails carving crescent moons into my palms. The scent of polished oak and stale coffee lingers, but all I can focus on is Claire, my warrior, my advocate, rising like a phoenix at the podium. Her voice is a blade, sharp and unyielding, cutting through the tension as she begins. "Ladies and gentlemen of the jury," she says, her eyes blazing with conviction, "today, you will hear the story of Jada—a young woman whose spirit was nearly crushed under years of control, manipulation, and violence at the hands of Don Blackwell." My breath catches, her words a spark igniting the fire in my chest. She doesn't just speak; she weaves a tapestry of Jada's life, not just the past few months but the decade of torment that began when Don's shadow first fell over her.

Claire's voice trembles with controlled fury as she describes Don's rules—ironclad, suffocating, designed to strip Jada of her voice, her dreams, her very self. "No friends unless he approved. No hobbies unless he permitted. No freedom," she says, and I see it all again: Jada at ten, her laughter fading; at twelve, her eyes dulling; at fifteen, her body bruised in ways I didn't see until it was almost too late. Claire's gaze sweeps the room, locking eyes with each juror, daring them to look away. "We will present evidence of physical and psychological harm," she declares, "supported by medical records, expert testimony, and Jada's own words, preserved in a diary Don tried to destroy." My heart lurches. That diary—pages I never read, pages Jada hid from me, torn to pieces by Don's hands but salvaged by a school counselor who saw the truth in my daughter's haunted eyes. I want to scream, to run to Jada, to hold her and beg forgiveness for not seeing sooner, but I stay rooted, my pain a silent storm.

The jury, eight souls—four men, four women—watches Claire with a mix of curiosity and wariness. I study them, desperate for a sign of empathy. The woman in the red sweater, her lips pursed—does she have a daughter? The older man with a weathered face—can he see Jada's fear? Their faces are a canvas of doubt, hope, and judgment, and I know they hold my daughter's future in their hands. I'm terrified they'll see her as others have: a rebellious teen, not a survivor fighting to be free. My nails dig deeper, a sharp sting grounding me as Claire steps back, her opening statement a gauntlet thrown down.

Then he rises—Hargrove, Don's lawyer, a man with slicked-back hair and a smile that could charm a snake. His voice is smooth as oil, sliding into the room like poison, and I hate him instantly. "Exaggerations," he calls Jada's claims, each syllable a dagger aimed at her heart. "A vindictive mother," he labels me, painting me as unhinged, a woman so consumed by spite she'd ruin a "successful businessman" to win. He drops the name of Don's company, Geaux Digital Branding, like a talisman, boasting of its contracts with local agencies, its polished reputation. It's a flex, subtle but deliberate, and my blood boils. I want to leap from my seat, to scream that Don's success is a mask, that behind his tailored suits and charming grin lies a monster who bruised my daughter's body and shattered her spirit. But Claire's hand grazes my arm, a quiet anchor—*don't react, not yet.* I bite my tongue until I taste copper, forcing myself to stay still.

Hargrove's lies are clever, a spider's web spun to trap the unwary. He paints Jada as troubled, me as obsessed, Don as a victim of our "hysteria." Every word is a calculated twist, sowing doubt in the air like seeds. I glance at the jury, my heart pounding. The woman in blue frowns, her brow creased—does she see through him? The man with glasses nods faintly, and my stomach churns—is he buying this? I pray they feel the truth, the weight of Jada's pain, the reality of her courage. My daughter is here today—I'm afraid she's too fragile, her testimony to be said not twenty feet in front of her abuser—but hopefully I can be the comfort she needs, her strength fuelling my resolve.

This courtroom is a battlefield, and I'm no bystander. I'm a mother, scarred and fierce, fighting for the girl I failed too long. Hargrove's voice fades, but his words linger, a challenge I'll meet with every ounce of my being. Claire leans close, her whisper a vow: "We've got this."

And I believe her, because I have to. For Jada, for the truth, for the chance to rebuild what Don tried to destroy. The jury watches, the war rages on, and I sit, heart ablaze, ready to fight until the end.

The first witness is Dr. Lena Patel, a pediatrician with graying curls and a calm that fills the room. Claire leads her through Jada's medical history, pulling out reports from my folder—bruises documented in 2020, unexplained weight loss in 2021, anxiety attacks by 2022. Patel's voice is steady, clinical but human, describing marks on Jada's arms, consistent with gripping, not play. "These weren't accidents," she says, holding up a photo, blurred for privacy but stark in its truth. My throat tightens, my eyes burning as I see Jada's skin, her pain inked in purple and yellow. The jury shifts, the woman in blue leaning forward, her lips tight. Hargrove cross-examines, suggesting "teen roughhousing," but Patel doesn't waver. "Not these patterns," she says, her gaze locking on him. "Not this frequency."

Next is Ms. Torres, Jada's school counselor, a woman with kind eyes and a binder of notes. She speaks of Jada's withdrawal, her sketches of locked doors, her whispers about "rules at Dad's." Torres found diary scraps in Jada's backpack—phrases like "he watches me sleep," "I can't breathe there." My heart cracks, each word a wound I couldn't shield her from. Torres chokes up, describing Jada's fear, her plea to stay at school late. Claire asks, "Did Jada name her abuser?" Torres nods, voice soft but firm. "Don. Always Don." Hargrove objects—

hearsay—but Harper overrules, her pen moving fast. The jury's eyes dart to Don, his jaw tight, his fingers drumming silently.

Hours crawl, the courtroom a pressure cooker. I testify next, my legs shaking as I walk to the stand, the folder left behind, my truth all I carry. Claire's questions are gentle, guiding me to 2011, when custody split us, to 2015, when I begged for justice, to 2022, when Jada slipped away. I speak of Don's threats, his voice low and cold: "You'll lose her for good." My voice breaks, but I push on, describing Jada's light dimming—her laughter gone, her hugs hesitant. "She's my daughter," I say, my green eyes wet, meeting each juror's gaze. "I failed her once by staying quiet. Never again." The room is still, my words hanging like smoke. Hargrove's cross is brutal, calling me unstable, a liar chasing headlines. "You've been after my client for years, haven't you?" he sneers. I lean forward, my voice steel. "I've been after my daughter's safety. That's all." A juror, an older man, nods, just once, and I cling to it.

The clock struck noon, but time felt like it had abandoned me, leaving me stranded in a haze of cold coffee and trembling nerves. Lunch was no reprieve—just a fleeting pause in the storm that had become my life. In a cramped side room, Claire, my rock, my confidante, leaned close, her hand enveloping mine with a warmth that fought against the chill in my bones. "You're doing it," she whispered, her voice steady but laced with an urgency that mirrored my own. "Jada's voice is next."

Those words landed like a lightning bolt, splitting my heart in two. Pride surged—my daughter, my brave, beautiful girl, was about to take the stand. But fear, that relentless shadow, clawed at me. I didn't want her in that room, under those piercing eyes, facing *him*. Don's stare, cold and unyielding, haunted me even in my dreams. The thought of Jada enduring it made my stomach churn, a violent collision of love and dread.

Back in the courtroom, the air had thickened, heavy with anticipation. The jury shifted in their seats, restless but alert, their faces a canvas of curiosity and judgment. The clock ticked mercilessly past noon, each second a hammer against my resolve. Judge Harper, her presence both stern and grounding, called a recess to prepare for Jada's arrival. I sat frozen, hands clasped so tightly my knuckles whitened, my breath shallow, each inhale a battle. The wait was torture, every tick of the clock stretching into eternity. My mind raced—images of Jada as a toddler, her blonde curls bouncing as she giggled, clashed with the reality of the young woman she'd become, forged in a fire I couldn't shield her from. I wanted to scream, to run to her, to wrap her in my arms and carry her far from this place. But I was rooted, bound by the weight of this moment, this fight, this truth.

Then, at 2 p.m., the doors swung open, and there she was—my Jada. My heart stopped, then thundered back to life. Almost sixteen now, taller than me, she carried herself with a quiet strength that both shattered and rebuilt me. Her blonde curls fell loosely around her shoulders, framing a face that held too much wisdom for her years. Her blue-green eyes, once so full of innocent wonder, now bore the weight of battles fought in silence. She wore a pale pink suit, simple yet radiant, a beacon of her resilience. Her hands were clasped tightly, her guardians a steady presence at her side. My chest ached, a visceral pang—she was still my baby, my little girl who once clung to my hand in the dark. But she was a warrior, too, carrying scars I would have torn the world apart to take for her.

Our eyes met, and for a fleeting moment, the world fell away. A flicker of a smile crossed her lips, fragile but real, and it was oxygen, life, everything. That smile was my lifeline, pulling me back from the edge of despair. Judge Harper's voice broke the silence, soft and measured, explaining the process with a care that felt like a small mercy. Claire approached, her presence a quiet force, her questions delicate, as if handling the most fragile glass. "Jada," she began, her tone a lifeline of its own, "can you tell us about living with your father?"

Jada's voice emerged, small at first, trembling like a leaf caught in a storm. But then, something shifted. Her words grew stronger, a river breaking free from its banks, rushing forward with a force that filled the room. She spoke of rules that weren't rules but chains—no friends, no phone, no privacy. "He'd check my room at night," she said, her eyes fixed on the floor, as if the weight of those memories pinned her there. “He’d stand there, watching. I’d pretend to sleep, holding my breath until he left. Some nights he would drug me. He would put it in my dinner. I’d wake up sometime in the night to use the restroom and it would burn, down there.” My tears fell silently, hot against my cheeks, my hands gripping the wooden bench until my fingers ached. Each word was a dagger, carving deeper into the wound of my guilt. I should have known. I should have saved her sooner.

She went on, her voice steady now, recounting moments that stole the air from my lungs. His hands—grabbing her arm, shoving her against a wall, all because she “talked back.” Then, in a moment that stopped time, she lifted her sleeve, revealing a faint scar etched into her skin. The jury gasped, a soft but sharp sound that echoed in the stillness. “He said it was my fault,” she whispered, her voice barely audible, “for making him mad.” The words hung in the air, a confession of pain that shattered the room’s fragile calm. My heart screamed; a primal wail trapped inside me. How could he? How could I have let her endure this?

Claire’s voice softened further, a gentle shift. “Jada, can you tell us about your mother?” At this, Jada’s face transformed. The hardness in her eyes melted, replaced by a warmth that pierced me to my core. “Mom fought for me,” she said, her voice steady, resolute. “Always. She’s why I’m here.” The words broke me. A sob tore free, loud and raw in the quiet courtroom, reverberating off the walls. Judge Harper’s eyes flickered to me, not with reprimand but with something softer, almost understanding. I covered my mouth, tears streaming, my body trembling with the weight of Jada's love, her trust, her truth.

In that moment, I was no longer just a mother sitting in a courtroom. I was a fighter, a survivor, a vessel for every sleepless night, every whispered prayer, every tear shed in the dark. Jada's voice was my redemption, her courage my salvation. She stood there, my daughter, my heart, baring her soul to a room of strangers, and I knew—whatever came next, we had already won. Because she was free. Because she was heard. Because she was mine, and I was hers, and together, we were unstoppable.

Hargrove's cross is a knife, probing for holes, suggesting Jada's "confused," her memories "coached." Her mother has been manipulating her feelings towards her father since she was a small child. "You love your mom, don't you? You would believe anything she tells you, wouldn't you?" he asks, his tone syrupy. Jada's eyes flash, her voice steady. "Yes. But I'm not lying. I lived it. My mom has only been there to comfort me. She's never once said a bad thing about Don." The jury leans in, the woman in blue wiping her eyes, the man with glasses writing fast. Harper watches, her face a mask, but her pen pauses, lingering. Jada steps down, her guardian guiding her out, and she looks back, our eyes locking—love, strength, a promise we're in this together.

The afternoon drags, witnesses piling truth on truth. A forensic psychologist, Dr. Ellis, testifies about Jada's PTSD—nightmares, hypervigilance, triggered by male voices. "Consistent with prolonged abuse," he says, his voice grave. Hargrove pushes back, citing teenage rebellion, but Ellis is unmoved. "Not like this," he says. A neighbor, Mrs. Kline, saw Jada crying in front of her bedroom window, locked in for days. "She was scared," Kline says, her voice shaking. "I should've done more." My heart twists, guilt and gratitude tangling.

By 5 p.m., I'm drained, my body heavy, my throat raw from holding back screams. Claire calls our final witness, the subpoenaed doctor, Dr. Marrow, a trauma specialist. His report, buried for years by Don's connections, details Jada's hospital visit in 2021—fractured wrist, "inconsistent with a fall." Marrow's voice is low, angry. "This was suppressed," he says, holding up the file. "Someone didn't want it seen." Harper's eyes narrow, her pen still. Hargrove objects—relevance—but Harper cuts him off. "I'll hear it," she says, and my hope surges, fragile but alive.

Don's side takes the stand, a parade of character witnesses—Geaux Digital Branding colleagues, a cop friend, all vouching for his "stability." They call Jada "troubled," me "obsessed." A social worker claims Don's home was "fine," but Claire tears into her—no home visits, no interviews with Jada alone. The jury shifts, restless, the woman in blue glaring. Don testifies last, his voice calm, practiced, denying everything. “I love my daughter,” he says, his eyes on Harper, not me. “Crysta’s unstable, always has been. Let’s Jada do whatever she wants, unsupervised.” Claire’s cross is fire, pulling up his threats, the churchyard arrest, Jada’s scar. “You struck Ms. Abelseth, didn’t you?” she asks. Don hesitates, a crack in his mask. “It was a misunderstanding,” he mutters. The jury’s eyes burn into him, and I breathe, just a little. “You knew how old she was the night Jada was conceived, didn’t you?” He denies, “I thought she was an eighteen-year-old college student.”

Night falls, the courtroom lit by harsh fluorescents, shadows pooling in corners. Closing arguments come at 9 p.m., Claire’s voice a clarion call. “Jada’s told you her truth,” she says, her eyes on the jury. “Medical evidence, witnesses, her own words—they don’t lie. Don does. Protect her. End this.” Hargrove spins his tale—doubt, family drama, a “good man” wronged. But his words falter, the jury’s faces hard, unmoved. Harper adjourns for deliberation, promising a ruling tonight. “Stay close,” she says, her voice heavy.

I wait in the hall, pacing, my sneakers squeaking, my heart a wild thing. Claire sits, calm but tense, her phone buzzing with updates—Chris Nakamoto’s crew outside, filming, waiting. Reporters linger, respectful but eager, their cameras a weight I feel but don’t fear. Jada’s with her guardian, safe, but I ache to hold her, to whisper she’s enough. My mind replays her voice, her scar, her strength, and I’m torn—proud she stood, shattered she had to. The clock ticks, each second a hammer on my nerves.

At 11:47 p.m., the bailiff calls us back, my legs lead, my breath shallow. The courtroom is hushed, the jury solemn, their eyes avoiding mine. Harper enters, her face carved stone, her papers neat. My heart stops, time suspended, as she speaks. "After careful review," she says, her voice steady, "this court finds credible evidence of abuse by Don against Jada Blackwell." My sob breaks, loud, raw, my hands covering my mouth. "Jada will remain with her third-party guardian," Harper continues, "with Mrs. Abelseth granted one weekend a month, unsupervised for now. Don is barred from all contact. If the minor child wishes, she can contact her father on her own free will." The gavel falls, a thunderclap, and I'm shaking, tears soaking my shirt, Claire's arm around me.

The jury files out, the woman in blue meeting my eyes, her nod a quiet vow. Don sits, head bowed, his empire crumbling, his lawyer whispering furiously. Reporters swarm, but Claire shields me, guiding me to a side room. "It's not everything," she says, her voice soft, "but it's a win." I nod, my voice gone, my heart full and broken. Jada's not home, not yet, but she's safe, her truth heard, Don's grip severed. I clutch her photo, tucked in my pocket, her smile holds me in place.

Outside, rain falls, soft at first, then a torrent, washing the night clean. I step into it, my blonde hair plastered, my green eyes wide, tasting salt and sky. Nakamoto's camera catches me, his voice distant: "Crysta Abelseth's fight continues, but tonight, a victory." I don't speak, don't need to—my tears, my stand, my daughter's voice says it all. The courthouse fades behind me, its weight lifting, not gone but lighter. I'm Crysta, mother, survivor, a woman forged in fire, and this battle, this bitter, bold war, has carved a path to dawn.

I drive home, the road blurred by rain and tears, my heart a symphony of ache and hope. Jada's face fills me—her courage, her light, her fight mirroring mine. The trial's over, but the war isn't—Don's appeals will come, Geaux's shadow lingers, my past a ghost that haunts. Yet tonight, I've won something unstealable: truth, laid bare, a beacon for Jada, for me, for every soul watching. My hands grip the wheel, steady now, my green eyes clear despite the storm. I whisper to the night, to her, "We're getting there, baby. Together." The rain answers, soft, relentless, a promise that we're not done, that bold beats bitter, always.

CHAPTER 13
FACING THE DARKNESS

It's late 2022, and the Louisiana night wraps my bedroom in a shroud, its darkness pressing against the window like a living, breathing thing, heavy with the weight of secrets I've carried for too long. I'm thirty-three, standing before my mirror, my blonde hair a wild, tangled cascade, falling in chaotic strands past my shoulders, no longer bound by the tight ponytail I wore like armor in courtrooms or knotted from nights spent wrestling with nightmares. My green eyes, raw and red from nightmares that won't stop, stare back at me, haunted by a truth I've dodged for seventeen years: I've been lying—to myself, to Jada, to the world—hiding the rape, burying the shame, pretending I could outrun the darkness that's been chasing me since I was sixteen. The air smells of rain, sharp and restless, seeping through the cracked window, mingling with the faint smell of Jada's shampoo, a ghost of her presence in this house now empty of her laughter. She's with Don, fifteen and fading under his control, her blue-green eyes dimming in my memory, and I'm alone, my bare feet cold against the hardwood, my heart a battlefield where guilt and rage wage a relentless war. After my story hit every local news channel, he blocked my number. I'll call relentlessly, but it won't ring.

I clutch the mirror's cold, unforgiving edge, my knuckles blanching, my fingers quivering with a tremor I can't suppress as I force myself to confront the reflection staring back at me. It's not Crysta the warrior, forged in battles of will and survival, nor Crysta the mother, who poured every ounce of her soul into shielding her daughter. No, it's Crysta the girl—sixteen, fragile, broken on a tattered couch in Ponchatoula, Louisiana, back in 2005, her world obliterated by Don's cruel hands, her innocence stolen in a single, merciless night that reshaped her forever. For nearly two decades, I've fled from that girl, building a fortress of lies, each one a heavy brick laid to entomb her memory. I told myself I was whole, unshattered; I spun tales for Jada, weaving a myth of a father who was never around; I convinced the world—and myself—that I could bear this burden alone, unyielding. But tonight, that carefully constructed wall crumbles, and she's here, that terrified girl, her green eyes wide with a fear that still feels alive, her silent scream a sound I smothered to keep breathing. My breath hitches, a scream clawing its way up my throat, and I collapse, sliding down to the floor, my back pressed against the wall. The wood's icy chill seeps into my spine, a stark reminder of the relentless coldness of this lifelong fight. "I'm sorry," I whisper, my voice trembling—to that girl I abandoned, to Jada, to the fragments of myself I've buried beneath years of denial. The words cut like a blade, slicing through the pretence I've clung to, and I'm bleeding now, exposed and raw, the bitter truth pouring out in a torrent I can no longer contain.

This house, our creaking haven perched on the quiet edge of Hammond, feels like a mausoleum tonight, its walls heavy with the weight of absence. Jada's room, just down the shadowed hall, stands as a silent shrine to everything I've lost. Her sketchpad lies closed on her desk, its pages brimming with intricate cityscapes she drew to escape the confines of our fractured reality. On the corkboard above, her dreams of LSU are pinned, a faded acceptance letter curling at its edges, yellowing like a promise left unfulfilled. The faint trace of her strawberry scent lingers on the pillow where she hasn't slept in months, a fading echo of her presence. I see her at five, her tiny hand nestled in mine, her laughter a bright, lilting melody that anchored me through the bleakest nights. I see her at twelve, her eyes shadowed with unspoken questions, her voice barely a whisper as she asked, "Why can't I stay with you?"—a question that pierced me deeper than any blade, her breath clouding in the frigid night air, her blue-green eyes—mirrors of my own—searching the darkness for a rescue I was powerless to provide. Each memory is a fresh wound, and I've been bleeding since 2011, when a paternity test, cold and clinical, tore Jada from my arms, forcing her into a life split between my desperate love and Don's suffocating dominion.

I fought for her—God, how I fought—through courtrooms that reeked of polished wood and betrayal, facing judges like Coyne, who dismissed me as a nuisance rather than a mother pleading for her child. But my silence, my refusal to speak the word "rape" until 2015, gave

Don's shadow room to grow, allowed his grip on Jada to tighten. I held that truth inside, locked it away, thinking it would protect us both, but it only fed the beast of guilt that now claws at my chest, its teeth razor-sharp with the undeniable reality: I failed her. That failure is a weight I carry every day, a relentless ache that pulses with every beat of my heart, a reminder that my love, though fierce, wasn't enough to shield her from the consequences of my choices, my silence, my fear. Tonight, as I sit here, broken open before the mirror, I am forced to face not just the girl I was, but the mother I became—and the daughter I lost to a battle I couldn't win.

I pull my knees to my chest, my nightgown damp with sweat, and let the memories flood in, unfiltered, unsparing. August 2006, Baton Rouge, a hospital room lit by dawn's first light. I was seventeen, my blonde hair matted from labor, my green eyes hollow from a secret that weighed more than the world. Cradling newborn Jada, her blue-green eyes locked onto mine, tiny and fierce, like she knew we were in this together. She was my salvation, her breaths a vow I made in blood: I'll keep you safe, baby. I'll give you everything. But the secret I carried—that Don's violence created her—poisoned that promise from the start. I lied to her, to everyone, spinning tales of a faceless father, hiding the rape to shield us both from the town's whispers and my own shame. I see myself at eighteen, working nights at a diner, my blonde hair tucked under a cap, my green eyes darting to Jada's crib in the corner, her coos the only thing keeping me from breaking. At twenty-two, in 2011, gossip forced the DNA test, and the truth erupted like a storm. Don, thirty-six then, a man with Geaux Digital Branding's police ties and a smirk that cut deeper than any knife, claimed her, and I was powerless, my screams drowned in a courtroom that didn't care.

The custody wars began that year, a blur of hearings that left me hollow. I see Jada at five, her blue-green eyes wide with confusion as she was ushered to Don's house, her small hand slipping from mine, her voice a whisper, "Mama, when am I coming back?" I see myself at twenty-three, learning to fight like Don, trained by necessity to hide my fear, to strike with words in court, my blonde hair pulled tight, my green eyes steel against his petty accusations—Jada's hair too messy, my job too unstable, my life too chaotic. By 2015, at twenty-six, I reported the rape, my voice trembling in the Sheriff's office, my green eyes blazing as I begged for justice. They shrugged— "Slipped through," they said, like my pain was a clerical error—and I stormed out, vowing to Jada's photo, "I'll fight for you." But Don's control tightened, his rules a vise around Jada's life: no friends allowed, no phone to reach me, her diary torn to pieces when she dared write her truth. I see her at twelve, her laughter dimming like a candle starved of air; at fifteen, her eyes dull, whispering to me in a stolen moment, "He watches me, Mom. I can't breathe." My heart broke, my resolve hardened, but the system shielded him, Geaux Digital Branding's ties to police a wall I couldn't breach.

In the late summer of 2022, the churchyard stood as a crucible, a place where memory seared itself into the marrow of my bones, vivid enough to pulse with a physical ache. The air hung heavy, saturated with the relentless drone of cicadas, their song a restless undercurrent to the tension that gripped the scene. My daughter, Jada, just sixteen, sat in the cab of Don's truck, her blonde curls half-hidden beneath the hood of her sweatshirt, her face a fragile mask of apprehension. We were at the church, the designated neutral ground where custody exchanges unfolded like a ritual, each one fraught with unspoken dread. I stood near the stone steps, my hands trembling as I clutched a single sheet of paper—a form for my attorney, a fragile gesture that carried no real authority but felt like a lifeline in that moment.

The world seemed to slow as Don's fist found me, a sudden, brutal strike to my chest that sent pain radiating through my ribs like wildfire. The impact stole my breath, but it was Jada's scream that shattered the twilight, a raw, desperate sound that pierced the haze of my shock. Through the truck's window, I saw her, her small hands pressed against the glass, her blue-green eyes wide with a terror so profound it seemed to anchor her in place, as if she could will herself to reach me, to undo the violence unfolding before her. The churchyard, once a place of quiet reverence, had become a battleground, its sanctity fractured by the weight of that moment.

A stranger, Stacie Triche, stood witness to it all, her presence an unexpected grace. She didn't hesitate, her fingers already dialing for help as she called the police, her voice a spark that ignited a chain of events that would alter the course of our lives. Don's arrest came swiftly, but it was fleeting—by nightfall, he was free, a deputy dismissing the incident with a shrug and a curt, "No restraining order." Yet that brief detention was enough to set something in motion, a slow-burning fuse that would soon erupt into something far larger than that single act of violence.

Days later, I received a call from Chris Nakamoto, a reporter with WBRZ, his voice calm but resolute, carrying the weight of someone who understood the power of a story. He wanted to tell mine, to shine a light on the shadows that had haunted us for years. I agreed, and when the cameras rolled, I poured out my truth—the rape in 2005 that had left scars deeper than skin, the grueling custody battle that followed, and now the churchyard assault, a public wound laid bare. My voice quavered but held firm, my blonde hair a wild halo in the studio lights, my green eyes burning with a defiance I hadn't known I possessed. I spoke for Jada, for myself, for every moment of fear and resilience that had brought us to this precipice.

The story didn't just air—it detonated. It spread like wildfire across screens and social media, a viral outcry that shook the foundations of the system that had failed us. The Sheriff, cornered by the public's fury, issued a rare admission: "We dropped the ball." Nancy Grace, her voice a sounding board on national television, called for Judge Coyne's disbarment, her outrage amplifying the chorus of demands for justice. And in the wake of that storm, the most precious outcome of all: Jada was placed with a third party, a safe harbor where she could finally breathe, free from the shadow of fear that had loomed over her for so long. The churchyard, that fleeting flashpoint, had become the spark that changed everything, a testament to the power of truth spoken aloud, no matter how trembling the voice that carried it.

But safety is fragile, and guilt is a relentless hunter. I crawl to my bed, the sheets cool against my fevered skin, and clutch Jada's old stuffed bear, its fur worn from her childhood hugs, its button eyes staring into the dark. My PTSD is a live wire, sparking nightmares where Jada vanishes, her voice calling from a darkness I can't reach. Therapy, started last year with Ms. Lena, a counselor with grey braids and eyes that see through walls, is peeling back the layers—paranoia, shame, the bone-deep dread of failing again. She asks me to name the girl I was, to forgive her, but it's like forgiving a stranger. I see her in flashes: sixteen, walking into a Ponchatoula bar, giddy with friends, my blonde hair loose, my green eyes bright with naive trust; sixteen, on Don's couch, my screams swallowed by his weight, my world collapsing; sixteen, pregnant, hiding in oversized sweaters, lying to my mama, my green eyes hollow as I whispered, "I'm fine." I hate her for her silence, her weakness, but tonight, I'm trying to love her, to hold her like I hold Jada's bear, soft and broken and mine.

The phone rings, shattering the quiet, and my heart lurches, dread coiling like a snake in my gut. It's my best friend, her sandy-haired, hazel-eyed warmth an ease through the speaker. "Crysta, you okay?" she asks, her voice thick with worry, cutting through the miles between us. She's been my rock since high school, the one who held me when I collapsed after Jada's birth, who was always on Jada's side when Don's threats spiked, who fought beside me when the world turned away. I sob into the phone, the words spilling like a dam breaking: "I lied to everyone. The rape, Jada's pain—I hid it, and it's killing me." My voice is raw, a scream muffled by years of silence, and she listens, her silence a blanket wrapping around my shaking soul. "I've got scars, too, Crysta," she says, her voice trembling, steady. "We all do. You're not alone." Her words are a spark, igniting something buried—a longing for connection, for truth shared, for a world where I don't have to hide.

She confides in me, unraveling a deeply personal tale, a burden she's borne in silence—not rape, but a different kind of abuse, a haunting shadow she's wrestled to escape. I can picture her vividly, sitting on her porch miles away, her hazel eyes glistening with unshed tears, her sandy hair tucked neatly behind one ear. She's opening her heart, laying bare her vulnerabilities to connect with mine. As we talk, our tears fall in unison, our shared stories forming an invisible bridge that spans the distance between us. In that moment, something shifts within me—a fracture in the oppressive darkness that has held me prisoner for so long. My pain, my trigger, ignites a fierce rage, a primal scream I muffle into my pillow. But it's more than just anger; it's a cathartic release, a solemn vow to stop shrouding my truth in silence. I still feel need to lie about anything and nothing, so people see someone of worth. Not the real me, of course, but someone worth loving, worth respecting.

I share my own story with her, the memories spilling out like a torrent. I take her back to 2015, when I was twenty-six, my blonde hair a wild halo, my green eyes burning with determination as I stormed into the Sheriff's office. I pleaded with them to investigate the rape, to bring justice for the violation that had shattered my world. Their response was a dismissive shrug, a cold "It slipped through the cracks," as if my pain were an insignificant oversight. I left that office with my fists clenched so tightly my nails dug into my palms, my heart whispering a fierce promise to Jada's photograph: "I'll keep fighting, no matter what."

I tell her about the grueling custody battles, the suffocating control Don exerted over every facet of our lives. His rules were ironclad: no friends, no phone, no semblance of freedom. I recount the day he found Jada's diary, her private sanctuary where she dared to etch her truth, and tore it to pieces in a fit of rage, leaving her words scattered like ashes. I share the memory of Jada at fifteen, her voice barely above a whisper in a rare stolen moment, her words chilling me to the core: "He watches me, Mom. I can't breathe." Those words broke my heart, but they also forged my resolve, tempering it like steel in a blazing fire, unyielding and unbreakable.

"I want to heal," I confess, my voice raw and trembling, both a desperate plea and a steadfast promise. "For Jada, for myself." Her response is immediate, unwavering—she swears to stand by me, to hold my hand through the pain and the healing, and I believe her. Those hazel eyes of hers, so vivid in my mind, become a guiding light, a beacon of hope amidst the storm. When I finally hang up, my chest heaves with the weight of our conversation, my breaths uneven but purposeful. I rise to my feet, my legs shaky yet undeniably my own, and I feel the cool hardwood floor beneath my bare soles, grounding me to the present.

I make my way to Jada's room, the door slightly ajar, as if beckoning me forward. I kneel beside her bed, where the moonlight spills through the window, casting a soft glow over the space where she should be. Her sketchpad lies open on the bed, revealing a cityscape she drew—jagged lines filled with raw emotion, yet infused with a quiet hope. In the center stands a solitary figure, arms outstretched, defying a sky that dares to dream of brighter days. I know instantly that it's us—Jada and me, captured in charcoal, embodying the fight we're still waging together. My fingers trace the lines of her drawing, smudging the edges of the charcoal, and I whisper into the stillness, "I'm coming for you, baby. I'm done hiding."

Outside, the stars blaze in the night sky, their light a testament to resilience—a reminder that though scars may be bitter, they carve the path for a bold, unyielding rise. I linger in her room, surrounded by the echoes of her presence, and feel a fire kindling within me, fierce and unrelenting, ready to face whatever lies ahead.

I return to my room, the mirror waiting, and face her again—the girl, the mother, the survivor. My green eyes are wet but fierce, my blonde hair a halo in the lamplight, catching the light like a fire I'm learning to wield. I see the rape, the lies, the years of silence, but I see more: the woman who fought, who stood in courtrooms, who spoke to WBRZ, who clawed her way to this moment, bloody but unbowed. I see Jada, her blue-green eyes, her courage, her love, and I know I'm not just fighting for her—I'm fighting for us, for every survivor, for a world where no one, no man or woman, no soul of any gender, has to hide their truth. Don's empire, Geaux Digital Branding, looms, its police ties a threat I can't ignore, its contracts a whisper in Ponchatoula's undercurrents. Coyne's bias, the Sheriff's excuses, the system's shield—they're still there, mocking my pain, but so am I, bolder than ever, my voice a flame that won't be snuffed out.

I think of the survivors I've met, their faces a chorus of pain and hope—men abused by those they trusted, women scarred by violence, souls of all genders carrying wounds no one should bear. Their stories echo mine, their strength fuels me, and I vow to speak for them, to fight for a world where abuse, sexual or not, has no place. I see my friend's hazel eyes, her shared scars, and I know connection is my salvation, the bridge from darkness to light. I climb into bed, Jada's bear tucked against my chest, its worn fur a reminder of her childhood, its button eyes a silent witness to my fight. I close my eyes, and Jada's laughter echoes in my heart, her smile a beacon in the dark. Tomorrow, I'll call Ms. Lena, dig deeper, name the pain with her gentle guidance. Tomorrow, I'll fight for Jada, for justice, for the girl I was. But tonight, I'm here, alive, unbroken, my heart a drumbeat of hope, my soul a fire that burns bold against the bitter dark.

As the night unfurls its quiet expanse, I surrender to its stillness, letting memories weave through the silence like delicate threads stitching together a tapestry of my life. Each recollection glimmers, vivid and sharp, pulling me back to moments that have shaped me, scarred me, and ultimately forged the woman I am now. I see myself at eighteen, a young mother with blonde hair tucked beneath a worn cap, my green eyes scanning the streets of Hammond for any hint of danger. My hands grip the stroller where Jada, my heart's anchor, sleeps, and my love for her burns fierce, a flame that no fear can extinguish. I see Jada at three, her tiny curls dancing as she toddles toward me, her giggle a radiant beam that cuts through the shadows of my worry, filling me with a joy so pure it feels like defiance. I see the courtroom in 2014, the air heavy with tension, my voice unwavering as I challenge Coyne's ruling, my green eyes fixed on Jada's small form, silently vowing, "I'll fight for you forever." I see the WBRZ studio, the camera's red light glaring like a dare, my blonde hair untamed, my voice quivering yet resolute as I bare my truth to the world: "He hurt me. He's hurting her." Each memory is a mark etched into my soul—a scar, a triumph, a step toward this moment of reckoning under the vast, starlit sky.

My thoughts drift to my mama, her absence a quiet ache in my chest. Her hands, rough from years of labor, were always gentle when they cradled baby Jada, her eyes softening as she whispered to me, "You're stronger than you know, Crysta." Those words echo now, a steady rhythm guiding me through the darkness. I think of my daddy, his deep, rumbling laugh once filling our home with warmth, his pride shining when I graduated high school early, pregnant but unyielding, my spirit unbroken despite the weight I carried. They never knew the full truth—the rape, the silent burden I bore—but their love was a bedrock, a foundation that steadies me as I build my life, brick by painstaking brick, from the ruins of pain.

Ponchatoula rises in my mind, its sprawling fields where I ran as a carefree child, its dimly lit bars where I sought escape at sixteen, its churches where I knelt in desperate prayer for strength, its streets where I marched, my voice joining a chorus of survivors who've become my family, my tribe. I think of Stacie Triche, her courage blazing in that churchyard, her bold call to the police a spark that ignited my own path forward, illuminating a way through the fog of despair. I think of Chris Nakamoto, his calm, steady questions in the studio, his commitment to amplifying my story, and gratitude swells within me, a tide that carries the weight of all those who've stood beside me, lifting me toward this moment.

The night stretches on, and I linger in these memories, each one a thread in the tapestry of my journey. They are not just fragments of the past but the very sinew of my resolve, binding me to Jada, to my truth, to the fight that has defined me. Here, in the quiet, I am not alone—my mama's whispers, my daddy's pride, the courage of my community, and the love for my daughter weave together, a constellation of strength guiding me toward dawn.

The rain slows, a soft patter now, and I open my eyes, the bear still against my chest. I see Jada in my mind, sixteen, her sketchpad her refuge, her blue-green eyes fierce despite the pain. I see her at five, braiding her hair, kissing her scraped knees, promising her the world. I see her at twelve, sneaking a text from a friend's phone, "I'm okay, Mom," her rebellion a spark that kept me fighting. I see her at fifteen, her scar—a faint line on her arm from Don's rage—hidden under sleeves, her voice a whisper, "I'm scared." I failed her then, stayed silent too long, but I'm speaking now, my voice a roar that shakes the heavens. I'll fight for her, for us, for every soul who's known this pain, until my last breath.

I rise, my legs steadier now, and walk to the window, the glass cool against my palm. The stars are out, bright and relentless, a canvas of hope against the night. I think of Jada's cityscape, that figure standing tall, and I know it's not just her—it's me, it's us, it's every survivor who's dared to rise. I whisper to the night, to her, to the girl I was: "We're not done. We're just beginning." The words are a vow, a fire, a promise that carries me forward. I climb back into bed, the bear beside me, and close my eyes, Jada's laughter a melody in my heart, her smile a light that no darkness can touch. Tomorrow's another battle—therapy, advocacy, the slow work of healing—but tonight, I'm enough. Tonight, I'm bold, my soul a flame that burns eternal, my scars a map of where I've been, my heart a compass pointing where I'm going.

I dream of Jada, her curls wild, her blue-green eyes bright, her hand in mine as we walk through a city of light, its towers built from our fight, its streets paved with our love. I dream of survivors, men and women, young and old, all genders, their voices rising with mine, a chorus that drowns out the pain. I dream of a world where no one hides, where truth is a shield, where love is a sword. And when I wake, the dawn is breaking, soft and golden, spilling through the window like a promise I'm learning to trust. I'm Crysta, survivor, mother, warrior, and I'm ready—ready to heal, ready to fight, ready to love, bold and unyielding, forever against the bitter dark.

CHAPTER 14
REBUILDING BONDS

August 2025, and the Louisiana dawn creeps soft over Hammond, its golden light spilling through my kitchen window like a promise I'm still learning to trust. I'm thirty-five, my blonde hair loose for the first time in years, not scraped into the tight ponytail of courtroom battles or knotted from sleepless nights, but falling in soft waves against my shoulders, catching the sun's glow like a halo I don't deserve. My green eyes, once hollowed by rage, guilt, and a decade of fighting, flicker with something new—fragile, tentative, but alive, like a seedling pushing through cracked earth. The air smells of coffee, bitter and grounding, mingling with the faint strawberry of Jada's shampoo, a scent that lingers from her shower this morning. It's a reminder, that smell, tethering me to this moment, this miracle: my daughter, my eighteen-year-old warrior, is home.

The air in our new house on the edge of town feels different, alive with a warmth I'd almost forgotten could exist. I have a full-time corporate job now, and I don't owe anyone a dime. It's not just that Jada is here—not as a visitor, not shadowed by some court-appointed stranger clutching a clipboard with cold, clinical detachment—but truly home, her presence filling the crevices of this place like sunlight after a long storm. Her laughter spills down the hallway, a sound so vivid and unguarded it catches me off guard, like stumbling across a song I thought I'd lost forever, its melody familiar yet achingly new. I stand in the kitchen, my hands curled around a chipped ceramic mug, the coffee's heat grounding me as I listen, marveling at how such a simple sound can carry so much weight—hope, resilience, the stubborn pulse of joy reclaimed.

It's been a couple years since the trial, that grueling 14-hour ordeal in the 19th Judicial District Courthouse back in July 2022. I can still see it so clearly: the crowded courtroom, heavy with tension, the air thick with the weight of years unspoken. Jada stood there, her voice trembling but resolute, each word a defiant act of courage as she laid bare the truth. When Judge Harper's gavel crashed down, it was like thunder rolling across a bruised sky, severing Don from her life with a finality that felt both victorious and surreal. That day, as I staggered out into the rain-soaked parking lot, water droplets streaming down my face and into my hair, my heart soared with a fleeting sense of triumph. I thought I'd won it all, that the war was over, the enemy vanquished. But life, I've learned, is rarely so tidy. The truth is rawer, more jagged, like a wound still knitting itself closed, tender and aching even as it heals.

Jada's emancipation at seventeen, granted almost a year after that courtroom battle, was a hard-won victory, carved from years of silent suffering and unspoken scars. She chose me, chose us—chose this life, in this house with me. Now, she's here, unpacking her life in the bedroom down the hall, her belongings spilling out of boxes as if staking a claim to this space, to this new chapter. On the fridge, her LSU acceptance letter hangs proudly, pinned there like a badge of her defiance, a testament to her refusal to be defined by the pain of her past. It's a quiet rebellion, that letter, a declaration that she's not just surviving but reaching for something more, something wholly her own. Don willingly signed off on the emancipation, tired of paying Jada's guardians child support each month. I didn't mind it as long as she was taken care of, but it was time. Time for her to come home so we could start living as mother and daughter completely again for the first time since she was five years old.

But healing? That's another kind of battlefield, one we're navigating with cautious, trembling steps. It's not a straight path but a winding one, strewn with moments of grace and the stubborn ghosts of what we've endured. Each day feels like a delicate dance between love and the shadows we both carry, a rhythm we're learning together. I lean against the counter, the mug's warmth seeping into my palms, and listen as Jada hums from her room. It's a tune I don't know, soft yet fierce, a melody that seems to capture her essence—fragile but unyielding, a song of survival and the slow, stubborn reclamation of joy. The sound tugs at something deep inside me, pulling me back to a moment long buried: August 2006, in a dimly lit Baton Rouge hospital room. I was seventeen then, barely more than a child myself, my world unraveling under the weight of a secret I thought I'd carry to my grave—a rape I'd buried so deep it felt like it belonged to someone else. Cradling newborn Jada in my arms, her tiny breaths were my only anchor, her blue-green eyes locking onto my green ones, wide with a tangle of terror and love. In that moment, I whispered a vow: *I'll give you everything, baby. I'll keep you safe.*

Nineteen years later, I'm still keeping that promise, though it's not the fairy tale I once envisioned. It's something realer, scarred and imperfect, a bond forged in the crucible of pain, tempered by loss, and now, slowly, beginning to bloom anew. Jada's humming grows softer, and I close my eyes, letting the sound wash over me. It's not just a melody—it's a reminder of what we've fought for, what we've survived. This house, with its sturdy foundation, is more than a shelter; it's a testament to our resilience, a space where we're piecing ourselves back together, step by trembling step. And as I stand here, coffee cooling in my hands, I know that this—our messy, beautiful, hard-won life—is enough.

The kitchen clock ticks, each second a reminder of time stolen and time reclaimed. I set the mug down, my fingers brushing the edge of the coffee table, its scratches a map of our life—spaghetti spills when Jada was five, marker stains from her doodles at eight, coffee rings from my late-night battles with legal papers. I let myself feel it all—the ache, the joy, the weight of what we've survived. The trial didn't erase Don's shadow; his appeals loom, Geaux Digital Branding's influence still whispers in the corners of this small town, its police contracts a quiet threat I can't ignore. My own guilt, that relentless beast, claws at me in the quiet hours. I failed her too long, stayed silent when I should've screamed, let her slip into his grip while I fought a system rigged against us. But Jada's here now, and that's a truth louder than any regret, a light brighter than any darkness.

I walk to her room, my bare feet soft against the hardwood, the floorboards creaking under my weight like they're whispering our history. I pause at the door, my hand resting on the frame, and watch her. She's sitting cross-legged on her bed, her blonde curls catching the sunlight, her blue-green eyes focused on a sketchpad. She's always drawn—since she was little, scribbling worlds where she could escape—but these lines are bolder, fiercer, a cityscape of sharp angles and soft curves, like her own heart laid bare. Her hands move with purpose, charcoal smudging her fingers, and I see the girl she was and the woman she's becoming, both fragile and unbreakable. "Hey, baby," I say, my voice catching, and she looks up, her smile small but real, a bridge across the years of distance.

"Hey, Mom," she replies, and that word—*Mom*—hits me like a wave, washing away the courtroom, the threats, the nights I cried alone. I sit beside her, the mattress dipping, and for a moment, we're just us, not survivors or warriors, but a mother and daughter stealing a moment from the storm. "What's this one?" I ask, nodding at her sketch. She tilts it toward me, her fingers smudged with charcoal, and I see it—a skyline, jagged yet hopeful, with a single figure standing tall, arms outstretched. "It's home," she says, her voice quiet but steady. "Not just this house, but… us. You, me, the fight. It's where I'm free." My throat tightens, tears prickling, and I reach for her hand, her skin warm against mine. Her fingers curl around me, strong despite the faint tremor, and I see it—her scars, not just the faint one on her arm from Don's rage, but the invisible ones, the ones we're both learning to name.

"I'm so proud of you," I whisper, my voice breaking, and her eyes meet mine, wet but fierce. "I'm proud of *you*, Mom," she says, and it's a lightning bolt, splitting me open. "You never stopped. Even when I pushed you away, you were there. When no one else believed me or cared, you did." The words unravel me, and I want to sob now, but I still can't feel all of my emotions. I want to in this moment, but I'm still numb. Once your body is in survival mode for so long, it takes just as much time to get out of it. She pulls me close, her arms stronger than I remember, and we hold each other, two souls battered but a little less broken, our sighs mingling, our breaths syncing in the quiet. Her strawberry scent wraps around me, and I'm back to her toddler years, braiding her hair, kissing her scraped knees, promising her the world. I failed that promise too many times, but here, now, I'm rewriting it, word by painful word.

The moment unfurls, sacred and heavy, suspending us in a quiet that feels like a prayer. I let myself sink into the memories, each one a shard of the years we lost, sharp enough to draw blood but too precious to release. The custody battles began in 2011, when Jada was just five, her blue-green eyes wide with confusion as she was ushered away to Don's house, her small hand slipping from mine. Those early days were a blur of courtrooms and hollow promises, each hearing a fresh wound. The nights she spent under his roof haunt me still—his rules were a vise, squeezing the light from her spirit. No friends allowed to visit, no phone to reach out, her diary ripped to pieces when she dared to write her truth. I can still see her at twelve, her laughter dimming like a candle starved of oxygen; at fifteen, her eyes losing their spark, dulled by the weight of his control; at sixteen, forced to live with strangers, a married couple always fighting, as she wept into the night wishing she could sleep in her own bed.

The memory of the churchyard in 2022 burns brightest, a flashpoint of rage and pain. He struck me over a form—a simple piece of paper that held no real weight, yet his fist came down like a hammer, a burst of pain blooming across my chest. Jada, fifteen then, sat in his truck, her face a mask of terror, her hands pressed against the window as if she could reach me through the glass. The media storm that followed was both a savior and a thief. WBRZ's exposé gave us a voice, amplifying Jada's story, but it stripped away our privacy, turning our private agony into public spectacle, our names splashed across headlines for strangers to dissect. The trial was its own crucible. Jada's testimony—her scar laid bare; her truth spoken in a trembling voice—shattered Don's carefully crafted lies. I see her at seventeen, whispering to her counselor about his watchful nights, her voice barely audible: "He stands there, Mom. I can't breathe." Each memory is a blade, slicing through the years, but it's also a vow etched into my bones: never again. I will spend every breath, every heartbeat, ensuring she is safe, loved, and whole.

"Mom," Jada says now, pulling back slightly, her eyes searching mine, blue-green depths holding both the child she was and the woman she's becoming. "I was scared you'd give up. When I was with him, I thought… maybe you'd stop fighting." Her voice fractures, a crack that splinters my heart, sending pieces scattering across the floor like broken glass. The weight of her fear, the idea that she doubted my resolve, is almost too much to bear. "Never," I say, my voice fierce, unyielding, as I cup her face, my thumbs brushing the soft curve of her cheeks. "Jada, you are my why. Every day, every tear, every scream in those courtrooms—it was all for you. I'd burn the world to ash to keep you safe." She nods, tears spilling over, and in her eyes, I see it dawning: belief, trust, the fragile but growing bond we're piecing back together, brick by painstaking brick. Her curls graze my wrist, a soft reminder of time's passage, and I'm struck by the duality of her presence—the child I once rocked to sleep, her tiny body curled against mine, and the young woman who stood in that courtroom, baring her soul to strangers, her courage a beacon in the dark. This moment, this connection, is our foundation, and I will build on it with every ounce of strength I have, for as long as I live.

We talk for hours, the sun climbing high, then sinking, the room glowing orange, then purple, then dark. She tells me things I didn't know—small acts of rebellion under Don's roof, like sneaking a friend's phone to text me, "I'm okay, Mom," or hiding her sketches under her bed, taped to the frame where he wouldn't look. I tell her my truths, too—the nights I drove past his house, my headlights off, praying I'd see her silhouette in the window; the therapy sessions where I learned to forgive myself, inch by inch, for not seeing his control sooner; the day I stood in the Sheriff's office in 2015, twenty-six and shaking, begging them to investigate the rape, only to be told it "slipped through." We laugh, we talk, we sit in silence, and it's enough. It's more than enough. It's everything.

By dusk, we're in the kitchen, cooking together, something we haven't done since she was little, when she'd stand on a stool, her tiny hands stirring pancake batter. Alfredo tonight, simple but hers, her hands steady as she stirs the sauce, the steam curling around her face. I chop garlic, my knife too fast, my laughter soft as she teases me, "You're gonna lose a finger, Mom." The radio plays low, some pop song she loves, and she sways, her hips bumping mine, a playful nudge that feels like a gift. "You're a terrible dancer," she grins, and I spin her in a clumsy twirl, my heart so full it hurts. "Learned from you," I shoot back, and her laugh—God, her laugh—is sunlight, warming every corner of my soul. I see her at six, twirling in a sundress, at ten, giggling as we danced to the radio, and now, eighteen, her eyes bright with a joy I thought he'd stolen forever.

The ghosts of our past still haunt us, their presence inescapable even in the quiet moments of our new life. When the phone rings, shattering the fragile calm, Jada and I both freeze, our eyes locking in a shared moment of dread. Her gaze flickers with that old, familiar fear, a shadow of the terror we thought we'd left behind. It's only Claire, my attorney, her voice warm yet edged with urgency as she delivers the latest blow: Don has filed another motion, submitted just yesterday. Jada's shoulders stiffen, her spoon hovering motionless above the pot she's stirring, and a surge of anger courses through me. I despise him—hate him for the way his influence still creeps into our lives, casting a long, oppressive shadow over the peace we've fought so hard to build. I hang up, my hand trembling, and muster a smile, forcing steadiness into my voice. "It's just Claire, baby. Nothing we can't face together." Jada nods, but the air between us feels fractured, a stark reminder of how delicate our hard-won sanctuary remains.

Don's relentless plays for control loom like storm clouds, his legal team circling like vultures, picking at the wounds we're still trying to heal. Geaux Digital Branding, his once-untouchable empire, still wields its insidious influence, its ties to law enforcement a whispered threat that lingers in the undercurrents of Ponchatoula's small-town gossip. The weight of it all presses against my own PTSD, a constant hum of paranoia that someone's watching, waiting. Nightmares plague me—vivid, suffocating visions of Jada slipping through my fingers, vanishing into the darkness again. I wake at 3 a.m., gasping for air, my heart pounding as I reach for her, needing to know she's still here. Therapy is a lifeline, but it's a grueling journey, each session peeling back another layer of guilt, rage, and the bone-deep fear that I failed her. My therapist wants to say things I'm not ready to say, and to feel things I'm not ready to feel. Jada carries her own scars—nightmares where Don stands at her door, his presence a violation of her fragile sense of safety. Her trust is a brittle thing, fractured by years of betrayal; she flinches at sudden movements, her anxiety spiking in crowded spaces where faces blur into potential threats. We both still search for him in crowds, searching for his truck in parking lots and streets we know he frequents.

Yet, despite the weight of our past, we are fighting—fiercely, together. Jada began therapy last week, stepping tentatively into healing with a counselor who's younger with braids and gentle demeanor seem to speak the language of trauma. This woman listens with quiet strength as Jada whispers of sleepless nights and the memories that still claw at her. Jada's resilience shines through in other ways, too. She's planning for college, her sketches—vivid cityscapes born from pain and hope—

forming a portfolio that's already drawing attention from LSU's art program. Each stroke of her pencil is a testament to her survival, a declaration that she is more than what was done to her. I, too, am carving out a new identity. I've begun speaking out, traveling to Baton Rouge, New Orleans, and beyond, standing before small groups of survivors who see their own stories reflected in ours. Their eyes glisten with tears as I share our truth, my voice steady now where it once faltered. I speak of the system's failures—the Sheriff's inaction, the judges who turned away, the police who shielded Don's empire under a veneer of untouchability. I am no longer just Crysta, the victim. I am Crysta, the advocate, the mother, the woman who clawed her way through the darkness to stand in the light of dawn.

Our fight is far from over, but it is ours, waged side by side. Each step forward—Jada's tentative trust in her counselor, my growing voice in the fight for justice—is a defiance of the shadows that still seek to claim us. We are rebuilding, piece by fragile piece, and though the ghosts may linger, we are learning to face them, together, with the strength of those who have survived the unimaginable.

We eat at the kitchen table, the single bulb overhead casting a warm glow, our plates piled with alfredo, the sauce creamy and perfect. Jada reaches for my hand across the table, her fingers threading through mine, and asks, "We're gonna be okay, right?" Her voice is small, a child's plea in a woman's body, and my heart aches for the years she had to doubt. I squeeze her hand, my green eyes locked on her blue-green, and I feel it—the strength we've built, the love that's carried us through. "We're already okay," I say, my voice steady, a vow. "We're *us*, baby. That's enough. Us against the world, remember? As long as we have each other, we're always okay." She smiles, a real one, her eyes crinkling, and it's a victory, brighter than any courtroom ruling.

After dinner, we wash dishes, her elbow bumping mine, our laughter soft as the water splashes. I tell her about my childhood, stories I've held back—running through Ponchatoula's fields at ten, my grandma's gumbo recipe, the way my daddy's laugh could fill a room. She tells me about her dreams—to travel, to paint, to build a life where no one controls her. "I want to go to Paris," she says, her eyes distant, sparkling. "Will you come with me?" I nod, with an of course look, and promise, "Anywhere, baby. We'll go anywhere." It's a dream, fragile but ours, a future we're daring to imagine.

Later, we sit on the couch, a blanket over our knees, watching some silly movie she loves. Her head rests on my shoulder, her curls tickling my cheek, and I'm struck by the weight of this moment—ordinary, yet extraordinary. I think of the survivors I've met, men and women, young and old, all genders, all scars, their stories echoing ours. No one should endure what we did, what they did—abuse, sexual or not, leaves wounds that linger, but it doesn't define us. We're more than our pain, more than our battles. Jada's hand finds mine, her fingers tracing the lines of my palm, and I know she feels it, too—the power of this love, this bond, this life we're rebuilding.

The movie ends, and she yawns, her eyes heavy. "Night, Mom," she murmurs, kissing my cheek, and I watch her pad to her room, her sketchpad tucked under her arm. I stay on the couch, the house quiet now, the cicadas humming outside. I think of the trial, of Jada's scar, her testimony, the way she said, "Mom fought for me. Always." I think of Don, his empire crumbling, his motions a desperate grasp at control. I think of Geaux Digital Branding, its name a stain on this town, its influence fading but not gone. I think of the system—Coyne's bias, the Sheriff's excuses, the police who looked away—and my resolve hardens. I'll keep fighting, for Jada, for every survivor, for a world where no one has to hide their truth.

I walk to her room, the door ajar, and peek inside. She's asleep, her sketchpad open to that cityscape—our home, our fight, her figure standing tall. The moonlight paints her face, soft and fierce, and I'm overwhelmed by love, by gratitude, by the weight of what we've won. I whisper to her, to the night, to the girl I was and the woman I'm becoming: "We're free." The stars answer, bright and relentless, a promise that bitter may scar, but bold always rises.

I climb into bed, the sheets cool against my skin, and close my eyes. Jada's laughter echoes in my heart, her smile a beacon in the dark.

Tomorrow's another battle—appeals, advocacy, the slow work of healing—but tonight, we're home. Tonight, we're enough. I dream of Paris, of her sketches, of a world where she's safe, and I know, deep in my bones, that we're getting there. Together, always, we're getting there.

The next morning, I wake to the smell of pancakes—Jada's up, flipping them in the kitchen, her voice calling, "Mom, you're gonna miss the good ones!" I laugh, pulling on a sweater, and join her, the sun streaming through the window, the day new and ours. We eat, we talk, we plan—college, trips, advocacy events. I tell her about the survivors' group I'm speaking to next week, about the men and women who've written to me, their stories a chorus of pain and hope. "No one should feel alone," I say, and she nods, her eyes fierce. "They won't, Mom. Not with you."

We spend the day together, simple things—gardening in the backyard, her hands in the dirt, planting marigolds; driving to the library, her picking out art books; sitting on the porch at dusk, her sketching while I sip tea. Each moment is a thread, weaving us closer, mending the tears of the past. I think of my own therapy, the way my counselor, Ms. Lena, helps me name my fears—paranoia, guilt, the dread of losing Jada again. I think of Jada's sessions, her slow trust in her counselor, her nightmares easing, her smiles growing. We're not whole, not yet, but we're healing, and that's a victory no one can steal.

That night, we cook again—gumbo this time, my grandma's recipe, the roux thick and perfect. Jada stirs, her laughter bright as I tell her about my first attempt at gumbo, a burnt disaster at sixteen. "You're hopeless," she teases, and I flick flour at her, her squeal filling the kitchen. We eat on the porch, the air cool, the stars sharp above. She tells me about a boy in her art class, her cheeks pink, and I listen, my heart full, knowing she's daring to dream again. I tell her about my first crush, a silly story from high school, and we laugh until our sides ache.

As the days gradually weave themselves into weeks, our lives settle into a comforting rhythm, a tapestry of small, meaningful moments that bind us closer. Each morning dawns with the rich aroma of freshly brewed coffee and the sizzle of pancakes on the griddle, golden and warm, shared over quiet laughter and plans for the day. Afternoons unfold lazily, filled with the soft scratch of pencils as Jada sketches intricate worlds on paper and I lose myself in the pages of a book, the stories offering solace and escape. When evening falls, we gather to exchange tales—some whimsical, some heavy with dreams—our voices mingling in the glow of lamplight, building a sanctuary of hope.

In Baton Rouge, I stand before a crowd at a survivors' event, my heart pounding but steady, Jada by my side. Her presence is a quiet, unshakable strength, an anchor in the sea of faces before me—men and women, young and old, people of all genders, their eyes glistening with shared pain and resilience. As I speak, my voice rises, clear and unwavering: "We are not defined by our scars. We are shaped by our fight, our love, our unyielding boldness." The room erupts in applause, hands clapping, hearts reaching out, and Jada's fingers tighten around mine, her pride radiating like a flame that warms my chest. Later, back in the safety of our home, she unveils a new sketch—a vibrant depiction of a woman and a girl, their hands clasped, standing before a city that pulses with light and freedom. "It's us," she says softly, her voice carrying a weight of certainty, and tears spill down my cheeks as I pull her into my arms, my heart so full it feels as though it might overflow.

Don's motions, as Claire had cautioned, continue to surface, but they grow increasingly feeble, his legal team grasping at straws while Geaux Digital Branding's contracts wither under the relentless glare of public scrutiny. The Sheriff's office releases a statement, a grudging admission of past failures coupled with promises of reform, but the words ring hollow to me, a half-measure in the face of deeper wounds. Undeterred, I press forward, my voice growing louder, my story transforming into a beacon that calls for change, for justice, for a world that listens. Meanwhile, Jada's art flourishes, her portfolio earning her a coveted spot at LSU, her dreams taking wing with a boldness that mirrors her spirit. In therapy, I find my nightmares receding, like shadows retreating before dawn, and my trust in the world begins to return, tentative but real. Jada, too, is healing—she flinches less often now, her laughter rings brighter, and her eyes shine with a spark of possibility, a promise of the future we're building together.

By September, we're planning a trip—not Paris, not yet, but New Orleans, a weekend of art galleries and beignets, just us. I look at her across the kitchen table, her curls wild, her smile wide, and I know we've won more than a trial. We've won *us*—a bond forged in pain, strengthened by love, unyielding in its bold. The ghosts will always linger, the scars will always mark us, but they don't define us. We're Crysta and Jada, mother and daughter, survivors and dreamers, and together, we're unstoppable.

I stand on the porch, the night thick with cicadas, the stars a canvas of hope. Jada's asleep, her sketchpad open to that woman and girl, hand in hand. I whisper to the night, to her, to the world: "We're free." The stars answer, and I step inside, locking the door, my heart steady. Tomorrow's another step, another fight, another dream, but tonight, we're home. Tonight, we're enough.

CHAPTER 15
THE BOLD PATH FORWARD

The dawn spills golden through Jada's bedroom window, a soft, molten light that bathes the room in a glow so tender it feels like a promise kept. It's early 2025, and I'm standing here, thirty-five, my blonde hair a tangled cascade falling past my shoulders, my green that don't burn anymore—they heal. The air carries the faint scent of strawberry from Jada's pillow, mingling with the bitter steam of coffee clutched in my trembling hands, a mug chipped from years of late-night talks. Jada, eighteen, sleeps in her bed, her blonde curls splayed across the pillow, her blue-green eyes closed in a peace I fought for with every fiber of my soul. She's home, emancipated, free from Don's shadow, her presence a miracle that stitches together the jagged pieces of my heart. I clutch her old stuffed bear, its fur worn thin from childhood hugs, its button eyes a silent witness to our war, and I whisper into the stillness, "We made it, baby. We're here." My voice trembles, not with fear but with a love so fierce it could shatter mountains, a love that carried me through the bitter dark to this bold, blazing dawn.

This room is a haven, a sacred space where the walls themselves seem to pulse with the rhythm of our shared existence. They are a canvas, painted with the vivid hues of our triumphs and trials, a living testament to the life Jada and I have forged together. On her desk, Jada's sketchpad lies open, its pages spilling over with intricate cityscapes—jagged towers that scrape against a sky brimming with the audacity to dream of brighter, bolder days. Each stroke of her pencil is a rebellion, a declaration of her spirit's refusal to be tethered by the weight of her past. Pinned to the corkboard above, a faded LSU acceptance letter curls at its edges, its ink softened by time but its significance undimmed.

It stands as a monument to her ambition, her fierce determination to carve her own path, to rise above the pain that once threatened to define her; a delicate ghost of her childhood, conjuring memories so vivid they pierce my heart. I see Jada at five, her tiny hand nestled in mine, her laughter a bright, cascading melody that tethered me to hope through the darkest, most desolate nights. I see her at twelve, her blue-green eyes clouded with unspoken questions, her voice a fragile whisper as she asked, "Why can't I stay with you?". Each memory cuts like a blade, sharp and unrelenting, yet today, they are also a triumph—a constellation of scars that map the journey to this moment, where Jada sleeps soundly, enveloped in safety, and I stand resolute, my heart a steady drumbeat of hope, unbroken and unyielding. I wanted to keep her here with me, but I knew that would be selfish. I wanted to make up for the years lost, but it was important to her to go to college out of town, so she's moved into the dorms with her friends. I miss her so much it hurts, but we speak on the phone every day and she comes home on some weekends and holidays.

I move to the window, the glass cool beneath my palm, and gaze out at the sprawling fields of Hammond, their emerald expanse stretching toward the horizon. These fields are more than land; they are the backdrop of my childhood, the crucible of my pain, the arena of my fight. The stars above are fading now, yielding to the soft blush of dawn, and in the window's reflection, I catch a glimpse of myself—not the shattered girl of 2005, crumpled on Don's couch, drowning in despair; nor the anguished mother of 2011, her voice raw from screaming in courtrooms as Jada was torn from her arms; but a survivor, a warrior, a woman whose blonde hair catches the early light like a halo, whose green eyes blaze with a fire no darkness can extinguish.

For twenty years, I've been running from that girl, burying her pain, her shame, her silence beneath layers of survival. But today, I stop running. I stand still, claiming every fragment of who I am. I am Crysta—mother to Jada, daughter of Ponchatoula's soil, sister to every survivor, regardless of gender, who has borne the crushing weight of abuse and dared to rise from its ashes. My story is not mine alone; it is theirs; it is ours—a tapestry woven from threads of anguish and resilience, a chorus that reverberates across Louisiana's winding bayous, across the vastness of the world. It is a solemn vow, etched in the marrow of my bones, that no one should endure the suffering we have known, that truth and love will illuminate the path forward, guiding us toward a future where hope prevails.

The mirror in the hallway waits, its silver surface a gauntlet I've faced before. I stand before it, my nightgown clinging to my sweat-damp skin, my blonde hair wild, my green eyes raw but fierce. The woman staring back isn't the broken girl of 2005, her innocence stolen in a single, merciless night, nor the defeated mother of 2011, her screams drowned in a courtroom that didn't care. She's Crysta, thirty-five, forged in fire, her scars a map of battles won, her heart a compass pointing forward. I trace the mirror's edge, my fingers trembling, and see the ghosts of my past flicker in the glass. There's sixteen-year-old Crysta, walking into a Ponchatoula bar, giddy with friends, her green eyes bright with naive trust, unaware that Don's shadow would shatter her world. There's seventeen-year-old Crysta, pregnant, hiding in oversized sweaters, lying to her mama, her green eyes hollow as she whispered, "I'm fine." There's twenty-two-year-old Crysta, in 2011, her blonde hair tight, her green eyes blazing as a DNA test confirmed Don's paternity, sparking a custody war that would define a decade.

In the twilight of 2022, the churchyard stood as a silent witness to a collision of anguish and fragile hope, a crucible where the weight of despair met the flicker of defiance. Jada, just fifteen, sat huddled in the passenger seat of Don's weathered truck, her blonde curls partially veiled by the dim light, her blue-green eyes wide with terror. The air was thick with tension when Don's fist crashed into my chest, a brutal strike that sent pain searing through my chest like wildfire racing across dry brush. Jada's scream pierced the fading light, a raw, desperate sound that seemed to fracture the stillness of the evening. Her small hands pressed against the truck's glass, a futile barrier between her fear and the violence unfolding outside. Her flinging the door open and rushing to my side to comfort me. In that moment, Stacie Triche, a stranger whose courage would alter the course of our lives, emerged as an unexpected savior. Her voice, steady and resolute, cut through the chaos as she dialed the police, her call a spark that ignited a chain of events no one could have foreseen.

Don's arrest that night was a fleeting reprieve, a momentary pause in a storm that refused to relent. The deputy's dismissive shrug—"No restraining order"—carried the weight of a system's failure, and Jada, still trembling, was sent back into Don's shadow before the stars had fully claimed the sky. Yet, that fleeting spark of intervention lit a fuse, one that would burn slowly but fiercely toward change. I can still see the WBRZ studio, its lights harsh against my weary face, my blonde hair a wild, untamed halo, my green eyes alight with a fire born of both pain and purpose. Chris Nakamoto's questions were calm, measured, but each one drew me deeper into the truth I had carried for too long: the rape that had shattered my world, the relentless custody battles that followed, and the churchyard assault that had finally broken the silence. As I spoke, my voice trembling but resolute, the story spilled out, raw and unfiltered. It caught fire, spreading across screens and airwaves, going viral in a way that felt both surreal and inevitable. The Sheriff, cornered by public outrage, admitted the system's failures. Nancy Grace's voice thundered across the airwaves, demanding Judge Coyne's disbarment, her indignation a rallying cry for justice. And Jada—brave, battered Jada—was finally placed with a third party, safe at last from the hands that had hurt her for so long.

The trial in July 2025 looms large in my memory, a grueling 14-hour marathon that tested the limits of endurance. By the end, I was dehydrated, my blonde hair hanging limp, my green eyes hollowed by exhaustion but unyielding in their resolve. Jada, then sixteen, took the stand with a courage that seemed to radiate from her very core. Her voice, steady and clear, named the years of physical and mental abuse she had endured at Don's hands, each word backed by a mountain of evidence—medical reports, a subpoenaed doctor's testimony, the weight of truth that could no longer be ignored. Judge Coyne, once untouchable, now sat under the unrelenting glare of public fury, his authority diminished by the collective demand for accountability. When the ruling came, it was imperfect but hard-won: Jada would remain with a third party, I was granted one weekend a month to rebuild the bond that had been so violently disrupted, and Don was barred from contact, his shadow finally banished from her life. It was not the full restoration we had dreamed of, but it was a victory carved from years of blood, tears, and unyielding determination.

Jada, who had claimed her emancipation at seventeen, came home to me, her spirit unbroken despite the scars she carried. Now, at eighteen, she stands on the cusp of her future, her blue-green eyes alight with dreams that refuse to be dimmed. She's in college, her cityscapes—vivid, intricate paintings that capture the pulse of urban life—serving as a testament to her resilience, her creativity, her refusal to be defined by the pain of her past. Those moments—the rape, the loss, the relentless fight, and the hard-won triumph—are etched deep into my soul, indelible marks of a journey that tested every fiber of my being. But they do not define me. They have shaped me, yes, molded me into someone stronger, fiercer, more acutely aware of the fragility and tenacity of hope. Yet I am more than the sum of those scars. I am bold, unapologetically alive, standing firm in the truth of who I am. And I am not alone—Jada's light, Stacie's courage, the voices of strangers who rallied to our cause—they remind me that even in the darkest moments, there is a constellation of souls ready to shine.

I see my best friend, her sandy-haired, hazel-eyed warmth a lifeline through countless nights. I see Stacie Triche, her courage in that churchyard a beacon. I see Chris Nakamoto, his commitment amplifying my voice. I see survivors—men abused by those they trusted, women scarred by violence, souls of all genders carrying wounds no one should bear. Their faces are a chorus, their strength my fuel, and I vow to fight for them, to build a world where abuse, sexual or not, has no place. My reflection nods, her green eyes fierce, her blonde hair a banner, and I whisper, "We're just beginning." The words are a vow, a fire, a promise that carries me forward, bold against the bitter dark.

Mostly, I think of my beautiful Jada today. Yesterday she moved out, and I saw her empty room. I felt that emptiness in my heart a little harder than I thought I would. I think of the kindness she shows to me and others on this day. I hope she always stays humble, shows up for others, extends grace, and loves selflessly. I'm so proud of her for staying true to who she is even when she's scared, even when she's hurt. She shows strength and courage and keeps her reactions full of dignity and poise. I've learned so much from her as we grew together. I like to think maybe she picked up a few things from me as well. Hopefully only the good stuff, although I know I haven't always been the best example. She got a version of me that wasn't always fair, or patient, or healthy, but I think there's a beauty in that and the closeness we have will never be the same or compare to anyone else. It was us against the world for so many years, and the world wasn't always kind to us. I always tried to make the best decisions for us at the time with the information that I had, but I still had so much to learn. I hope she continues to seek wisdom all of her life, and she has a child one day that is to her what she was tome. My anchor, my center, my ultimate test, and my ultimate love. Of everything and everyone that has come and gone, she has been my constant.

I lived in fear for many years, yet now, I speak, my voice a thunderous roar that reverberates through the heavens, demanding justice, proclaiming love. Jada's return to my arms is nothing short of a miracle, her emancipation a victory forged in fire, her journey to college a radiant testament to her unyielding courage. As she sleeps, I brush her curls, my fingers trembling with the weight of our shared past, and whisper, "You're my everything." My green eyes linger on her peaceful face, her own blue-green eyes closed in rest, and I know this bond—our love—is an unbreakable force, fiercer than any pain, brighter than the darkest night.

The trial's echoes still ripple through my soul, a tempest that reshaped the contours of our lives. It was July 2025, in a Baton Rouge courtroom that felt like a crucible, its air thick with the scent of polished wood, stale coffee, and the nervous sweat of those who filled its pews. I sat there, my body dehydrated from sleepless nights, my blonde hair hanging limp, my green eyes hollowed by months of fear and fight. My fists clenched so tightly that my nails bit into my palms, drawing tiny crescents of blood, a silent testament to the stakes. Jada, now eighteen, stood before the court, her presence commanding despite the weight of her story. Her blue-green eyes, so like mine yet uniquely her own, held steady, her voice clear and unwavering as she recounted Don's abuse—the physical blows that left bruises, the mental cages that sought to break her spirit, the diary she poured her heart into, only to see it torn to shreds when she dared to claim her truth.

The evidence was undeniable: medical reports detailing her injuries, a subpoenaed doctor's testimony, and Jada's own words, each one a brick in the wall of her truth. Chris Nakamoto's camera, ever-present, captured the marathon battle, his lens a silent witness to our anguish and our resilience, broadcasting our story to a world that could no longer look away. The public's outrage, a tidal wave of support, cornered Judge Coyne, who had no choice but to act. His ruling was not the complete triumph I had dreamed of in my sleepless nights, but it was enough: Jada was placed with a third party, safe at last; I was granted one precious weekend a month to hold her close; and Don was barred from contact, his shadow banished from her life. It was a hard-won step toward freedom—Jada's voice had been heard, her safety secured, her future reclaimed, a canvas now hers to paint with the colors of her dreams.

Advocacy is my fire now, a blaze that burns in Baton Rouge, New Orleans, in survivor groups and lawmakers' offices. I stand before crowds, my blonde hair a banner, my green eyes fierce, naming Don, Geaux Digital Branding, Judge Coyne, the system that shielded them. I speak in church basements, community centers, state capitals, my voice raw but steady, a survivor's roar that shakes the silence. I hold survivors—men, women, all genders—their stories echoing mine, their strength my fuel. There's a man, forties, his voice trembling as he speaks of his father's fists, his shame a mirror to my own. There's a woman, twenties, her eyes like Jada's, scarred by a partner's control, her courage a spark that lights my own. I say to them, "You're bold. Your truth is enough." Their tears, their hugs, their whispered thanks—they're my tribe, my family, my reason to keep fighting.

In the heart of Baton Rouge, I step into the modest offices of LFASA, the Louisiana Foundation Against Sexual Assault, a steadfast group that stood shoulder-to-shoulder with me in the fiercest battles of my life. Their space is more than walls and desks—it's a sanctuary where I learned to unearth my voice, to speak my truth with unyielding courage. The air hums with purpose, a quiet strength that binds us, survivors and advocates alike, in our shared mission. From there, I travel to New Orleans, where I join forces with SAVLIV35, a vibrant coalition dedicated to shattering the chains of abuse. Their banners ripple in the humid breeze, bold declarations demanding an end to violence, their voices rising in a powerful chorus that drowns out the echoes of suffering. Together, we are a force, a collective roar that refuses to let pain have the final word.

Before lawmakers, I stand resolute, my green eyes alight with righteous fury, my blonde hair untamed like the fire in my soul. I speak not just for myself but for every survivor, my words a clarion call for transformation—stronger laws, judges trained to understand the weight of trauma, a system that doesn't just hear but truly listens. In my heart, I carry Jada, her memory a guiding star, and every survivor whose story fuels my resolve. I dream of a world where no one—man, woman, or soul of any gender—endures the torment we've known. Abuse, whether sexual or otherwise, has no place in the future we're building, and I pledge to fight with every ounce of my being until that vision becomes reality. The crowds respond, their cheers a thunderous affirmation, their raised hands a testament to their strength. Their scars, visible and invisible, map a journey of resilience, and in their unity, I feel the pulse of a movement—a rising tide, a bold path we're forging together toward justice and healing.

Yet, amid the fervor of advocacy, therapy remains my anchor, a sacred space where I confront the depths of my wounds. Ms. Lena's office is a haven, its walls steeped in quiet compassion, the lamplight casting a warm glow on her gray braids as they shimmer with wisdom. Her eyes, sharp and knowing, seem to pierce through the barriers I've built, and her question lingers in the air: "Who's Crysta now?" I sit, my blonde hair a flowing cascade, my green eyes brimming with unshed tears, and I begin to name the fragments of my pain. There's the PTSD that shadows my steps, the nightmares where Jada slips through my fingers like smoke, the guilt that gnaws at my chest, relentless and raw. Memories surface, vivid and unbidden: 2006, when I was pregnant, my body hidden in oversized sweaters, my green eyes hollow as I wove lies to shield my mama from the truth. Then 2015, storming into the Sheriff's office, my blonde hair wild, my green eyes blazing with desperate rage, pleading for justice only to be dismissed with a cold excuse—a "clerical error" that erased my cries. And 2022, the churchyard, where Don's fist met my flesh, Jada's scream slicing through the twilight, my heart fracturing as she was torn from me and sent back to him.

Each session with Ms. Lena is a step toward reclaiming myself, peeling back the layers of trauma to find the woman beneath. The fight outside—before crowds, lawmakers, and systems—is mirrored within, a battle to heal, to redefine who I am beyond the pain. With every word spoken in that quiet office, with every tear shed and truth named, I grow stronger, more whole. And as I stand with LFASA, rally with SAVLIV35, and speak truth to power, I carry this inner work forward, weaving it into the movement we're building—a world where survivors are not just heard but honored, where justice is not a dream but a reality, and where no one ever has to walk the path of suffering alone.

Lena asks me to love the girl of 2005, to forgive her silence, and it's like forgiving a stranger. I see her, sixteen, giddy in a Ponchatoula bar, her green eyes bright, unaware of the nightmare waiting. I see her on Don's couch, her screams swallowed, her world collapsing. I see her pregnant, lying, hiding, her green eyes hollow but fierce with a mother's love. I hate her for her silence, her weakness, but today, I'm learning to love her, to hold her like I hold Jada's bear, soft and broken and mine. "You did your best," I whisper, my voice trembling, and Lena nods, her eyes warm, her hand on mine. Therapy is slow, painful, but it's freedom, a bold step toward healing, toward a Crysta who's whole, not just surviving but thriving.

Connection is my salvation, a bridge from darkness to light. I call my best friend, her sandy-haired, hazel-eyed warmth a lifeline through the phone. "You're changing the world," she says, her voice thick with pride, and I laugh, "I'm just keeping up with Jada." We share scars—her abuse, not rape but a shadow she's wrestled, my rape, my silence, my fight. Her hazel eyes, vivid in my mind, are a beacon, her tears a mirror to mine. I see Stacie Triche, her courage in that churchyard, her call to the police a spark that changed everything. I see Chris Nakamoto, his calm questions in the WBRZ studio, his commitment amplifying my voice. I see my mama, her hands gentle as she cradled baby Jada, her eyes soft as she whispered, "You're stronger than you know." I see my daddy, his laugh a rumble, his pride shining when I graduated early, pregnant but unyielding.

I see survivors, their faces a chorus—men, women, all genders, their stories a tapestry of pain and hope. A man, fifties, speaks of betrayal by a trusted friend, his voice a tremor I feel in my bones. A woman, thirties, shares her escape from a violent home, her eyes like mine, fierce with survival. A nonbinary soul, twenties, whispers of rejection, their courage a light that burns bright. They're my family, my tribe, and I vow to stand with them, to fight for a world where no one hides, where truth is a shield, where love is a sword. Connection is our power, our bold defiance against the bitter dark, and I'm not alone—I'm surrounded, lifted, loved.

The porch calls me, dawn's light soft and golden, coffee steaming in my chipped mug. I sit, Jada's bear in my lap, its button eyes staring into the fields where I ran as a child, where I fought as a mother, where I rise as a survivor. I see Jada's cityscape, that solitary figure standing tall, arms outstretched, defying a sky that dares to dream. It's her, it's me, it's every survivor who's dared to rise. I see Ponchatoula's bars, where I sought escape at sixteen; its churches, where I prayed for strength; its streets, where I marched with survivors, our voices a chorus that drowned out the pain. I see Jada, her curls wild, her blue-green eyes bright, her hand in mine as we walk through a city of light, its towers built from our fight, its streets paved with our love.

I dream of a world where no one hides, where survivors—men, women, all genders—stand tall, their scars a testament to their strength, their voices a roar that shakes the heavens. I dream of a system that listens, judges who care, laws that protect. I dream of Jada, her architecture reshaping the world, her laughter a melody that never fades. And when I wake, the dawn is breaking, spilling through the window like a promise I'm learning to trust. I'm Crysta, survivor, mother, warrior, and I'm ready—ready to heal, ready to fight, ready to love, bold and unyielding, forever against the bitter dark.

I rise, my legs steady, my blonde hair catching the light, my green eyes a flame that burns eternal. I whisper to the dawn, to Jada, to the girl I was, to every survivor: “We’re not done. We’re just beginning.” The words are a vow, a fire, a promise that carries me forward. I climb back into bed, Jada’s bear beside me, and close my eyes, her laughter a melody in my heart, her smile a light that no darkness can touch. Tomorrow’s another battle—therapy, advocacy, the slow work of healing—but today, I’m enough. Today, I’m bold, my soul a flame that burns eternally, my scars a map of where I’ve been, my heart a compass pointing to where I’m going.

EPILOGUE

November 12, 2025. The Hammond night presses close, air thick with summer's pulse, my porch lamp casting shadows across my bare feet. At thirty-eight, my blonde hair falls in loose waves, my green eyes tracing the horizon where lightning flickers, a storm brewing like the one in my chest. Don's name, once a chokehold, fades under fraud indictments, his Geaux Digital Branding a rotting shell, but the rape case—mine, ours—sits frozen in the DA's desk, a wound that won't close. Logan's voice, warm and gravelly, drifts from the kitchen, his presence a spark I'm terrified to touch. For the first time, love beckons, a fragile flame in my scarred hands, and every step toward it drags me through the ashes of 2005. I'm Crysta, mother, survivor, a woman daring to want more, the bitter a weight, the bold a fire I'll fight to keep.

The concrete burns beneath my weight as I stand motionless, my coffee mug abandoned on the railing, its contents long gone cold. The humid Hammond air clings to my skin, heavy with the weight of memory. Logan, a man I first met under the bright lights of a buzzing bar in this very city, carries his own burdens—ghosts of parents stolen by violence, a life forged in the relentless pursuit of justice. His brown eyes, warm and unwavering, seemed to see through me from the moment we met, as if he understood the cracks in my foundation before I ever uttered a word. It was his question one night, simple yet piercing— "How do you keep going?"—that unravelled a truth I'd buried deep, a truth I hadn't dared voice until he asked.

For months, we've talked—long, winding conversations that stretched late into the night, his patience a quiet anchor in the storm of my past. His voice, steady and thoughtful, became a lifeline, pulling me through moments when the weight of my memories threatened to drown me. But tonight, everything shifted. His hand brushed mine, a fleeting touch meant to comfort, and my body betrayed me. The world tilted, and suddenly it was 2005 again—Don's breath hot against my ear, the suffocating weight of the couch pinning me down, the jagged edges of that night slicing through me. My heart thundered, palms slick with sweat, and I stumbled back, the words "I can't" choking out of me like a plea. Logan didn't move, didn't reach for me. His voice, low and calm, cut through the panic: "I'm not him, Crysta." Shame flooded me, hot and relentless—why can't I just feel what I want to feel? Why can't I let him in? But Logan stood there, steady as ever, offering no demands, just space for the trembling truth I couldn't yet name.

In therapy, Ms. Lena's words echo like a mantra: "Trauma rewires the mind, but you're rewiring it back, piece by piece." I'm trying—God, I'm trying—clawing my way through the triggers that ambush me without warning. His touch, his closeness, the way he leans in when he listens—they all scream danger, even as my heart aches for the safety I sense in him. Logan is different. His stories of battling depression, of standing up for those the world has cast aside, mirror my own fight in ways that make me feel seen. We're two souls shaped by loss, by the relentless grind of seeking justice in a world that so often turns its back. And yet, trust remains a knife's edge, sharp and unforgiving. I want to cross it, to reach for him, but every step feels like a gamble with my own survival.

Last night, sleep brought no reprieve. I dreamed of Don's smirk, his allies' whispered conspiracies, and a crisp letter from the DA warning of new motions to bury the case that has haunted me for two decades. The dream clung to me when I woke, its claws sinking deep, and for a fleeting moment, I ached for Logan's arms around me, for the warmth of his presence to chase away the chill. But fear surged, my PTSD snarling that love is a trap, that letting him close will only betray me in the end. Still, I see it—the quiet curve of his laugh, the way he listens without judgment, the way his eyes hold mine with a gentleness that feels like home. I want it, all of it—a life where I'm not just surviving, not just piecing together the fragments of who I was, but whole, fully alive, and unafraid to love again. The path to that life is treacherous, lined with the ghosts of my past, but Logan's patience lights the way, and maybe, just maybe, I'm learning to walk it.

Inside, the house hums, alive with small sounds, a world I've built from ruins. The fight's not done—Don's shadow lingers, his allies circling, the DA's inaction a slap. Next month, a new hearing looms, a chance to push the case forward, to demand justice not just for me but for every voice silenced. Logan's offered to help, his mind sharp, his heart steady, and I'm learning to let him in, to believe I deserve this. My green eyes lift to the storm, rain starting to spit, and I feel it—a shift, a daring. Love's a battle, each touch a step through fire, but I'm thirty-five, scarred, fierce, ready.

Logan steps out, his silhouette soft in the lamplight, and my pulse spikes—fear, want, hope colliding. "You okay?" he asks, voice a deep connection to my soul. I nod, throat tight, and take his hand, my fingers trembling but holding on. The rain falls harder, washing the night clean, and I stand, green eyes blazing, blonde hair wet, a woman stepping into the unknown. The next fight's coming—courts, ghosts, my own heart—but I'm here, bold against the bitter, a spark that won't die.

RESOURCES FOR SUPPORT

If this book stirs pain or memories, reach out. These lifelines caught me when I was falling—use them, please.

- **RAINN (Rape, Abuse & Incest National Network):** 1-800-656-HOPE (4673), www.rainn.org – 24/7 support for survivors of sexual assault. They listened when I was drowning in 2015.
- **National Domestic Violence Hotline:** 1-800-799-SAFE (7233), www.thehotline.org – Help for those facing abuse or control. They armed me with steps in 2022 when Don's threats closed in.
- **Louisiana Foundation Against Sexual Assault (LFASA):** www.lafasa.org – Advocates who fight for survivors in Louisiana. They linked me to warriors like Stacie Triche in 2022.
- **SAVLIV35:** stacie@savliv35.org – Stacie's group, born from my fight, supports moms losing kids to abusers. They sparked the media storm that shook the courts.
- **Louisiana Legal Services:** 1-800-310-7029, www.louisianalawhelp.org – Free legal aid for those in custody wars. They gave me a voice when I had nothing.

- **National Crime Victim Law Institute (NCVLI):** www.ncvli.org – Legal resources for survivors. They showed me I could still fight in 2023.

You're not alone. Call, click, reach out. I'm Crysta, still here, still bold, and I'm with you.

www.ingramcontent.com/pod-product-compliance
Lightning Source LLC
LaVergne TN
LVHW050909210926
848482LV00012B/381
* 9 7 9 8 3 4 9 3 2 2 9 6 9 *